The Practice of Psychoanalyti Parent–Infant Psychotherapy

C000259443

This is a distinguished book

Dilys Daws, Hon. Consultant Child Psychotherapist, Tavistock Clinic and Adviser to Association for Infant Mental Health

This extraordinary volume, written by master clinicians at one of the leading international centers in child development, offers an effective therapeutic model that is solidly grounded in very recent advances in attachment theory and developmental neuroscience. Yet at the same time it is brimming with evocative clinical vignettes that outline practical therapeutic techniques in remarkable detail. More than simply positively affecting the baby's developing psychological abilities, these interventions are directly impacting the early developing right brain, and therefore the consequences of such treatment are long enduring. This work makes an important contribution towards creating effective early interventions that can reduce the risk of the intergenerational transmission of a predisposition to psychopathology. I predict it will become a gold standard in the cutting edge field of parent–infant psychotherapy.

Allan N. Schore, University of California at Los Angeles David Geffen School of Medicine. Author of *Affect Dysregulation and Disorders of the Self* and *Affect Regulation and the Repair of the Self*

This comprehensive handbook addresses the provision of therapeutic help for babies and their parents when their attachment relationship is derailed and a risk is posed to the baby's development.

Drawing on clinical and research data from the psychological and biological sciences, this book presents a treatment approach that is comprehensive, flexible and sophisticated, whilst also being clear and easy to understand. The first section, **The theory of parent–infant psychotherapy**, offers the reader a theoretical framework for understanding the emotional-interactional environment within which infant development takes place. It draws upon psychoanalysis, attachment and developmental research to describe how babies' minds and development are sculpted by the dynamics of the relationship with their primary love figures. The second section, **The therapeutic process**, invites the reader into the consulting room to participate in a detailed examination of the relational process in the clinical encounter. The third section, **Clinical papers**, provides case material to illustrate the unfolding of the therapeutic process.

Written by a team of experienced clinicians, writers, teachers and researchers in the field of infant development and psychopathology, *The Practice of Psychoanalytic Parent–Infant Psychotherapy*, is unique in its systematic approach to describing the theoretical rationale and clinical process of therapy. It will be of great interest to all professionals working with children and their families, including child psychiatrists, psychoanalysts, psychotherapists, and clinical and developmental psychologists.

Tessa Baradon developed and manages the Parent–Infant Project at The Anna Freud Centre. She is a practising child psychotherapist and supervisor and writes and lectures on applied psychoanalysis and parent–infant psychotherapy.

Contributors: Carol Broughton, Iris Gibbs, Jessica James, Angela Joyce, Judith Woodhead

The Practice of Psychoanalytic Parent–Infant Psychotherapy

Claiming the Baby

Tessa Baradon with Carol Broughton, Iris Gibbs, Jessica James, Angela Joyce and Judith Woodhead of the Parent–Infant Project at The Anna Freud Centre

Routledge
Taylor & Francis Group

LONDON AND NEW YORK

First published 2005 by Routledge
27 Church Road, Hove, East Sussex, BN3 2FA

Simultaneously published in the USA and Canada
by Routledge
270 Madison Avenue, New York, NY 10016

Routledge is an imprint of the Taylor & Francis Group

© 2005 selection and editorial matter, Tessa Baradon; individual chapters,
the contributors

Typeset in Times by Garfield Morgan, Rhayader, Powys, UK
Printed and bound in Great Britain by TJ International Ltd, Padstow,
Cornwall
Paperback cover design by Lisa Dynan

All rights reserved. No part of this book may be reprinted or reproduced or
utilised in any form or by any electronic, mechanical, or other means, now
known or hereafter invented, including photocopying and recording, or in
any information storage or retrieval system, without permission in writing
from the publishers.

This publication has been produced with paper manufactured to strict
environmental standards and with pulp derived from sustainable forests.

British Library Cataloguing in Publication Data
A catalogue record for this book is available from the British Library

Library of Congress Cataloging in Publication Data
Baradon, Tessa.
    The practice of psychoanalytic parent infant psychotherapy : claiming the
baby / Tessa Baradon with Carol Broughton, Iris Gibbs, Jessica James, Angela
Joyce and Judith Woodhead
        p. cm.
    Includes bibliographical references and index.
    ISBN 1-58391-760-8 (hbk) – ISBN 1-58391-761-6 (pbk) 1. Parent-infant
psychotherapy. 2. Infants–Development. 3. Infant psychology. 4. Infant
psychiatry. 5. Parent and infant. 6. Parenting–Psychological aspects. I. Anna
Freud Centre. Parent Infant Project. II. Title.
    RJ502.5.B37 2005
    618.92'89–dc22

                                                                    2005006152

ISBN 1-58391-760-8 hbk
ISBN 1-58391-761-6 pbk

Contents

SECTION II
The therapeutic process

SECTION III
Clinical papers

Foreword

This book provides an invaluable theoretical tool and clinical instruction for those working in the burgeoning field of parent–infant psychotherapy. It offers a clear, comprehensive and sequential account of the therapeutic encounter while explicating the rationale for intervention and discussing techniques for doing so. In addition, this book is distinctive in providing real case examples of work, tracking the unfolding therapeutic processes between individual families and babies, and in a group context with mothers and babies. It therefore constitutes an essential source of both psychodynamic thinking and technical guidance for the rising number of parent–infant psychotherapy practitioners.

There are, in my view, two main reasons for the rapid increase of parent–infant therapy in recent years: One relates to today's *psychosocial conditions* leading to greater prevalence of disturbance in the early parenting period. The other, to the growing realisation that primary relationships are not only systemic and intersubjective, but for the large part sub-cortical and non-symbolised – consisting of highly emotional exchanges between two or more reciprocally influential beings, who intuitively register and react to each other's feelings. Therefore, when things go wrong, the primary 'patient' is neither parent/s nor baby, but the *relationship*. Hence the importance of joint psychotherapy.

This book offers a model of parent–infant therapy that works with the baby as an active and creative partner in the therapy. It focuses on techniques to promote this, building on a growing field of neonatal and neuro-scientific research that has established that even newborns are far more capable and discriminating than previously suggested, endowed with exquis-itely sensitive feelings and an innate ability for accurately reading and responding to the emotions of others. This corresponds with a shift in psychoanalytic theory from a focus on the singular Oedipal individual, to 'object relations' between pre-Oedipal baby/mother, and beyond that, to a gradual acknowledgement of interpsychic 'subject relations' between a com-petent infant and carers, who are real (and fallible) subjects in their own rights (rather than fantasy figures or inexhaustible providers). Precursors to this new view were introduced through clinical observations of gifted early psychoanalysts whose work with infants taught them to see development not as a pre-programmed unfolding of cognition but a gradual evolution of innate capacities for sociability, thought and language within the matrix of a specific 'facilitating environment'. However, as this book illustrates, there are many ways in which this intricate process of development can become 'derailed'.

It is necessary to remember that, today, parent–infant disturbances occur within the context of rapidly changing patterns of family relationships, with few support networks and intense emotional reliance between sexual partners. This leads to inevitable destabilisation of a couple's relationship during and after the transition to parenthood. Smaller nuclear units, dispersed extended families and social stratification by age when growing up, result in both lack of experience with babies and less parenting guidance from experienced others. More importantly, parents were once babies themselves and carry unprocessed residues of their childhood experience. As clinical practice reveals, today's social conditions provide few opportunities for people to work through infantile experience in the presence of newborn siblings and cousins before becoming a parent with exclusive responsibility for a baby of his or her own.

This renders new parents vulnerable to *reactivation of their own unprocessed passions at the very time when their adult capacities are most needed.* Unremitting exposure to the raw emotions of the infant and to primal substances (such as urine, faeces, lochia, breast milk . . .) revitalises unintegrated, denied or disavowed experiences of being parented in one's own childhood. This *'contagious arousal'* (Raphael-Leff, 2005) engenders a sudden release of unconscious forces, flooding some susceptible new parents with traumatic flashbacks, overwhelming feelings of rage, guilt or self-hatred and/or terrifying helplessness, which inhibits their adult capacities and may unconsciously trigger archaic re-enactments with the baby, with detrimental and long-lasting effects. It is here that therapeutic intervention becomes essential.

Psychoanalysis has long been aware of the cross-generational interpenetration of internal worlds. *In psychoanalytically oriented parent–infant therapies there is an assumption that the baby's experience of self comes into being through interaction with primary others, and their behaviours reflect interactive inner realities.* When primary health carers, GPs or parents refer babies with a variety of complaints this indicates *family* disturbance. In the first year of life these problems may manifest in a variety of ways. The book's detailed consideration of attachment issues and psychosocial factors underpinning presenting difficulties enables the reader to see beyond the referral to unconscious conflicts and representations. It then provides guidelines for working with defences and resistance as they emerge in the therapeutic process, noting that 'the effectiveness of a therapeutic treatment is contingent with the balance it provides between containment of anxiety and disruption of typical and pathological ways of being' (Chapter 2, p. 30)

The transition to parenthood, with its emotional vulnerability and economic dependence, is also associated with its raised tensions, increased domestic conflicts and violence. Sadly, many treatments still tend to focus on mothers rather than both parents, neglecting the psychodynamics between them as parents. However, the model described in this book addresses the parents' functioning as a couple and advocates engaging the father in the therapeutic process. There are also few procedures in place to identify problems antenatally. Again, the theoretical and clinical frameworks explicated in this book set guidelines for understanding and identifying risk. When therapeutic resources are scarce, identification of high-risk groups and early intervention are crucial preventive measures. Perinatal therapy can reduce the potential for cross-generational transmission and perverse enactments with the baby, when pregnancy and reproductive events revitalise people's unresolved traumatic experiences with their own carers, including incestuous abuse, cruelty and violence, loss, neglect, abandonment or invalidation (Raphael-Leff, 2000). Given a young baby's sensitivity to the feelings of others, developmental processes are affected by emotional or personality disorders in the parent/s such as postnatal depression or persecution, narcissistic or borderline states. But, not only is the baby affected by the adult – the parent too, is deeply affected by the infant. Adult capacities for nurturing are embedded in an unconscious schema of a benign or damaging baby-self seen through the eyes of an internalised carer. Unprocessed, this representation is acutely reawakened by close contact with a real baby

As so clearly described in this book, observing the moment-to-moment give and take in the treatment sessions, the parent–infant therapist speaks the infant's feelings while also voicing connections with the emotional climate of the parent's own childhood as remembered and reported. The therapist often evolves emotional understanding of intergenerational transmissions of which the family members themselves may be unaware. This is partly achieved through the therapist's own countertransference feelings during the sessions, in which the therapist with the family, like the parent with an infant, experiences intuitive responses to non-verbal, implicit emotional cues. Therapists, therefore, have to remain receptive to distress in both parent/s and baby, while also fine-tuning awareness of their own motives, emotions and attitudes.

The psychoanalytic model of parent–infant psychotherapy described in this book is a remarkably effective form of treatment. It capitalises on rapidity of change due to the plasticity of development of the baby within primary relationships, which may serve as an incentive for growth even in unlikely mothers and fathers. The therapy enables primary relationships to run a healthier course by enhancing the carer/s' capacity for reflectiveness and by fostering faith in interactive repair, based on their own internal resources and the baby's resilience.

In true scientific tradition, this therapeutic model presented has been subjected to an outcome study and is now the basis for a systematic evaluation of intervention. As such it is a fine product of The Anna Freud Centre – with its historical tradition of excellence in clinical work and research. I have no doubt that this will become a classic handbook for practitioners.

Joan Raphael-Leff

Preface

Someone would like to have you for her child
But you are mine.
Someone would like to rear you on a costly mat
But you are mine.
Someone would like to place you on a camel blanket
But you are mine.
I have you to rear on a torn old mat.
Someone would like to have you as her child
But you are mine.

Lullaby, Kwabana Nketia, Ghana

This book is about laying claim: the parent/s' claim of their baby, the baby's 'possession' of his parent/s: 'You are mine!'

Sometimes this process goes awry. A variety of emotions, experiences, expectations can get in the way of the bonding between the new dyad or triad of mother–baby, father–baby, mother–father–baby. When, for whatever reason, the attachment is threatened, the baby and his parent/s need urgent help to restore them to the course of mutual cherishing and claiming. The urgency derives from the baby, as evidenced by current research and clinical knowledge about early development. Namely, that the interactions between socioemotional environment and genes bias brain structuralisation and that evolving mental structures influence later development[1]. Neuropsychological plasticity, the relative fluidity of relationships in formation, allows deficits to be addressed more effectively than at later stages[2].

In the domain of infant mental health, parent–infant psychotherapy is gaining recognition as a method of early intervention to promote infant development within a failing primary relationship[3]. Different models of

---

1 This issue is discussed and referenced in Chapter 1.
2 See Balbernie (2002) for evidence regarding early interventions.
3 Daniel Stern (1995) addresses the 'ports of entry' in early interventions.

intervention have been developed within different disciplines; even within the applied psychoanalytic field there are variations in emphasis[3]. The model of the Parent–Infant Project at The Anna Freud Centre has been developed over the past seven years. The specificity of this model lies in the direct psychotherapeutic work with the baby in the room alongside the work with the representational world of the mother and with their attachment relationship. The urgency imposed by timetables of development is supported by the tenacity of the developmental pull in infancy. Babies make such good patients. 'By and large', Winnicott (1962, p. 169) wrote, 'analysis is for those who want it, need it, and can take it'. When an infant is trapped in a derailed attachment with his parent, he will want, need and take the therapy for himself and for his parent. In the clinical material presented, the babies can be seen modifying their own schemas of being with their parent/s, already shaped by experience but also still being formed.

While this model has drawn from the work of many innovators in the field, e.g. Fraiberg, Stern, and Cramer and from discussion with valued colleagues, it is contextualised by its development within a team of child, adult and group analysts at The Anna Freud Centre.

The Parent–Infant Project at The Anna Freud Centre

In their seminal work with young children in the war nurseries, Anna Freud and Dorothy Burlingham laid the basis for psychoanalytically informed observation and intervention in relation to the young child's ties to his parent or primary caregiver (described in *Infants without families*, 1944). With the establishment in 1950 of the Hampstead Child Therapy Clinic (later renamed The Anna Freud Centre) their approach was carried forward in the training of child psychotherapists and in the model of a well-baby clinic, which brought together the physical and psychological care of the infant and his parent in a community setting. In 1997, the Parent–Infant Project took over from the well-baby clinic, to address psychological disturbance in the parent–infant relationship. The Parent–Infant Project integrates clinical services for infants and their families where there are attachment disorders, training of professionals working with infants, and research of populations at risk and efficacy of intervention.

The development of this book

In 2003 the Parent–Infant Project clinical team started manualising the psychotherapeutic model of parent–infant psychotherapy; an adapted version of the manual forms the basis for this book. The systematic approach of describing the process of the therapy, with an emphasis on the 'how to do it', is unique in current publications in the field. Contrary to the usual style of clinical papers for professional and academic audiences, the challenge was to observe, step-by-step, *what the therapists do, why, and when. And when it doesn't work!* This necessitated thorough discussion of shared theoretical assumptions and clinical practice, areas of difference and/or disagreement, and an exploration of what lies within the model and where individual style takes over. The book aims to present the overarching model, while at the same time to maintain, in the individual chapters, the particular style and personality of each therapist.

Structure of the book

For heuristic purposes, the theoretical and clinical process chapters have been separated, although in practice there is a dialectical relationship between theory and practice in that each derives from, and informs, the other.

The first section of the book sets out the theoretical framework in terms of the parent–infant relationship and parent–infant psychotherapy. In Chapter 1, Angela Joyce distils consensual understanding regarding the infant's pre-wired capacities to relate, 'good enough' parenting and the risks to developmental outcome for the infant of failures in the early relationship. In Chapter 2, Tessa Baradon and Angela Joyce present the theory and aims of parent–infant psychotherapy and the attachment problems that can be addressed. In Chapters 3 and 4, Tessa Baradon discusses the clinical frameworks for parent–infant psychotherapy and key techniques of intervention. These chapters also examine the role of the network and processes for assessment of risk.

The second section of the book includes the chapters on clinical process in parent–infant psychotherapy with individual families and in a group. The process chapters cover the stages from engagement to termination. They address the fundamental issue of establishing the baby as a partner in the therapeutic process, and the role of the therapist in this. They highlight the aims of each stage in the therapeutic process and the techniques applied in relation to the aims. As well as discussing the unfolding of the therapy the authors address problems, possible resolutions and possible failure to resolve difficulties, resulting in the break-down of the therapy. In Chapter 5, Iris Gibbs describes the therapeutic approach to engaging a family in the work. She discusses the processes of introduction, intake and choice of treatment modality. In Chapter 6, Carol Broughton discusses the elaboration of the therapeutic process in the middle phase of therapy, and consolidation of therapeutic gains. Chapter 7 addresses the process of ending. Here Judith Woodhead looks at signs of readiness to begin to end, and the therapist's understanding and working with the dynamics of ending. Chapter 8 completes the process chapters in describing group psychotherapy with mothers and babies. In this chapter, Jessica James discusses the particular contribution of the group as a treatment modality in parent–infant psychotherapy and details the process of setting up and running such a group.

The third section of the book includes clinical papers, selected to present a range of work illustrating different topics. Chapter 9, by Angela Joyce, describes a brief intervention with a mother and baby, who were able to use a consultation to explore unconscious contributions to their difficulties. Chapter 10 by Tessa Baradon and Carol Broughton, attempts to describe how changing psychodynamic formulations of the therapist are titrated into the therapeutic encounter. Chapter 11, by Judith Woodhead, discusses the importance of the 'third' – father/analyst, and the move from the dyad to the triad in an emotionally enmeshed mother and son. In Chapter 12, Jessica James illustrates the maturation of a mother–baby analytic group and possibilities for change therein.

Readers and how to use the book

The book is directed to a varied audience. Prior knowledge is not assumed and the authors have tried to write in an accessible style, clearly and reflectively. Anyone working with infants and their families may find it a useful resource in thinking about the parent–infant relationship. Professionals trained in early intervention may gain insight into the psychodynamic approach to unconscious processes between infant and parent.

It is envisaged that the book can be used flexibly, according to the interests of each reader. Chapters can be read independently to enhance understanding of a particular topic – theoretical or clinical. As a whole, the book could serve as a handbook for psychoanalytic practitioners.

To facilitate ease of reading we refer to the parent as she, the baby as he, the therapist as she. However, the book pertains equally to fathers, female babies and male therapists!

Tessa Baradon

Contributors

The contributors, trained in individual or group psychoanalysis, have all worked in the Parent–Infant Project for extended periods and contributed to the development of the intervention model.

Tessa Baradon has a Masters degree in Public Health, and trained at The Anna Freud Centre. She has worked in the National Health Service and consulted to social service and voluntary child-care organisations. She teaches and supervises in child analysis and psychotherapy, and infant mental health. She developed the Parent–Infant Project at The Anna Freud Centre and is manager and lead clinician.

Carol Broughton has a Masters degree in Psychoanalytic Developmental Psychology and trained at The Anna Freud Centre. She works as a Child and Adolescent Psychotherapist in the National Health Service. She is researching into the clinical assessment of parent–infant interaction as part of her work in the Parent–Infant Project and as a clinical doctorate with University College London. She is a member of the editorial board of the *Journal of Child Psychotherapy*.

Iris Gibbs trained as a Child and Adolescent Psychotherapist with the British Association of Psychotherapists and works, supervises and teaches in the field. For the past ten years she has worked with 'looked after' children and their carers in the Integrated Support Programme and has a special interest in race and cultural issues and their impact on child rearing.

Jessica James trained as a group analyst at the Institute of Group Analysis. In the Parent–Infant Project she conducts a therapeutic group for mothers and babies and an outreach group in a hostel for homeless families with babies. She conducts analytic groups at the Women's Therapy Centre. She works with non-clinical groups of parents preparing for birth and the transition to parenthood, also supervising and publishing in this field.

Angela Joyce worked as a psychiatric social worker in the Child Guidance
Service before training as an adult and child psychoanalyst at the British
Psycho-Analytical Society and The Anna Freud Centre. She works in the
Parent–Infant Project and is an honorary lecturer at University College
London. She teaches child and adult psychoanalysts in the UK and
abroad. She is an editor with the Winnicott Trust and is Deputy Director
of the Squiggle Foundation.

Judith Woodhead, MA, is an adult Jungian analyst (Society of Analytical
Psychology). She specialises in work with young vulnerable patients and
migrant families in the Parent–Infant Project and has developed ante-
and post-natal groups in primary health settings. She teaches and
publishes in the field.

Acknowledgements

Our thanks to:

Our patients, who have given us their trust and inspired our work.
Our families, who supported and encouraged us, especially when the going got hard.
Professor Peter Fonagy and **Dr Mary Target**, for consulting to us on manualisation and supporting this project.
Dr Liz Allison for her very helpful editing comments.
Lynne Pressnell for her patient secretarial assistance.
British Journal of Psychotherapy and *International Journal of Infant Observation* for permission to reprint abridged versions of published papers.
Each other, as colleagues, fans, critics and friends!

Key terms

Affects/affective states The emotions and feeling states that parents and babies experience and that can explain their behaviours and give subjective meaning to them.

Ambivalence The co-existence of loving and hating feeling towards the same person, which characterises all intense human relationships. Parents, consciously or not, feel ambivalence towards the baby and the developing baby feels ambivalence towards the parents.

Anxiety The experience of anxiety is thought to be qualitatively different in a human infant compared to a child or adult. In a baby a state of extreme apprehension arises when he feels that his survival is threatened. The source may be the parent, which can generate relational trauma, or the parent can be experienced as failing to protect the baby from other sources of external danger. Cumulatively unmodulated internal affective states can also create 'anxiety'. 'Falling forever', 'unthinkable anxiety' and 'annihilation anxiety' are descriptions of such extreme experiences of anxiety.

Attachment The primary affective relationship between parent and infant that becomes structured through development as internal templates of expectations in relationships.

Containment The mental stance of the parent/therapist, which gives the infant/patient the experience of being understood and thus emotionally safe. Lack of containment implies an experience of emotions being out of control, generating a sense of being overwhelmed.

Contingent responsivity The provision of a response that corresponds to the baby's specific emotions and needs such that the baby has an experience of control over the environment, making him feel effective and safe. It is assumed that such experience of control can serve to regulate emotional arousal. This is why responding contingently (sensitively) to the baby appears often to soothe the infant.

Counter-transference The largely unconscious feelings and thoughts evoked in the therapist by her experience of being with the patient/s. The therapist uses the range of her emotional responses to understand the depth and complexity of the communications from the patient, including their need for her to take a specific position in relation to them. The replay of therapist's own past relationships (her transference) in the therapeutic encounter are also important as the re-activation of problematic aspects of her own history might interfere with her capacity to engage effectively with this work.

Defences   The mechanisms a person employs, either knowingly or unknowingly, to avoid conscious recognition of their thoughts and feelings that provoke anxiety and are experienced as threatening to get out of control. In the parents' relationship with their baby the range of defences used may be especially constraining as the mother's fear of thoughts and feelings somehow damaging the baby can be intense. The baby can only resort to action as he has little capacity for psychological defence. When threatened, and without the necessary parental support, the infant may use pathological defensive actions such as freezing, and gaze avoidance.

Dependency   The state of need for an attentive, intimate other – parent, caregiver – for survival and development in earliest infancy. The baby moves from absolute to relative dependency in the context of contingent parental responses.

Disassociation/Dissociation   The process by which overwhelming experience may be defended against by the mind cordoning it off so that it is not accessible or felt. This then creates unintegrated and fragmented states of mind. When faced with overwhelming negative affect the baby appears to adopt ways of 'not being present', such as blanking out or sleeping, and the consequent unintegration risks becoming structured into his developing personality.

Disorganised attachment   One of the categories of attachment identified in attachment research, describing the absence in a child of a coherent strategy for dealing with anxiety provoking situations relating to attachment relationships. Disorganised attachment appears to be related to internal relational models in the parent – of fear, hostility and helpless – which are frightening to the infant.

Emotional dis/regulation   The process by which the levels of positive and negative emotions are kept within bounds, so that they are registered but not overwhelming. The regulation of the baby's emotions takes place within the co-constructed contingent interactions with the parents. If these interactions are not successful, or are in themselves distressing, the baby risks becoming disregulated, overwhelmed by his emotions or defending against them by blanking them out altogether. Parents may be in similar states in relation to their own emotional arousal and thus risk disregulating their babies.

Facilitating environment   The primary loving attachment that supports the development of the infant.

Ghosts in the nursery Negative and painful feelings from the parent's past that are associated with early relational disturbance, that are transferred into the relationship with newborn baby and can potentially significantly distort it. When in the past the parent's defences rendered negative feelings of pain, helplessness, hostility, unconscious and the parent identified with the aggressor (the grandparent of the baby), the parent may repeat this role in relation to the baby in the present.

'Good enough' Describes the position of the observer in relation to the parenting and therapeutic environments, whereby 'perfection' is not expected. Nor is perfection seen to lead to healthy development and change. 'Good enough' suggests imperfect but sustainable and therefore stable and predictable parent–infant relationships where mistakes can be made and mended. This dialectic process is seen as critical to healthy growth.

Interaction The to and fro of emotionally laden interpersonal behaviours between the infant and parent (or therapist). This is a verbal or non-verbal phenomenon that each participant simultaneously contributes to, and can be thought of as co-constructed by the pair. In real-time, such interaction can serve to regulate reciprocally the contribution of both partners in the interaction. Each adjusts the timing, rhythm, approach/avoidance, and level of arousal in tune with the others. These processes may take place outside of awareness and constitute the emotional regulatory system.

Internal working models The representations of interactions between the baby and his caregivers that become structured in the mind over time as general expectancies concerning the reactions of the other. They are relatively enduring but are open to the influence of new experience and subject to change as new experience accumulates.

Internal world The psychological narrative of the relationship with oneself and between oneself and others. This narrative is both conscious and unconscious. The internal world evolves during infancy and early childhood in the context of the emotional relationship with the caregivers.

Mentalisation/reflective function The psychological capacity to make sense of actions and behaviours in oneself and in others in terms of underlying feelings and thoughts. Without this process human behaviour can be experienced as meaningless and random. Attributing mental states as guiding the actions of others adds meaning to social interaction. The mentalising stance is one of creating psychological meaning in the relationship with the other. The therapist's mentalising stance in relation to the parents and the baby support the parent/s in reflecting on the meaning of their baby's experience and actions.

Motherese The special style of 'language' adults use all over the world to emotionally engage the baby. This includes exaggerated facial expression, lilting tone of voice, words.

Object A mental representation of a significant other figure (the object). This mental representation is based on the perception of the external figure and shaped by the subject's phantasy wishes, fears, feelings concerning that person and their relationship to him/her.

Oedipal situation This is the phrase used by psychoanalysts to describe the triangular relationship the baby has with his parents in which he comes to recognise that they are a couple in relation to him as the child. As the child develops Oedipal triangulation he comes to be able to hold complex emotions of desire and rivalry.

Phantasy An unconscious construct of the imagination that relates to wish fulfilling or destructive aspects of a relationship. Phantasy imbues experience and actions with individual, context-specific meaning.

Primary maternal preoccupation and maternal reverie States of mind in the parent, beginning in late pregnancy, whereby the infant is the focus of the mother's emotional investment. This enables the mother to imagine the baby's needs and elaborate on the baby's emotional experience and give it psychological meaning. The baby can in this way have an experience of his bodily and emotional states being held and contained. For both mother and baby much of this process of preoccupation is unconscious.

Procedural memory Experiential memory available from earliest infancy that is stored and retrieved in mainly non-symbolic (action) form. Procedural memory can be seen to include patterned ways for being with another person. It may reflect the quality of relationships with the caretakers. This aspect of memory may account for the impact of early relationships on later relationships as procedural memories are expressed throughout life in action sequences.

Projection and attribution The defensive process whereby the individual ascribes qualities of the self (projection) or another person (attribution) to the infant. In early relational process projections can distort the parent's perception of the baby as he actually is.

Protoconversation The preliminary forms of intentional affective communication constructed between parent and pre-verbal infant that includes turn taking and assumes careful observation of, and accommodation to, the other's response.

Psychodynamic formulation The working hypotheses by the therapist bringing together the psychological aspects of the parent–infant relationship, its maladaptive aspects, its implications for the therapeutic encounter, and the ongoing processes of the therapy.

Reality testing A psychological process of examining the extent to which internal and subjective experiences match or differ from external reality, or from the subjective reality of the other person/s in the relationship. Parents' experiences of their baby may be distorted by powerful feelings or defensive processes that prevent them from relating to their baby as he really is.

Representations   Initially these are bodily based, pre-symbolic images and sensations in infancy, created out of repeated patterns of experience of interpersonal interaction. These mental structures come to shape later experience and expectations in relation to both self and other, and self and other in relationship. Eventually it comes to be structured as the individual's representational world.

Risk   The probability of unfavourable developmental outcome associated with aspects of the infant's experience. In the present context this usually refers sub-optimal outcomes to the baby where the parent's difficulties in their past come to be woven into the affective and behavioural interactions with the baby.

Scaffolding   The process whereby the parent/therapist recognises, labels and structures the baby's/patient's motor, mental and emotional experiences ahead of the baby's capacity to do this himself. The baby/patient is able in time to do this for himself.

Self   The person's subjective sense of who he is, which has coherence over space and time. The parent's self-representation is changed with the birth of a child. We assume that the baby's sense of self is constructed through an experience of feeling known in the mind of his parent/s.

Therapeutic alliance   The establishment between therapist and patient/s of a commitment to work together in a clinical setting to address the difficulties the patient/s bring. In parent–infant psychotherapy a therapeutic alliance is built with the baby as well as with the parents.

The therapist as a 'new object'   The experience of the therapist as an attachment figure that can be different from habitual experiences with disappointing attachment figures in the past and present. This has the capacity to modify the parent/s' set expectations of relationships (templates), e.g. with her baby, partner and therapist.

Transference   The repetition in the present of significant aspects of a person's relationships with earlier attachment figures, usually but not exclusively, parental figures. In parent–infant psychotherapy the raw emotions of the parents' earliest relationships with *their* parents (the baby's grandparents) are often expressed in their relationship with their baby.

Transitional space   An aspect of the relationship between the baby and the mother wherein the beginnings of separateness and differentiation between 'me' and 'not me' take place. It is a twilight area where playfulness and imagination probably originate.

Unconscious   The large area of experience that is not readily available to conscious thought. In cognitive terms it describes 'non-conscious' states; in psychoanalytic terms it describes thoughts and feelings deliberately rendered unconscious (dynamic unconscious) because of the anxiety potentially generated by conscious contemplation of these mental states. Much of the parent/s' feelings and phantasies about the baby are dynamically unconscious.

Unresolved trauma   Preoccupied states of mind which are unremitting in relation to overwhelming negative experiences, and which are likely to distort the way in which current situations are responded to. Parents who have experienced overwhelming trauma may unwittingly recreate a traumatic experience for the baby.

Angela Joyce and Tessa Baradon

The theory of parent–infant psychotherapy

Introduction

Angela Joyce

These chapters outline the conceptual and technical foundations of this model of parent–infant psychotherapy. It is a fundamentally psychoanalytic model, which stresses the centrality of unconscious processes in mental and relational life while also drawing on other traditions of thought about development[1]. The model adapts the technical aspects of the psychoanalytic setting to make it suitable for work with young infants and their parents together. It can be used in brief therapy and also in longer-term, more open-ended therapy.

All clinical practitioners draw on a range of pre-consciously held theories that underpin their practice and which may be to some degree in contradiction with each other. Although these theories are relatively unexamined in the minute-by-minute unfolding of the therapeutic work (Sandler, 1983), nevertheless they affect the way the clinician relates to and thinks about the work with the patient. Elucidating the theories that we hold in the Parent–Infant Project has revealed a slant towards psychoanalytic object relations theory. Particularly useful are the ideas of the paediatrician and psychoanalyst D.W. Winnicott, where the adaptation of the 'good enough' mother to her infant is at the root of healthy development. We link this up with the research prompted by John Bowlby's theory of attachment, which has so enriched our understanding of the interpersonal processes central to the development of the child. Similarly, the explosion since the 1970s of developmental research into early relational capacities of the infant, itself much influenced by psychoanalytic ideas and in turn influencing it, has found its way into our pre-consciously held theories. Lastly, the much more recent work from the 'decade of the brain' (the 1990s) has given us 'hard

---

1 Pioneers of psychoanalytically informed psychotherapy with infants and their parents include Selma Fraiberg and Alicia Leiberman in the United States, and Bertrand Cramer in Switzerland. For current writing in the UK on this subject, see Daws, Hopkins, Aquarone and Barrows, amongst others. There are references at the end of the book should you wish to read some of their contributions.

science' evidence for our clinical findings regarding the role that early life plays in the developmental outcomes of children.

Putting such diverse theories together inevitably reveals contradictions and gaps. We follow Anna Freud's suggestion of roaming between traditions and using each as convenient. Therefore, what we offer here is our own synthesis. Some of the concepts we use are broadly defined and, to some degree, adapted to fit what has emerged in the clinical work. Indeed, the ideas that are outlined in these chapters are clinically determined.

This section also describes the adaptations of the psychoanalytic setting to create a therapeutic milieu in which to address the early relational disorders that constitute the focus of parent–infant psychotherapy. They reflect the rawness of the emotions to which everyone involved in the work, therapists as well as families, is exposed. The therapeutic setting is considered in different ways: primarily the setting is embodied in the person of the therapist and her personal qualities, sustained by sound training and ongoing support from the team. This personal setting is reflected in the reliability of the physical arrangements of the room and the timing of sessions. The clinical problems that are dealt with are further elaborated in a consideration of how the therapist assesses risk in the parent–infant relationship. The thread that runs through all these issues is the therapist's thinking as she considers her understanding of the problems presented, and how they should be responded to within the treatment frameworks available. Finally the key components of the therapeutic intervention are outlined.

These chapters are best read together as a unit. They describe the why, how and when of the therapy in principle, and are a preparation for the process chapters that follow.

Chapter 1

The parent–infant relationship and infant mental health

Angela Joyce

OVERVIEW

Why intervene in the parent–infant relationship?

Development, and therefore mental health and disturbance, takes place within the context of the care-giving relationships children have with their parents. Early care has a decisive, lifelong influence on how children learn, form relationships, experience and regulate their emotions and their behaviour (Belsky, 2001; Melhuish 2004). The majority of parents, the 'ordinary devoted mothers' (Winnicott, 1949) and fathers, provide their children with a loving, safe home. 'Good enough' parents protect and comfort their babies, play with, praise and enjoy them. They also sometimes 'get it wrong' but try to rectify this in relation to the baby. Their babies respond, initiate, interact, explore and show pleasure. However, some parents find it very difficult to provide their children with conditions for this rounded development. In more extreme circumstances of hostile, neglectful environments, babies fail to thrive and their normal development is severely compromised or interrupted.

There is mounting evidence for the severe long-term effects of disturbed early relationships and those characterised by neglect and abuse (Fonagy et al., 1994; Glaser, 2000; Lyons-Ruth & Block, 1996). Recent neuroscientific research has shown that brain development is affected as neuronal pathways 'fire' in response to the baby's experiences of being cared for. For instance, babies and young children who are repeatedly exposed to violence and other trauma, such that they feel severe and unmitigated distress over sustained periods, tend to become chronically anxious. This results from emotional experiences being 'hard wired' into the developing brain so that states of distress become characteristic features of the person's disposition or ways of being (Perry et al., 1995).

Where the infant is at risk, early intervention can prevent later disturbance. Once a child's development has been derailed, it is important to intervene before maladaptive patterns of relating become set, because later intervention can only modify an already existing situation. Thus, early intervention will lead to more adaptive development and less disturbance in the first place (Balbernie, unpublished data).

KEY CONCEPTS AND COMPONENTS OF EARLY DEVELOPMENT

Attachment

Attachment is the unique and powerful relationship that develops between an infant and caregiver during the child's first year of life (Bowlby, 1969, 1973; Carlson & Sroufe, 1995). It is the outcome of the response of the parent to the absolute dependency of the infant at the beginning, and of the baby's propensity to relate. The history and quality of that relationship influences all aspects of development. A positive attachment is essential to establishing the child's sense of safety and security, and influences his fundamental modes of regulating thoughts and feelings, the quality of his relationships, his self-esteem, and his capacity to explore the world productively and autonomously. The child's earliest relationships with his primary objects also influence his eventual ability to take on parenting roles in the future (Carlson & Sroufe, 1995).

Dependency

Babies are absolutely dependent on their parent/s at the beginning of life. This dependency is not just for physical care, without which they would die, but also for the emotional care and relating that implements and then helps sustain mental and psychic development. On the basis of his emotional, social and physical needs being adequately met in this state of absolute dependency, the baby moves to a state of relative dependence and eventually he becomes relatively independent and self-reliant in the context of predominantly loving and reliable family relationships (Winnicott, 1945). Thus the helpless neonate becomes the baby who can signal his desires and goes on to become the junior toddler who, still needing his parent/s, explores the world beyond his mother's lap.

Relating

Babies come into the world primed for affective interactions with others. They are specifically receptive to feeling states in other people and sensitive to the emotional tone of interactions with the people who care for them. They are specifically motivated to respond and communicate with 'rhythms of interest and feeling displayed by other humans' (Trevarthan & Aitken, 2001).

After the first few weeks, during which the baby and parents are getting used to each other, infants simply want to relate to the other and in turn to be related to. This can be increasingly observed as the sleepy baby of the first weeks gives way to a more wakeful one. At this time the parent's emotionally expressive face is the most powerful stimulus for the baby and he tracks it, searching out connection. Mutual gazing soon includes smiling and cooing, with signs of turn taking. The baby is able to initiate a particular sequence of interaction, or bring it to an end through averting his gaze or becoming quiet. Mothers and fathers naturally adjust their voices to a higher pitch with a rhythm at approximately adagio (walking pace in music) termed 'motherese' (Trevarthan & Aitken, 2001). They actively seek and engage in 'proto-conversation' (Trevarthan et al., 1979), the form of discourse with babies (cooing, talking, gesturing) that engages attention, communicates feelings and facilitates social interaction and, ultimately, language acquisition. The quality of relating in these early weeks is intensely social, with the baby being deeply interested in the connection with the mother as an end in itself for the very pleasure it brings (Lyons-Ruth, 2004).

The baby responds preferentially to those nurturing him, as his perceptual capacities enable him to recognise and distinguish his mother's voice, smell and face from birth (Karmiloff-Smith, 1995). By the middle of the first year he demonstrates his preferences in the emotional quality of his relating: he will keep his most beaming smiles for his mother and father and siblings if they have established positively hued interactions with him.

During the second half of the first year of life, the baby will actively use his primary caregivers to guide his decisions about what feels safe, e.g. by looking at his mother's emotional expression in order to decide if a new person is safe to interact with (Klinnert et al., 1983, 1986). This 'joint attention' (Bretherton, 1992) and 'emotional referencing' are indicative of the baby's coming to sense, in a very basic way, that the mother (and others) has a mind with mental contents such as feelings and intentions, which are important and of use. The corollary of this is that the infant begins to realise that he, likewise, has a mind (Mayes & Cohen, 1996).

The dyad and the triad

Although in Western cultures it is likely that the young baby is cared for primarily by his mother, their dyadic relationship takes place within the context of a more complex three-person relationship, which includes the father. The triad of mother, father and baby is recognised as being there right from the beginning of life (Green, 1986), and fathers can and do have a direct relationship with their infants from early on. Yet the 'place' of the father is understood to be not just a literal relationship (with a father present), but includes the meaning of the place of that father even if he is absent from the family. The representation of the 'father' in the mother's mind, and the 'mother' in the father's mind, are crucial factors in the way the baby incorporates and functions in a relational space that includes the triad 'mother', 'father' and 'self' (Trowell & Etchegoyen, 2002; Von Klitzing et al., 1999).

And yet, developmentally, it seems that the baby relates initially in a dyad, within the triangle or triad of mother, father and baby. It is a developmental shift for the baby to relate in a threesome with both his parents. The baby is then faced with the parental couple, either as a 'concrete' entity in his family, or as an idea embodied in the very fact of his conception and birth. The Oedipal situation, involving the central dyad of parental couple and the couple of mother and baby, constitutes a tension in the family that has to be worked through by all concerned. In some families the parental couple is replaced by the mother–infant couple; if this becomes a permanent feature of the family structure it compromises the developmental environment (see Chapter 11).

Earliest anxieties and primitive defences

A baby is extremely vulnerable in his state of absolute dependency . The input from those who care for him is crucial in protecting the baby from harm that may threaten him from the outside, and from anxieties that emerge internally when the protective parental environment fails. Failure, or not good enough caregiving (see below), exposes the baby to states of overwhelming helplessness. These have been described as experiences of 'falling forever', 'unthinkable anxiety' and 'annihilation anxiety' (Bion, 1962; Winnicott, 1962). These earliest anxieties, which occur within the relationship with the primary caregivers, can be provoked by volatile parenting where the baby cannot anticipate what parental mood and behaviour he will be faced with at any moment. He may be frightened by certain mental states or behaviours in the parent, or be left too long in a state of distress. The situation is particularly complex if the baby is in the care of a parent who poses a threat to the baby, as in abuse and neglect. In circumstances of extreme anxiety the baby employs his most effective, but still developmentally primitive, defences in the bid to keep himself safe (Fraiberg et al., 1975). These defences can often be seen in action, as when a baby habitually averts his gaze from the parent's eyes, suggesting that to look into those eyes is very frightening. He may learn to inhibit his attachment needs and become a baby who demands little of his caregivers and develops a precocious capacity to soothe himself. The baby may express inconsolable distress and, when his cries do not bring the comfort and safety he needs, may become dissociated from his surroundings. Dissociation is expressed by the baby holding his body very stiffly or being in a frozen, unresponsive state, as though 'playing dead'. From this we may infer that the baby is struggling to get rid of states of mind that are intolerable and which are not being adequately attended to by a responsive, reflective mother or other person who is able to console and render these states endurable.

Emotional regulation

Babies experience a range of states of arousal. Without the contingent presence of the parent who can accurately perceive and respond to his emotional states, the baby will experience his emotions as overwhelming and disrupting of his developing sense of self. Regulation of emotional states is a fundamental ingredient of early development (Fonagy et al., 2002a; Schore, 1994).

The parent's function as a moderating, regulating other is linked to the capacity to mentalise – that is, to consider the baby as a person with a mind and with feelings, and to relate to the baby's behaviours as intentional attempts to communicate these feelings (see below). The parent/s remain the primary resource for helping the baby to regulate his states of emotional arousal, as his ongoing development will face him with situations in which this is constantly affected. Through repeated experiences of his parent/s as regulating others, the baby comes to feel varieties of emotions and levels of arousal without being overwhelmed.

The self

The infant's evolving sense of self, his subjective sense of who he is, is the central organising process in psychic development (Stern, 1985). The sense of self has its origins in this earliest phase of development. It develops in relation to another (or other) human person and is utterly dependent upon their interactions and the emotional hue of these interactions. The nature of this relating will lead to the child feeling loved and cared for, worthy of affection, able to manage his wishes and anxieties, effective and confident in himself; or its opposite.

The minutiae of interactions make up the baby's daily experience of his parent/s and family members. The baby increasingly may extend his relating to include these others and with this his sense of his self will grow in complexity. Dyadic, triadic, quadrangular relating require the infant to integrate different ways of being, which in turn promotes a more multi-faceted sense of self in relation to these others. However, where the baby is required to accommodate drastically different ways of being with others, for example a baby who has volatile parents or who perpetrate abuse against the baby, the task of integration may be impossible.

It is also important that the infant is cared for in ways that fit with his experience of himself, in order to form a core sense of himself that feels real. This will be the basis for experiencing his inner urges as part of himself rather than external, random and inexplicable (Winnicott, 1945) and contribute to him developing his own individual personality (Bollas, 1989).

The representational world

The social–emotional relatedness of the early environment is the milieu in which the baby's 'inner world' is constructed. The concept of the 'inner world' explains the way in which experiences of the self in relation to others in the external world are eventually 'represented' in the mind. Characteristic patterns of interaction between the baby and those who care for him form the basis for 'self and other (object) representations' (Beebe et al., 1997). These representations are pre-symbolic, emotionally laden and bodily based. They are in a constant state of revision and transformation as experience is accrued, and are gradually elaborated with wishes, fantasies, fears, to create the 'representational world' (Sandler & Sandler, 1998; Steele, 2003). The child's representations, which thus derive both from real experiences with his parents and from his own mental functioning, are active in the way he thinks, feels and acts in relation to others. Eventually these interactional expectations will be represented in the mind as non-conscious templates that organise the characteristic ways the child relates.

The attachment concept of 'internal working models' (Bowlby, 1969) – representations of the relationships that build up in infancy and young childhood – also recognises the enduring quality of internal representations and their tendency to repetition. This concept has proved very useful in research into intergenerational transmission of patterns of relating (Ainsworth et al., 1978; Fonagy et al., 1991a; Main et al., 1985).

The concept of procedural memory, taken from cognitive psychology, throws light on the representational world of psychoanalysis and internal working models of attachment theory. Procedural memory refers to the knowledge that is learned in 'how to do things' and can be extended to include how the self relates to others. It is a generalised representation of repeated experiences that are non-verbal, automatic and cannot be easily consciously recalled (Clyman, 1991). For example, a baby may come to feel that physical proximity to his mother is uncomfortable because he senses her anxiety. He may habitually avoid such closeness but feel easier about connecting from a distance. This characteristic way of being with his mother may become a significant feature of how this baby relates to other people, even in intimate relationships. Early experiences of the self in relation to others are embedded in the procedural memory as 'body memory'. Such memories can be triggered into action and repeated unconsciously in the way the person interacts with others later in life, for example they are enacted when the person becomes a parent with his or her own baby.

Transitional space

The shift the baby makes in the way he relates, from the very early close-ness with the mother to a more differentiated relating, is complex. The space opening up between the mother and baby in which the baby begins to experience 'me' and 'not me' is an important developmental step. In this space the capacity for play emerges, drawing on the baby's innate creative potential and on the contribution the mother makes in allowing her baby to move away from her (Winnicott, 1971a). This process contributes to the baby's developing ability to regulate intimacy and separation in relation-ships and also to his emerging sense of self. The mother's ability to tolerate – without intrusion or retaliation – the baby's spontaneous drive to be himself, including all his passions, love, hate, aggression and destructive-ness, is fundamental to his achievement of this developmental step.

Separation—individuation

As the baby becomes adept at moving around, discovering the world out-side the orbit of close protective relationships, his progressive develop-mental push towards separation and individuation becomes more apparent (Mahler et al., 1975). The potentially stormy times of toddlerhood – often referred to as 'the terrible two's' – reflect his internal conflict about wanting to be a separate person growing up, and at the same time remain a baby. His growing ability to take possession of his own body – through his motor development and bowel and bladder control, are a source of both pleasure and conflict in the relationship with the parents. It is within these relationships that the toddler will experience the most profound passions of love and hate, as his emotional life becomes more complex. The strength of his feelings continues to be a source of anxiety for the young child and the threat of being overwhelmed is frequently present. The parents' capacities to tolerate their toddler's predicament continues to be of central importance in enabling the child to keep these feelings within manageable bounds, so that they can be a helpful contribution to his development rather than a possible source of it being derailed.

WHAT DO PARENTS BRING TO PARENTING?

Conception, pregnancy and birth

The immediate past of the conception and pregnancy influences the parents' relationship with this particular child – whether it was planned, positively anticipated, uncomplicated, full of difficulty, guilt or compromised by trauma. The birth may have been straightforward and satisfying or painful, dangerous and frightening. The social and cultural environment will be significant: for instance, whether one or other gender was desired, or perhaps the family moved from one geographical location to another and this pregnancy was imbued with hopes and wishes as well as fears consequent upon these changes. Difficult experiences in the pregnancy, birth and post-partum period can be exacerbated by the unconscious elaboration in the parents' minds of the meaning of these events.

The past

Past experiences give complex meaning to the present. Parents bring to parenting unconscious and sometimes conscious memories of having been a baby themselves, of what it felt like having been parented in the way they were, of having been a sibling or an only child, of their history. These past experiences can consist of a range from very good to traumatic. How individuals represent their experiences, the sense that is made of personal history and the narrative constructed around it, are important.

Attachment research has demonstrated that the parents' patterns of attachment – their habitual modes of relating – shape their mode of relating to the baby and predict the baby's attachment pattern with them (Fonagy et al., 1993). Many parents have a good internal model of attachment relationships on the basis of which they are able to provide a secure emotional environment for their baby. Others want to give their children a better start in life than they felt they had. A question then arises about the repetition of painful experiences from a parent's past in the relationship with the baby. Sometimes a parent, unconsciously and against all their conscious intentions, inflicts disturbing experiences similar to their own on the child of the next generation. Why and how does this happen? A central concept from the pioneer of psychoanalytic parent–infant psychotherapy, Selma Fraiberg, is that of 'ghosts in the nursery' (1975). The 'ghosts' that hover in the nursery are the painful remnants of the parents' past – the unresolved feelings associated with early relational disturbances and trauma in their childhood. The defences put in place against the overwhelming experiences are then challenged by their newborn's helpless dependency. Unable to feel for or identify with the pain of their baby, which so resonates with their own repressed pain and helplessness from the past, the parents protect themselves by unconsciously identifying with the perpetrator of the original trauma and inflict a similar experience on their child.

The parents' representational worlds

Parents bring to the parenting of each of their children specific unconscious and conscious expectations of how this new relationship is to be. For example, the birth order of this child will resonate with the meaning of the birth order of the parent in their family of origin, or that of a favoured or hated sibling; the sex of the child will have deeply personal meaning for each of the parents as well as cultural significance; the baby may be born in the context of a bereavement (early or recent) and there may be hope for repair of the lost relationship. The baby may unconsciously represent part of the parent's own self, a loved or a hated part (Brazelton & Cramer, 1990). This is the basis upon which projections and attributions of characteristics of the self or of a person from the past may interfere with the baby being seen as himself.

The position the baby has in his parents' minds is linked with the representational worlds of mother and father. These representations not only reflect the parents' 'real' experiences from the past, but are also highly coloured by feelings, wishes and fantasies that have accrued over the course of their development. Representations unconsciously guide expectations of relationships with others and have a tendency to repetition, the creation with others of what is familiar. In their couple relationship, the parents will be playing out versions of their internal world with each other (Cowan & Cowan, 1992). In some couples, these ways of relating will be flexible and adaptive; in others rigid and excessively controlling. In such situations parents are often repeating with their partners earlier patterns of abusive relationships; these then form part of the family situation into which the baby is born.

The wider social context

Parents and babies live within a wider familial and social network that contains the sources of their cultural, class and religious affiliations. The degree of integration or isolation from their culture and community is significant. Parents may have a sense of being part of a coherent and cohesive social environment and this will filter down to the baby and form part of his experience of growing up with this family. However, increasingly this experience of social cohesion is absent, as social and international mobility has increased. As well as being geographically dislocated, a parent may also have a history of discord and disruption in their family. Parents who do not have an adequate support network around them are more prone to phenomena such as postnatal depression (Brown & Harris, 1978).

WHAT DOES THE BABY BRING TO THE RELATIONSHIP WITH HIS PARENTS?

Healthy newborn babies evoke in their parents the most profound feelings. Babies' warm soft skin, smell, intense gaze, their unique openness and appetite for primordial connection, their attachment behaviours such as smiling, cooing and clinging, invite the parents to respond and engage with them. Responding to the baby's communications potentially gives the parents immense pleasure and satisfaction, thus promoting the ongoing maintenance of the appropriate environment for the unfolding of the infant's developmental programme.

The maturational base

The baby has an in-built developmental programme, which is the matura-tional base for his potential to unfold. This will meet the environmental provision, upon which it is dependent and by which it is shaped, beginning with the environment of the mother's womb. The unfolding of the matura-tional base, the developmental trajectory, in the first year is dramatic: from lying to sitting to crawling and perhaps walking, through the unfolding of emotional and psychological capacities such as 'protoconversation' to 'joint attention' and 'emotional referencing'. By the end of the first year the baby will have established the basic templates of his sense of self and other. The essential mental structures of expectations of relating will have coalesced into symbolic representations around which phantasy will be beginning to be woven. His emotional connections with his primary attachment figures will be more apparent and differentiated. Early brain development is fundamental to this maturational unfolding. At birth, the baby's brain is 25% of its adult weight, and by the time the baby is two years old it has increased to 75% of adult weight (Ashe & Aramakis, 1998). These early years constitute a 'critical period' (Spreen et al., 1984) as the connections between neuronal pathways are established in accordance with the stimu-lation received from the environment. This stimulation essentially involves all aspects of the relational connection – physical, cognitive and emotional – with the parental environment (Gerhardt, 2004; Schore, 2001).

Prenatal life and the birth

The baby's development begins prenatally and there is a continuum between pre- and postnatal life (Klaus & Klaus, 1998; Piontelli, 1992). The prenatal environment provides not only the nutritional lifeline to the baby, but may contribute to characteristics in the newborn such as greater sensitivity to sound and touch that require more adaptation on the part of the parents (Stechler & Halton, 1982; Glover & O'Connor, in press).

The birth itself has an impact on the baby, and can help set up a good or less good bonding process (Klaus et al., 1995). Whether it was easy, difficult, traumatic or premature, will be significant for the beginning of the infant's postnatal life. Complications at birth will put a strain on an already highly vulnerable situation. With the transition to postnatal life the baby relies on his own bodily functions, supported by his parents, to remain alive and adapt to the environment. This is part of the bodily base of his unfolding psychological development.

The baby's health

Whether the baby is healthy or not is of major significance. Prematurity and/or ill health or abnormality pose difficulties for baby and parents in their adaptations to each other and challenge the establishment of their attachment relationship. Physically vulnerable babies may not be well prepared for life outside the womb, and will not have the same immediate contact with the mother and father if medical interventions are needed. Moreover, they may be less responsive and alert than full-term healthy babies and may not be able to use the array of behaviours and cues normally available to contribute to the relationship with their caregivers. However, research on prematurity shows that, unless there are other adverse circumstances, the majority of parents are able to compensate for the limitations imposed by premature birth and the infants become securely attached to their mothers by 12–18 months (van Ijzendoorn et al., 1992). Research also suggests that babies that go on to be learning disabled, such as those with Down syndrome, form attachments more slowly but in line with their developmental trajectory. By the time they are developmentally functioning at the one-year-old level, secure Down syndrome infants will be using their caregivers as a safe base for exploration (Cicchetti & Beeghly, 1990).

The baby's temperament

The baby's temperament and match with his parents will impact upon their relationship. All babies require adaptation from their parents to their individual characteristics. For most parents that will be part of the exciting discovery of who their baby is. There may be elements of the baby's temperament and/or earliest experiences that predispose him to be difficult to soothe, or easily upset or startled. For some mothers it might feel too much of a challenge; with a postnatally depressed mother, a fractious oversensitive baby can contribute to her depression, compared to a baby who is more easily comforted (Murray, 1997; Murray et al., 1999). On the other hand, a parent who is herself securely attached and well supported may be able to adapt to and meet her baby's sensitivity effectively.

Developmental stage

The rapidity and complexity of change in the first eighteen months of life is enormous and the different stages of the baby may pose different challenges to his parents. For example, some parents feel easier with tiny babies but are anxious about the move to toddlerhood, or vice versa. Babies, sensitive to their parents' needs and expectations from them, may unconsciously adapt to fulfil these, such as some babies who are precocious in their development. The baby and his parents are able to rejoice in his age appropriate developmental achievements as long as the parents can respond with flexibility and adaptability. Where the infant's developmental stage evokes conflict in the parent, difficulties may arise.

COMPONENTS OF GOOD ENOUGH PARENTING

It is important to recognise that parenting is always an approximate process; there is no possibility of 'perfection'. Indeed, parents who seek to provide a seamless experience for their children find it either impossible or in fact detrimental to their ongoing development (Hopkins, 1996). Winnicott emphasised the 'good enough' nature of ordinary devoted parenting. 'Good enough' relates to the parents' capacity to tolerate the infantile state of their baby, to identify with the baby sufficiently to imaginatively understand their needs, to see their baby as a human person with feelings and intentions and to possess reflective functioning in relation to the baby. 'Good enough' parents respond contingently to their baby's communications so that he experiences a sense of being understood and contained. By this we mean that the baby feels that his physical and mental states have been responded to in such a way as to make him feel safe[1].

Primary maternal preoccupation

As pregnancy advances, the mother to be – and often the father – becomes highly sensitive to and preoccupied with the bodily and psychic experience of the baby growing in the uterus (Winnicott, 1956). This heightened sensitivity lasts in its most acute form into the first months after the baby's birth. It relies on the mother's capacity to identify positively with her baby and enables her to adapt to the baby's absolute dependency in the first weeks and months of life. The mother who is in this state of 'primary maternal preoccupation' is much more likely to be in tune with her baby's various states of feeling, including his neediness and potentially profound anxieties if his needs are not met in a timely way. Through this largely unconscious process she will gradually be able to intuit the different meanings of her baby's communications and adapt herself to them. Her contingent responses then enable the baby to feel that his states of being are recognised.

1 We use this term loosely, not in the very specific way that Bion used it in relation to processes of projective identification from the baby at the beginning of life.

A mentalising stance

The capacity for a mentalising stance refers to an overarching position of the parents in which they consider the baby as a person with a mind and feelings, and see their baby's behaviours as attempts to communicate these feelings. The mother receives the baby's inchoate communications and in her own mind makes them meaningful. She registers them as intentional and intensely personal communications to her. She weaves 'stories', unconsciously and consciously, about what is going on for her baby and for herself in relation to him and between them. This can be described as a state of 'maternal reverie' (Bion, 1967). These processes are reflected in her ordinary care of the baby as she tends him in his dependency upon her, feeding, holding, handling and playing with him (Winnicott, 1960). Parents who are able to understand their unfolding relationship with their infant in terms of feelings, beliefs and intentions, that is in terms of the mental states that underpin behaviour, are more likely to respond to their infant as an experiencing, feeling, intending person (Fonagy et al., 1991b, 1997). The parents' 'reflective function' or 'mentalising stance', expressed in the way they reflect upon their own and their baby's inner experience, is linked to secure attachment in their infants, even in adverse conditions (Fonagy et al., 1991b).

Mirroring and attunement

In the interaction between the baby and mother, the baby needs to feel that her responses to him fit what he feels in himself. The mother's ability to 'mirror' (Winnicott, 1971b) the baby's emotional experience enables him to find a faithful reflection of himself in her mind – the feeling of being seen and recognised in the eye/mind of the beholder. Through the experience of being mirrored the baby can learn to know about his own feelings. Attunement describes how the mother shares her baby's feeling states from a position of separateness. Through experiencing the parent's attunement with his emotions, the infant learns that mental states can be shared. Thus mirroring and attunement are ways of conveying to the baby that his affective states have been recognised by the parent.

In both mirroring and attunement, the mother needs to distinguish sufficiently between her own mental states and his. For example, if she is flooded with anxiety and panics when the baby is upset, neither she nor the baby will know whose feelings are being registered. The mother marks her difference from the baby, for example by exaggerating her voice or widening her eyes, at the same time as communicating to the baby her registering of his state (Gergely & Watson, 1996). Thus the baby experiences a sense of being known as his upset is attended to, and ownership of the upset as his.

Scaffolding the baby's experience

The architectural metaphor of 'scaffolding' is used to evoke the ways that parents help the baby experience and tolerate a range of states of being. 'Scaffolding' includes recognising and containing, explaining, supporting and extending the baby's motor, mental and emotional experiences (Tronick, 1998). This allows the baby to have emotional states that do not become overwhelming or severely inhibiting. It may be particularly challenging for some parents when it comes to scaffolding anger and frustration in the baby. A parent who, for example, is frightened of angry feelings may find their baby's anger intolerable, and may behave in ways which lead to the baby being frightened to show anger. Another parent may be able to empathise with the baby's expressions of rage, thus enabling their baby to experience their own spontaneous responses in the context of the parents' toleration. This kind of scaffolding leads to a more complex level of brain and mind organisation where a broad range of experiences can be sustained and elaborated, and incorporated into the baby's sense of self.

Interactive repair

The capacity to tolerate disruptions and to repair them is central in relationships. The mutual synchronicity of the parent–infant interaction is subject to ebbs and flows, disruptions and repairs. In contrast to what might be expected, good enough mother–infant pairs frequently miss each other in their quest to connect. Approximately half of attempted communications between ordinary mother–infant pairs result in mismatch (Tronick & Cohn, 1989). What is important is that these misaligned interactions are repaired quickly and satisfactorily through the minute-to-minute adjustments parent and baby make to each other. The repair of an interactive mismatch conveys to the baby a sense of his efficacy as partner in the interactions, a belief in the reliability of his parent, a pleasure in the attunement achieved (Beebe, 2004). For example: a baby becomes upset as his nappy is changed. His mother efficiently cleans and oils him, but does not closely attend to his upset and his cries become very loud. Mother then realises that she has not attended to the upset and holds him, softly speaking to him. His cries stop, and they gaze at each other intensely. His body moulds into mother's embrace, conveying much needed emotional anchorage.

Tolerating mixed feelings towards the baby

Parents also need to be able to tolerate the inevitable mixed feelings that go with being a parent. This includes the times when their emotional response to the baby's neediness and dependency might be one of hatred, as well as the profound feelings of tenderness and love that are evoked. When these ambivalent feelings of love and hate can be borne and kept within tolerable limits, they are less likely to be acted upon with consequent damage to the emotional connection between the parent/s and the baby (Winnicott, 1947). If the hostile feelings are sensed as being too dangerous, they may be rendered unconscious where they will remain active, but outside the possibility of conscious modification. Further, in tolerating this broad range of feeling towards their baby, the parent is more able to tolerate the range and intensity of feelings in the baby.

Promoting separateness

While parents need to be able to meet the baby's total needs in the earliest period, with development and as his innate capacities for agency and intentionality are supported, this changes. Paradoxically the parent/s become able to 'fail', that is not to meet their baby's needs so promptly (Winnicott, 1988). He becomes able to wait, perhaps now using his emerging memory traces and expectations to evoke in his imagination what he desires, to begin in his own mind the uniquely human capacity for making meaning out of experience (Bion, 1962; Freud, 1920). It could be said that 'mind' emerges in the gap between good enough experiences of connection. These processes slowly open up the beginning of separateness and relative dependence (Mahler et al., 1975; Stern, 1985; Winnicott, 1988) as well as promoting the baby's use of his developing mental capacities to think and imagine. Inevitably this will involve the baby having to bear more frustration as both parent and baby adapt to this expansion of their relating. The parents' ability to adjust to their baby's development in this area also depends on being able to bear their baby's potential rage in the face of frustration.

WHAT COMPROMISES GOOD ENOUGH PARENTING?

Parents who are not able to make space in their minds to become 'preoccupied' with their baby are often not able to adapt adequately to their particular early needs and to engage in the subtle emotionally charged relationship with their baby. It limits the parents' ability to intuit and imagine their baby's inner experience, to respond from a place of 'reverie' (see p. 17) in their own minds, and restricts their capacity to relate to their baby as an experiencing feeling person requiring response (Fonagy et al., 1991b; Hughes & McGauley, 1997).

The components that underpin good enough parenting are largely unconscious and are subject to being undermined by repressed or split off aspects of the parent/s' feeling that cannot be consciously tolerated. Difficulties that parents have in parenting their children stem from impingements from unresolved conflicts from their own past or from the present. In situations where there is significant interference with the parenting function it is often the case that these parents' thoughts and feelings are infused with anxiety, guilt, grief and lack of confidence. When called upon to comfort and console, or play with or set limits for their children, they inevitably rely upon habitual expectations formed long ago. They may also be in current relationships with partners where these early relational traumas are re-enacted, as in situations of domestic violence, or perhaps caught up in political situations of war and dislocation. Parents may be suffering from mental illness, or states of mind that interfere with their parenting capacities. Individual children need their parents to adapt to their own specific personalities, and sometimes the expectations laid down from the past and other issues alive in the present are at odds with the baby's needs being met.

Unresolved issues from the past or present

Parents may have unresolved issues around fundamental aspects of babyhood, such as dependency and helplessness, which makes them dread ordinary infantile states and makes it very difficult to tolerate these states in their baby. 'Ghosts in the nursery' (see p. 12) may infuse the parent's response to the infant. It might mean the parent finds it difficult to keep the baby and his needs in mind such that the baby experiences the parent's fluctuating attentiveness as impingements. The parent/s may feel that the baby is demanding too much of them, that infantile states of neediness are devouring and evoke rage and aggression that is difficult to modulate. This may lead to the neglect of the baby's emotional needs for interaction, holding, comfort, play or to more active abusive responses. Alternatively, parents may express such unresolved issues by maintaining their infant's dependent states and subtly preventing their baby from moving. Either way the baby's experiences of dependency and neediness will be distorted and his development impaired. Precocious independence may follow where the child does not seek comfort or express neediness to the parent, or his ordinary developmental moves towards independence may be disrupted and he may fail to acquire competencies that reflect his potential for separateness.

Trauma and loss

Parents who have experienced trauma and loss may lack mental representation and integration of those events and be in a state of denial or dissociation or perseverative preoccupation. This affects their care of the baby because it interferes with the parents' capacity to be emotionally present to him. Moreover, the emotionally overwhelmed, grieving and frightened parent can be frightening for the baby (Lyons-Ruth & Jacobovitz, 1999; Main & Hesse, 1990). Developmental research shows that emotional disregulation in the parent is disregulating for the baby (Schore, 2001) and attachment research has shown that parents who are unresolved as regards past trauma or loss are likely to have infants who develop 'disorganised' attachments. These children fail to develop an organised way of responding to stressful situations and are frequently overwhelmed by unmodulated affect. This has a cascading effect upon their social emotional and cognitive development.

Mental illness

Parents may be suffering from a mental illness such as depression, psychosis or borderline personality disorder. The impact of parental mental illness on children is a very complex phenomenon, involving the nature of the diagnosis, co-morbidity, severity of illness and the child's exposure to unpredictable mental states in the parent. However, in varying degrees mental illness will interfere with the parent's capacity to be emotionally available to their baby, will lead to difficulty in regulating their own emotional states and scaffolding their baby's experience. In more extreme situations it will seriously impair or disrupt their care of the baby (Marks et al., 2002).

Emotional and behavioural unpredictability

Emotional unpredictability and unmodulated affect and behaviour in the parent engender lack of safety in the child. Parents who are sometimes loving but, unpredictably, at times hostile and frightening to their infant raise the child's anxiety and need for defence. Unpredictability includes situational volatility, such as domestic rows, and emotional lability such as uncontrolled rages in a parent. In such circumstances the parents' ordinary functions of protecting the infant and helping him regulate his affective states will be absent – at the same time as the infant is in a state of fearful arousal. In the face of these experiences, the baby will be in states of extreme emotion that will feel overwhelming and require defensive activity for self-protection (see p. 8).

Unhelpful ways of being with the baby

The parent/s may be unable to make the important shifts in adaptation that promote separateness and individuation in the baby. They may be unable to give their developing infant experiences that are necessary to learn to tolerate and deal with frustration, limit setting, and boundary creations. The parent/s may pre-empt the baby's own capacity for agency and intentionality, always 'knowing' what he wants and preventing him from discovering for himself so that he can truly own his impulses (Bollas, 1987). Alternatively, the parent may subject the baby to too much frustration, which also interferes with his developing capacities. The baby is then subjected to overwhelming affect from within that cannot be adequately regulated.

The parent/s may be overly intrusive, invading the baby's bodily or mental space, and unaware of the anxiety this creates for their baby (Schore, 2001). For example a parent may have been interacting with the baby having a 'proto-conversation', and the baby turns away. Anxious parent/s may either turn away themselves or pursue the baby in an intrusive way. This may escalate so that the baby becomes distressed, not being able to regulate the closeness and distance between himself and the parent (Beebe et al., 1997). Alternatively, the parent may avoid physical contact with the baby so that his needs for touch and holding are not adequately met. In these customary ways of being with their baby the parent/s may contribute to his experiencing escalating states of anxiety and negative emotional arousal.

THE OUTCOME OF GOOD ENOUGH EXPERIENCES FOR BABIES' DEVELOPMENT

> In our clinical experience parenting that is good enough is associated with security of attachment and good social, emotional and cognitive developmental outcomes.
>
> (Fonagy et al., 2002b)

Parents who are predictable and contingent in their interaction with their baby provide him with a sense of:

- safety and an expectation of help and comfort when he needs it
- his dependency needs being recognised and met
- security and creativity in exploring and playing
- being able to begin the process of separation.

Parents who scaffold their baby's emotions and provide regulated pleasurable stimulation enable him to develop:

- a relatively stable coherent sense of self
- a sense of ownership of his body, his feelings and experience
- an expectation of pleasure in himself, his body and his relating to others

- a capacity to experience a wide range of emotions without being over-whelmed, encompassing pleasure, affection, anger, rage, desire.

Parents who allow graduated frustrations and are able to repair disruptions that occur within their relationship with the baby, enable him to develop:

- a sense of evolving difference and separation so that boundaries of the self and other can be established
- a sense of hope that connections can be re-established when broken
- a sense that frustration is bearable and will be productive
- a sense of awareness of and concern for those taking care of him, the basis of empathy.

THE OUTCOME OF NOT GOOD ENOUGH EXPERIENCES FOR BABIES' DEVELOPMENT

Parenting that is not sensitive to and contingent with infants' needs is associated with insecure patterns of attachment and poor developmental outcomes (Goldberg, 1997, 2000; Lyons-Ruth, 1996; van Ijzendoorn & Bakermans-Kranenburg, 1996). In our clinical experience, babies who have not had good enough parenting experiences respond in a variety of ways, and there will be a wide variation of degree in the following characteristics.

Babies with parents who are unpredictable and not contingent in their interactions with him:

- do not feel safe and do not develop a sense that help and comfort can be relied upon when needed
- may be excessively fractious and difficult to soothe
- are unable to explore and play
- may become vigilant out of anxiety
- may be withdrawn and show intermittent or pervasive patterns of disconnecting from the parents
- in extreme situations may go into dissociative states.

Babies of parents who do not scaffold their emotions and provide regulated pleasurable stimulation:

- may frequently be disregulated
- will be prey to anxiety that feels overwhelming
- may develop inflexible and rigid ways of being in order to deal with the threat of being overwhelmed
- may show little pleasure in themselves or their relationships

- may habitually resort to self-soothing
- may develop an unstable sense of self that does not feel real
- may habitually interact with negative emotion, or harm themselves to indicate need.

A baby whose parents have unhelpful ways of being such that they do not regulate frustrations, are intrusive and are unable to repair disruptions that occur within their relationship:

- will be unable to bear frustration
- may find it very difficult to 'know' his own mind
- will feel unable to regulate closeness and distance
- may have a confused sense of boundaries around his sense of self
- will be prone to feel hopeless that connections can be adequately re-established after a breach.

Chapter 2

The theory of psychoanalytic parent–infant psychotherapy

Tessa Baradon and Angela Joyce

THE AIMS OF PARENT–INFANT PSYCHOTHERAPY

Parent–infant psychotherapy is a therapeutic modality that works to promote the parent–infant relationship in order to facilitate infant development. 'Infancy' is defined as birth to two years of age and 'parent' refers to either or both mother and father of the child or the primary caretaker and attachment figure. The therapy addresses a range of conscious and unconscious factors that shape the individual parent's and infant's specific modes of 'being' with each other.

The practice of parent–infant psychotherapy needs to take account of differences in culture, religion and class (Berg, 2002) as they affect child rearing and family interactional patterns, and at the same time maintain a view of core infant developmental needs.

The parent–infant relationship can be addressed directly or via each of the participants. Thus some of the aims of the therapy focus more on enhancing parental functioning in relation to the infant and some focus more on promoting the infant's developmental moves.

Aims that focus more on the parent

To enable parents to reflect upon states of mind in themselves, in their infant and in the relationship between them. The capacity to be thoughtfully aware of different states of mind and how they are manifested in a variety of behaviours and actions within the parent–infant relationship has a crucial bearing on how parents will respond to their baby. In turn, this will influence to what extent the baby will feel that his inner states are recognised and attuned to, which is linked to the baby's evolving sense of self (see Chapter 1). The therapist will attend to the states of mind the parents and infant bring to, or which develop within, the session, always keeping in mind how these interact and their impact upon the baby. Her interventions will be focused on extending the capacity of the parents to recognise and think about the states of mind thus engendered, and respond to their baby in a more emotionally contingent way.

To enable parents to regulate their own and their infant's emotional states. Emotional regulation is a crucial component of development and for much of infancy and early childhood babies are dependent upon their parents to scaffold this unfolding capacity. The provision of modulated stimulation, of comfort and the repair of disruptions within the parent–infant interactions are significant ways parents enable their baby to keep their emotional states within manageable bounds. The therapist will attend to disregulated states in the infant when the parent is unable to respond, and to such states in the parent which will affect both the baby directly and the parents' capacities to help their infant regulate his emotional states.

To enable parents to recognise their infant as a dependent person with a developing mind. This involves helping parents differentiate their own mental states from those of their baby and to take into account their infant's age-appropriate emotional, cognitive and motor capacities. This may involve helping parents to observe their baby in a different way, to tolerate their extreme dependency in the earliest months and eventually to enable the baby to initiate and implement the process of separation–individuation.

To interrupt the repetition of negative intergenerational patterns of relating and diminish traumatic impact on the baby. Rigid, non-adaptive repetitions of patterns of relating across the generations interfere with the parents' relating to their baby as a person in his own right. The precedents for what is observable in the here and now, for instance in the history of the parents' own infancy and childhood and also the earlier history with this baby (see Chapter 1), may be a focus of the therapeutic discourse, although this will be thought about in relation to the evolving parent–infant relationship.

To facilitate the couple's parenting of the baby. The infant's development is supported by coupled, collaborative parenting between mother and father. Difficulties involving severe conflict, and even violence between the parental couple, will negatively impact on their care of their baby. Often, the pregnancy or birth of a baby highlights more hidden fractures in the relationship and this might be reflected in difficulties in cooperating in the care of their baby. The therapist might focus on this in the treatment in the context of the interactions in the room between the family members.

Aims that are more focused on the infant

To promote positive attachments behaviours between the baby and his parents. Babies' innate capacities for attachment can be inhibited in the face of lack of contingent response from his caretakers, and/or affected by particular vulnerabilities of the baby. Met by a withdrawn or intrusive parent, a baby may himself withdraw or give up attempts to become engaged. The therapist's interventions will aim to stimulate the infant's interest in his parents and to reinforce both his attachment behaviours and his parent's contingent responsiveness.

To promote the baby's coherent sense of self. The baby's sense of self develops in and through interactions with others. As a consequence of the contingent responses of the adult, the infant learns to register his different mental states so that they are felt to be a part of him rather than random and alien. The therapist will help the baby and his parents to recognise, acknowledge and scaffold his emotional states to promote the development of a coherent sense of self.

To facilitate the infant's age-appropriate dependency and moves towards separation and individuation. The baby's absolute dependency at the beginning of life has to give way to a more relative dependency on his parents so that gradually the child can become more psychologically separate and his individuated sense of himself established. The therapist addresses the difficulties that can inhibit both the experience of dependency upon reliable adults and the age-appropriate separateness that emerges out of dependency. This will include recognising the development of maladaptive defences in the baby and promoting ways of being that are more conducive to the establishment of relative independence as childhood proceeds.

To assess and address risk to the baby's safety and development and where necessary act towards the provision of alternative care for the baby. This is an ongoing aspect of parent–infant psychotherapy because of the vulnerability of babies and the profound effect of their early experiences upon their future development. Such assessment is best conducted in the context of the relationship the therapist builds up with the family, and involves sensitive discussion with the parents about these concerns. Involvement of the statutory agencies may be required in more extreme circumstances when the needs of the baby and parent do not mesh and additional support or action to facilitate the baby's safety (see Chapter 3).

Theory of the therapeutic process in parent–infant psychotherapy

Parent–infant psychotherapy provides a safe relational and physical space to explore and facilitate the emerging meaning of the parent–infant interactions, the building blocks of their relationship.

The patient is the relationship between the parents and their infant and therefore both parents and the infant will be present in the sessions. When this is not possible, the absent parent is still 'present in their absence' and from time to time this 'presence in absence' will be a focus of the therapeutic endeavour.

The therapist will work towards all the participants in the room becoming engaged in the therapeutic process. This will be through a variety of measures

– such as actions, play and verbalisation – which seek to elucidate the underlying meanings of the interactions that are taking place in the session. The focus can move from the parents to the baby and back again, and to the interaction between them, depending upon where the focus of the affective experience is at any given moment. This will involve being sensitive to and working with possible conflicting tensions between the parents' and the baby's interests as the session moves along.

The therapist seeks to create a facilitating environment for the therapy to take place. A facilitating environment is one in which the family can feel safe enough to address the painful difficulties that have brought them into treatment. Components of such a setting are the regularity and frequency of the sessions, their location and meeting the same therapist. Often when such reliability has not been part of the parents' own early experiences, they find it difficult to provide this for their baby. Thus the reliability of the setting is provided also as a source of identification for the parents and baby. Disruptions in the frame, such as holiday breaks and missed sessions, are thought about and understood in the context of the unfolding therapeutic relationship.

Establishing a working alliance as the basis for the therapeutic work. The therapist and family reach a basic agreement as to the nature of the work being undertaken. This agreement may involve a measure of exploration with the parent/s; without it there is the probability of the therapeutic work failing because the different parties are at cross-purposes with each other. This 'alliance' is a significant component in sustaining the therapeutic work during phases of the treatment that might be particularly difficult or painful for the parents.

Everything that takes place in the room is taken as an intentional communication and therefore is seen as a legitimate focus of enquiry in the therapy. This intentionality is not necessarily consciously determined, and each communication can be expressed in any modality. Indeed, as processes in infancy are so profoundly non-verbal, much of the significant communications will be conveyed in body language, gesture and the language of emotions. Particularly significant moments in a session that offer openings for change take place in any of these modalities.

The interactions between the parents and their baby represent their unfolding relationship, and include enactments of past situations. The therapist will be mindful of those components of the relationship that facilitate progressive development in the infant, and those that might be repetitions of the past or current situations that will militate against this. In attending to these as they unfold in the session, the therapeutic focus can be brought to bear upon them and understanding and repair made possible in an emotionally immediate way.

Working with disruptions and repairs in the ongoing therapeutic relationship. The therapist's attention to the minutiae of the interactions helps her to focus on disruptions in the relationship between a parent and infant, as well as sometimes analogous disruptions in the relationship with the therapist. These, and the way that they are repaired, are significant elements of parent–infant interaction. Addressing these transactions as they occur in the therapeutic discourse brings them into focus so that a better way can be found for repair to take place.

Working directly with the baby to promote the baby's efficacy in engaging parental care. Having the baby present in the therapy enables the therapist not only to observe and intervene in the interactive processes between baby and parents, but also to have a direct therapeutic input with the baby himself. Through the therapist's interventions with the baby, she can represent the baby's experience of himself and the other and help to promote the baby's efficacy in engaging his parents' care. Sometimes the therapist offers herself as an object to the baby for stimulation and/or emotional regulation if this is not within the parent's capacity at that time in the session, in the context of re-establishing that primary relationship.

Working with the positive and negative transference matrix, predominantly in the parent–infant relationship. The range of feelings and fantasies as represented in the mind, press to be made real in interactions with other people in the external world. The residues of the earliest relationships with their own parents can be apparent in the parents' relationship with the therapist but are most often expressed in their relationship with their baby. These processes will be apparent as the therapeutic work unfolds and will be the focus of the therapist's interventions, judiciously interpreting the transference elements in that relationship as it is apparent between parent and baby in relation to herself.

As with the transference, the therapist uses the counter-transference as an essential tool for attending to the unconscious transactions between the participants in the therapy. The feelings and thoughts evoked in the therapist by the experience of being with the patient are largely unconscious. However, the therapist attempts to reflect upon and use the range of responses evoked in the therapeutic situation to understand further the depth and complexity of the communications. The therapist must also be mindful of her own transferences to the situation she is dealing with, and the re-activation of problematic aspects of her own history that might interfere with her capacity to engage effectively with this work.

Provision of new object experience to each of the participants in the treatment. The therapeutic relationship encompasses the range of feelings and meanings, whether linked to the repetition of the past or the experience of a new relation in the present. The therapist responds to the parents and infant in ways that do not further the actualisation of the transference situation but which bring something new into the interaction. This provokes the patient also to respond in a new way, with a probable cascading effect in their relationship with the baby. As well as providing a different set of experiences that can be internalised, this process facilitates the ongoing negotiation of containment and disruption.

Attending to the emotional and phantasy aspects of behaviour and communications, including conscious and unconscious components. The interactions between parents and babies are taken to be the outward manifestation of layers of meaning and emotion that constitute the complex tapestry of their relationship. The therapist seeks to uncover these textures of feeling and fantasy with the parents and baby, especially where they are problematic and conflictual, and interfere with the good enough environment necessary for healthy development. This process of uncovering is the body of the therapeutic work and will probably form the bulk of the therapeutic discourse as the therapy moves along.

Working with defences and resistance as they emerge in the process. The range of defences used in the parents' relationship with their baby may be especially restricting as a consequence of the fear of hurting or damaging the baby in some way. Alternatively, the baby may be caught up in the parents' defences in a potentially malignant way, for instance if the baby is the recipient of distorting projections from the parent. Just as important is attending to pathological defences in the developing infant that may be observed and attended to in the here-and-now of the session.

Attending to the balance between containing and challenging in therapeutic technique. The effectiveness of a therapeutic treatment depends on the balance it provides between containment of anxiety and disruption of typical and pathological ways of being. For the parents to be able to take the risk of changing from compelling and detrimental ways of being with their baby, the therapist has to provide a measure of safety and repair. This is also a model for the repair of inevitable disruptions in relating between parents and baby.

Promoting reality testing within the parent—infant relationship. The therapy will promote the exploration of the distorting effects of fantasies, defences and transferences to the baby so as to enable the parents to be more aware of their infant as a person in his own right. The baby will thus have a better chance to develop a coherent sense of self without impingement from the parents.

Working with the therapist as a part of a 'geometrical structure'. The presence of the therapist with the parents and baby brings new complexity into their relatedness. The dyad of mother and baby may become a triad; the parental couple and baby becomes a quad; the therapist may symbolise another generation – such as the grandparents to this new family. For a time, the therapist may provide the 'other' in the dyad when the parent is unable to do this for the baby. These geometrical metaphors reflect the potential complexity of relatedness within the family structure, and the potential mental functioning of each individual within it. The therapist promotes the ability to relate in a group who are emotionally invested in each other, sponsoring attachment and commitment at the same time as differentiation and separateness.

Creating an understanding of cultural and religious influences. The therapeutic holding space involves a consideration of cultural and religious aspects of the family. These are an intrinsic part of the tapestry of relatedness between family members and have a profound effect upon their interaction and the meanings ascribed to these interactions. It is central to the respect towards an individual family that the therapist is open to these cultural differences, is prepared to enquire into them and explore them respectfully as she observes the family interaction.

Provision of guidance to parents where appropriate. Occasionally the therapist may find it necessary to provide guidance to the parents about their care of their baby, when they are not yet able to create solutions for the baby's well-being. This would take the form of exploring different alternative possibilities for action with the parents in the broader context of the exploration of these difficulties. Parent guidance may enhance the parents' working alliance with the therapist when they are feeling especially helpless.

Bringing the treatment to a planned ending, the significance of which is understood as far as possible. The ending of the therapeutic relationship with both parents and baby is a significant part of the work. As in many aspects of this work, endings provoke powerful feelings at a conscious and unconscious level and the elucidation of these is likely to reinforce the efficacy of other work done in the treatment. It also offers the opportunity to rework previous losses and provides a model for future separations and losses within the parent–child relationship.

Working with the network of other professionals linked with the family. The professional network provides a broader holding environment for the family and the therapeutic work to proceed. The therapist ensures that the family is involved in and knows about the links with the professional network and that issues of confidentiality are clear.

THE THERAPIST: TRAINING AND EXPERTISE

Who can practise psychoanalytic parent–infant psychotherapy?

The ties between infants and their parents are characterised by powerful primitive emotions on both sides. Working with a dyad/triad where emotions are raw, and may be passed back and forth, is psychically challenging to the therapist – in relation to the family and in what it may evoke from her personal history and current attachments.

In addition to an intense interest and pleasure in babyhood, early relationships and development, the potential parent–infant psychotherapist requires certain personal capacities in working with the mental states of infancy and parenthood. These include an ability to recognise and tolerate states of dependency, helplessness, rage, 'unthinkable anxiety' and a capacity to work with unconscious processes of defence against overwhelming affects and emerging phantasies. In part, the ability to hold such emotions is dependent on the therapist's ability to think about her own childhood and the accommodations she has made in relation to her own parents' 'failures'. This is important in preventing the therapist from being retaliatory towards the parents with whom she works.

Formal training and experience necessary for the practice of parent–infant psychotherapy would cover the following fields:

- psychoanalytic clinical practice
- infancy and early childhood development
- observation skills
- adult mental disturbance.

A personal experience of psychoanalytic psychotherapy is seen as a necessary condition for this work. It is assumed that this would contribute to the potential parent–infant psychotherapist's ability to understand the importance of early attachment relationships, the working of unconscious processes in relation to this, and to an understanding of the challenge of the therapeutic process to the patients.

Further professional skills include:

- good team-working skills
- the ability to assess and work with risk within the legal and organisational framework
- skills in assessing and working with complex relationships within the family.

The practice of parent–infant psychotherapy requires a structured programme of continuing professional development, which would include regular clinical supervision, learning events in the fields of infant development and psychopathology, and changing risk assessment procedures.

THE THERAPEUTIC STANCE

All clinical interventions are shaped by the over-arching therapeutic stance of the therapist. The therapist's attitude to her patients, and her observational and mentalising stance, introduce different 'ways of being' with each other to the parents' and baby's repertoire. The aim is to validate and make the parent's experience coherent and to acknowledge and respond to the baby's requirement for an attentive, reflective adult mind to meet his developmental and attachment needs.

Use of the psychoanalytic framework

The psychoanalytic model is the frame of reference for understanding experience, activity and development in the parent and infant, their relationship with each other and their relationship with the therapist. The therapist works concomitantly with what is observed in the room, that which is conscious to the parent, and with the hypothesised unconscious phantasies and defences that underpin the affects and behaviours. Transference and counter-transference also inform the therapist about emotions, anxieties, conflicts that are shaping the interactions observed but are unavailable as part of the parent's or infant's conscious mental experience because of their defensive manoeuvres.

It is a primary therapeutic assumption that the unconscious material is to be addressed because it shapes the pathology and, unless worked through, will continue to irrupt in forms and contexts beyond the parent's control. At the same time, the infant's internal world is constructed out of the real experiences with his parent (and other primary figures) and shaped, too, by desire, disappointment and emerging phantasies. While support of positive affect and pleasurable interactions is built into the therapeutic work, the bulk of interventions will address impingements of conflict, phantasy, negative affect and maladaptive defences.

Although the psychodynamic model of functioning is privileged, the therapist also uses other theoretical knowledge bases to understand the patients' material (see Introduction to this section) and inform her responses.

The underlying attitude of the therapist

The therapist's approach to the patient/s is crucially important. In her facial expressions, tone of voice, body cues as much as what she says, the therapist will be communicating her attitude to her patients. Interest, respect, empathy and lack of judgement are necessary to help the patient build up trust in her and their work together. Similarly, attention to the patient/s verbal and non-verbal communications, her attempts to understand and elucidate areas of obscurity, and her ability to reflect on the patients' and her own feelings before making an intervention, will model her therapeutic stance.

The role of observation

Observation, as a mental stance and as a technique, plays a central role. The therapist observes the back and forth of interactions that take place between parent/s and baby and herself. This includes the details and nuances of facial expressions, body tone, emotions and behaviours. With experience the therapist will become more adept at observing and recalling swathes of interaction; these inform and refine her understanding.

The mentalising stance of the therapist

A primary therapeutic activity is that of creating meaning. The infant is entirely dependent on the adult to structure his experience through meaning, and many parents come for therapy without having had this done for them in their childhood. In the absence of such scaffolding, feelings and behaviours are felt and perceived as random and disorganised, and where there is recognition of intentionality, and thus meaning, they are experienced as hostile. For example, a baby reaching to the mother's face may be seen as 'he can use his hands now' (concrete and devoid of meaning) or 'trying to hurt me' (hostile). The therapist's enquiring, reflective and explanatory stance conveys to the parent and to the infant a view that what they feel and think is important and valid and, in due course, as trust and safety become part of the patient's experience in relation to the therapist, that there may be other positions to be considered.

Maintaining the therapeutic stance

The therapeutic stance of the therapist may be greatly challenged, since emotions and behaviours in either the parent or the infant can provoke responses in the therapist that cut across her intended professional stance. The therapist is more likely to react outside of the therapeutic stance if she has become over-identified with the patients or their problem. In such case the therapist may experience unusually strong feelings, similar to those of her patient. There is also a danger of identifying with either mother or baby, and thereby being drawn into taking sides. Impatience with either baby or parent, or with both, a lack of empathy, apathy or withdrawal, are all feelings which should alert the therapist to examine the transference and counter-transference in order to locate the sources of these distortions in her relationship to her patients and work through them. Situations can also arise where the therapist feels, or is pushed to act precipitously, perhaps as a result of heightened emotional state in herself and/or because she has been 'prodded' into a particular course by the patient (Sandler, 1976). It is important that when the therapist feels 'swamped' by the patient or overwhelmed by her own responses, to the point where her capacity to reflect is affected, she takes 'time out' before intervening. This respite-as-mental-space is necessary for processing the situation. However, sometimes the therapist is aware of the breach only subsequent to its occurrence, and will need then to examine what has taken place and what needs working through with the patients. Consultation in all these circumstances is often appropriate.

WORKING ACROSS CULTURES

It is becoming increasingly common for the family and therapist to come from different cultural, racial or religious backgrounds. This raises the issue of feelings about difference, and phantasies and preconceptions about specific classes, skin colour, cultures and religions. Working with differences requires sensitivity on the part of the therapist to the family's, and her own, experiences and feelings about the other's race, culture. Differences need to be understood at a psychological level in terms of their personal meaning to each participant in the therapy. However, engaging in exchanges about difference and diversity can be intimidating to the therapist and family as it touches upon core self-representations and possible prejudices.

In the first instance, the therapist needs to acknowledge the family's own ideas and frames of reference. These would have been built up over a period of time and may play an essential part in how the parents' perceive the referral difficulties and the therapeutic process. The necessary frame of mind is one of 'respectful curiosity' and the therapist probes unclear statements rather than glossing over them as a given part of the presented culture. The therapist also needs to build up an understanding of how she, representing her class or culture, is perceived by the family and what attributions are being made to her. In situations where differences feature strongly, an important but more difficult aspect may lie in the therapist's capacity to distinguish between what may be cultural or religious and what belongs to personal pathology in the parents. Teasing-out a formulation may take time and will need revisiting as the therapy unfolds.

Mother referred herself and seven-months-old son because of his poor eating. The mother was of West African origin and had lived in the UK for several years. She was trying to wean her baby but he was not eating the food provided for him. In the session, the therapist observed that he backed away in fear when mother approached him with food. Mother told him sternly that he had to get used to eating this food.

In exploring this comment, the therapist learned that this food, pepper stew, was important to mother's culture. Baby had not taken to the peppery food, which mother saw as weakness in him and a rejection of her. The therapist acknowledged the cultural aspects of the food as an important part of mother's identity and her wish to instil this appreci-ation in her son. As the therapy progressed, however, additional information emerged which suggested that aspects of this mother's culture were being used to justify behaviour which overlooked the effect on her son. In describing her early experiences, mother spoke of her step-mother's harsh parenting, which she saw as instilling a steely resili-ence in her that had helped her to manage life in hostile environments.

In the example above, the therapist needed to understand the contributions of cultural and personal factors on the parenting of the baby. It was important to acknowledge the positive meaning of mother's cultural heritage that the sense of belonging the food bestowed. However, the stern attitude in insisting baby take the food seemed to stem from mother's own experiences of being parented, which had been adopted in an identification with the parent/aggressor. Mother was behaving with her son in a way that suggested she had not processed her childhood experiences. Her feelings as a child in response to the harsh parenting she received appeared to be 'forgotten' (repressed). Therefore she was not able to recognise her baby's upset and fear and was repeating her own childhood experiences with her infant. In this way, 'culture' was also used defensively, to mask intrapsychic difficulties that were being played out in the relationship with her baby, and that needed working through in the therapy. This is crucial in terms of unravelling the parent's difficulties from cultural identifications and intro-ducing new thinking about themselves and their baby. Being able to talk about these issues can also cement the mutual trust and respect that underpin the therapeutic alliance and the relationship with the therapist as a new object.

COMMON CLINICAL PROBLEMS

We distinguish between presenting problems, which is the initial language the family brings, and possible underlying unconscious and symbolic factors that organise the presenting symptomatology, and which are the basis for the therapeutic work.

Categories of problems at referral

The presenting problem is the problem that the family or referrer describe as the reason for seeking help. The way the problem is formulated by the parent/s is influenced by how urgent, upsetting and/or shaming they feel it to be. It may also be influenced by cultural mores.

Problems located with the baby. This category refers to problems that are directly attributed to the baby. Regulatory problems, e.g. in feeding, soothing or comforting, and problems in establishing a routine, as in sleeping for example, are common in the referral of very young babies as well as older babies and toddlers. Behavioural difficulties, tantrums and clinging characterise the referrals of toddlers.

Problems located with the parent. Referrals are made of families where problems relating to the parent's health and/or mental state are seen to potentially affect the baby. These include postnatal depression or other mental health problems, and situations in which the parent is intensely preoccupied with a loss and/or trauma. In addition, parents who experienced difficult relationships with their own parents or had problematic childhoods may be afraid of the impact of these on their parenting of their baby.

Problems in the relationship with the baby. This category refers to instances where the relationship with the baby has already run into trouble, for example a parent may report that she has not bonded with the baby or a health-care professional may be concerned about attitudes and behaviours towards the baby.

Relationship problems. The relationship between the parents may be the initial reason for referral, e.g. with questions about the impact of separation on the infant. In other instances, information about a troubled relationship may emerge in the course of the intake as an underpinning factor for the referral.

Psychodynamic factors underpinning the referral problem

There is usually a complex interplay of psychological anxieties, adaptations and defences underpinning any presenting problem. A state of emotional turbulence – disregulation – often characterises the parent and baby at the point of referral. The following is a list of central factors that are associated with attachment difficulties that may be considered:

Emotional disregulation in parents can often be associated with the following:

Unresolved trauma and/or loss which continue to overwhelm the parent and sap their caretaking and bonding capacities. These include referrals where the parent has recently lost his or her own parents or other significant attachment figures, or where the birth of the baby has rekindled an unresolved separation/bereavement from the past. Asylum seekers and political refugees often fall into this category, usually having abruptly lost their attachment network under traumatic circumstances.

Fear of mutual damage, where the parent carries strong destructive feelings towards the baby (conscious or unconscious) and experiences the baby as potentially harmful of them. Parents in this referral category find the boundaries between thought and action frighteningly fragile, and therefore need to constantly monitor the well-being of their baby. In a similar vein, projection of hostility onto the baby results in a perception of ordinary attachment behaviours in the baby, such as crying or reaching out, as dangerous to themselves. These parents are in a state of vigilant hyper-arousal much of the time.

Re-evocation of traumatic attachment experiences from their own child-hoods. Faced with their vulnerable, dependent infant, a parent's habitual defences against their own thwarted attachment needs may break down. Ordinary needs and behaviours in the baby, such as hunger and crying, may resonate with the parent's long-buried helplessness and pain and their repudiation of these states, resulting in emotional turmoil – anger, resentment, pain, guilt.

Conflict in the parental relationship is often an intensely destabilising situation in relation to bonding with the baby. Even where the parents actively try to protect the infant from exposure to the conflict, the baby is invariably affected through the parent's preoccupation with the relationship with their partner and feelings of sadness and anger. Moreover, the baby may become associated in the parent's mind with the partner, to the detriment of the parent's representation of his/her baby as individual and unique.

Infants may present as emotionally disregulated as a consequence of:

Fragility in the infant. This can be related to constitutional factors or, for example, to prematurity or a traumatic birth.

Disregulation of their parents. Parents who are in a state of turmoil communicate their high arousal to their babies. Touch, handling, facial expression, smell – the ordinary modes of contact and regulation – become the vehicles for transmission of the parent's disregulation. The baby then serves as a barometer for the parents' mental state as much as communicating about his/her own state of distress.

Intrusive parental projection. The parental projection impinges on the baby's ordinary experience of going along and acts as an alien intrusion into, and thereby disruption of, the baby's sense of self. Unable to achieve internal coherence, the infant may seem fractious, prickly and difficult to settle.

Whereas temporary states of emotional disregulation in the infant are to be expected given their state of immaturity, prolonged states of disregulation are indications of failure on the part of the adult to help the baby regain a state of emotional regulation through providing safety, comfort and interactive repair (see Chapter 1).

PSYCHODYNAMIC FORMULATIONS OF THE PROBLEM AND FOCUS OF INTERVENTION

The psychodynamic formulation is the therapist's hypotheses about the unconscious and conscious constituents of the parent–infant relationship and pathology, the task of the therapy and the interventions she may use. These working hypotheses are underpinned by knowledge, theory, experience, intuition, and may be skewed by the therapist's counter-response and blind spots. Moreover, not all aspects of the therapist's thinking will be consciously defined from the beginning. Some of her hypothesising may remain latent for some time, as she unconsciously processes the cues from the family, her observations and counter transference.

The psychodynamic formulation is inherently refined and redefined in the process of the therapy, thereby always carrying the status of a partial hypothesis. Another way of seeing it is to view the process of therapy as constantly producing psychodynamic formulations.

There are a number of temporally overlapping steps in the process of reaching a formulation. Any new referral will trigger in the therapist a network of implicit and explicit ideas, however full or sparse the information given in the referral. For example, the surname of the family can suggest racial and cultural origins. The date of birth will suggest the infant's level of dependency and how long-standing or recent the problems may be. The therapist brings her ideas, hypotheses and expectations to her first contact with the family and these are, in some measure, tested out in relation to the 'real' family. At this point, she may be surprised by the many assumptions she had not consciously registered. This can assist the therapist in differentiating what she brings of herself from any counter-transference evoked by the family material.

In the initial contact with the family the therapist's observing stance is primary. The communications from parent/s and infant are emotional, behavioural, physical and symbolic, and need to be taken in at all levels. The therapist, at the same time, will be observing how the family manages the complexity of feelings around seeking help; anxiety, shame, anger, hope and trust. Baby and parent/s will each, in their own way, show adaptive and defensive responses to her as stranger. The therapist will also be attentive to what she does not observe in family communications and interactions, such as the mother who does not smooth the way for her baby, or a baby who does not express caution to the therapist as an unfamiliar person. The absence of expectable affects and behaviours can indicate unconscious defensive manoeuvres that are contributing to the problem/s.

Some of what is observed may be processed in the first meetings, and used in building the therapeutic alliance and engaging the family in the therapeutic work. Anchored in her observations, the therapist and family will look at the networks of associations and meanings linked to the difficulties they have presented. The personal histories of the parents and intrusions from the past, and current psychic and relational functioning, have bearing on the meaning of the problem to the parent/s and the way the problem is woven into the family dynamics. The therapist also holds in mind a theoretical framework of 'good enough' functioning of the parent–

infant relationship and of infant development and the problems, presented and observed, are referenced to this framework.

However, much is inevitably left for processing after the session through writing up, viewing the videotapes, clinical discussion, reading and thought. Conscious processes of reflection and analysis are often complemented by less conscious processes of assimilation, free association, the ticking over 'at the back of one's mind' and, during sleep, dreams.

As the therapist becomes more acquainted with the family she is able to take an internal 'step back' to reflect on the process she has engaged in with the family at this early stage. This includes some processing of the impact of the family upon her, her response, her communications to them, the emotional tone of the transactions between them all. The therapist needs also to review the hypotheses she has been formulating. This is an opportunity to think through the assumptions she has made and to be alerted to the impact of her counter-transference.

Although not a linear process, these steps of observing, hypothesising, testing and reviewing, and the concomitant network of associations and assumptions that both enrich and confound the more analytical processes, are the basis for the psychodynamic formulation of the problems and interventions.

If the work progresses, the meanings created between family and therapist are elaborated upon and the psychodynamic formulations reach greater complexity at each stage. If the work is shorter term, there may be less unravelling of the multiplicity of meanings and the initial formulation will inform the intervention. Where there is an abrupt withdrawal of the family from the therapy, the psychodynamic formulation will need to include an understanding of difficulties in engagement, taking account of the interplay between the parental pathology and the therapist's techniques of engagement and therapeutic stance.

Chapter 3

The clinical framework

Tessa Baradon

THE SETTING

Establishing and maintaining the framework – the setting, participants and boundaries – is crucial to the therapeutic alliance and work. The setting provides the framework within which the patient/s will be building up their trust and attachment to the therapist and therapeutic process. As in other analytically based therapeutic encounters, emphasis is placed on the reliability and predictability of the setting. Although not predicated on 'sameness' as in individual therapy, e.g. the parent–infant psychotherapy sessions may not be held on the same day/time each week, when change is introduced, such as a change in frequency of sessions, there will be adequate discussion and preparation for this. Reliability is introduced by the therapist's availability at the set times and her mental stance (see Chapter 2).

The physical setting

The therapy room is arranged to be welcoming and comfortable while being sensitive to people who may feel envy as well as satisfaction. It contains large cushions on the floor for the adults, set around the baby mat. The video equipment is set unobtrusively although not hidden. Age-appropriate toys are set out for the infant. Toys are selected to meet emotional–developmental needs, e.g. for mouthing and biting, and that can stimulate curiosity and phantasy in the developing infant. In line with the aim of providing a predictable, reliable framework, the room is set up in the same way for each session.

Frequency of sessions

Frequency impacts on the sense of continuity and holding on to the possibility of change. Families may be seen weekly or at longer intervals. Considerations in determining the frequency include factors related to the particular family and sometimes organisational factors. The therapist, in discussion with the family, has regard for the urgency of the problem, the age of the baby (younger babies may need to be seen more regularly and frequently because of their vulnerability), concerns about 'at-riskness' in the parent–infant relationship and/or of the baby, the parent/s' ability both to attend regularly and to straddle the gaps between sessions, the stage they are in the therapy. A family may be seen more frequently at the beginning so as to establish a relationship with the therapist and start the therapeutic process; the frequency of sessions may be changed once the family has internalised aspects of the therapy, has accomplished more positive patterns of relating between them, and feels ready to pace the work with the therapist at longer intervals.

Use of videotaping

The videotaping of each session is an integral part of the work. The videos may be used for clinical discussion, clinical audit and research, teaching and training.

Parental consent is sought at the beginning of the first session. The aims of videoing are explained and each parent is asked to sign a consent form. The proposed uses of the tapes are listed and the parent may refuse to be videoed, agree to only some or agree to all possible uses. Refusal to be videoed does not jeopardise the patients' entitlement to therapy in any way. However, the refusal may be indicative of the parents' perception of the therapist/therapy as intrusive or judgemental, or carry other transference meanings that are important to explore, for example a fear that the therapist could use the material to have the baby removed from their care.

Changes to the setting

Conducting therapeutic sessions outside the consulting room

In certain instances the therapy may begin or be temporarily maintained outside the regular setting. When a parent is unable or unwilling to attend the centre, e.g. a housebound parent or one who is frightened of the professional setting, the therapist may consider that a home visit or conducting sessions in the patient's local setting, e.g. a health centre, holds a better chance of setting up the therapy and engaging the patients. Where the therapy has already commenced but there is a change in the patient's circumstances, e.g. physical illness or a mental breakdown, the therapist may wish to maintain the contact with the patient until regular sessions can be resumed and will visit the parent in the current setting, e.g. on the ward.

Suspension of therapy

There may be a break in the therapy, anticipated or unexpected, for a longer than usual period, for instance when the family visits their country of origin or moves home. These occurrences are common in mobile and immigrant populations, especially when there is a new baby to be introduced to the family network. As far as possible, the therapist will ensure that if the family members wish to resume therapy upon their return, they will be able to meet with her.

While it is important for the therapist to be flexible in finding ways to engage and maintain the therapeutic contact with the patients, it is equally crucial that boundaries are maintained. Thus, each contact outside the regular setting should be considered afresh.

PARTICIPANTS IN THE THERAPY

Who may attend a session

In parent–infant psychotherapy the primary patient is the relationship. As the parent–infant relationship develops within the context of past and current familial and social relationships, the therapy may need to include all supports and agents for change.

The baby is the 'entry ticket' to the therapy, and the caregiving parent and baby almost always attend together. The exceptions to this are: when the woman is still pregnant, where the baby cannot attend, e.g. is ill, situations where a parent has material to disclose and it would be counterindicated to discuss this material in front of a toddler, e.g. rape.

Father

Although the referrals often focus on mother and baby, engaging the father in the therapeutic process, where possible, is encouraged. The father's attachment relationship with his baby and his role in relation to the mother–baby dyad (see Chapter 1) can be central to progressing the work. When there is a lot of acrimony between the parents it may be necessary to work first with mother and baby towards including the father. In exceptional situations, for example of breakdown between the couple, it is possible to work separately with mother and baby and father and baby. The question will then arise as to when, clinically speaking, the family can be brought together in the therapeutic work.

The following are considered as potential participants in the therapy for limited periods of time. Their inclusion is recommended when the parent and therapist have discussed their role with regards to the parent and baby and their contributions, positive and negative, to the relationship.

Older children

Sometimes older children may also attend, either because they are in the therapeutic spotlight or simply for expediency, as when school holidays may mean the parents will bring an older child to the session. When this happens that child will be incorporated into the therapeutic situation because they are members of the family and are therefore involved in its emotional matrix.

Other family members

When the parent/s are reliant on the presence of other family members for the care of their baby, they may wish to include these others in the therapy – for a period or a one-off session. Alternatively, the parent may feel that the involvement of another member of the family is impacting negatively on their relationship with the baby and may wish to use the therapeutic setting to clarify unresolved issues between them. The therapist needs to be aware of the parent/s' dependency on, or enmeshment with, these significant others as well as the need for the parents to be able to separate and establish their nuclear family. The pros and cons of including the other family members will be discussed with such considerations in mind.

Professionals

When the parent has a good relationship with another professional, particularly the referring professional, they may wish to use that other person to bridge the early period with the therapist they do not yet know and trust. The 'use' of the support of the referring professional is encouraged, although the issues of confidentiality and of handing over need to be clarified.

Interpreters

Working with interpreters in psychotherapy is not straightforward because of the multiple relationships in the room. The interpreter may have a significant relationship with the parent as she represents their culture and country of origin and all that means to the parent. In such cases their relationship can be an important resource and can help the family present the cultural and religious framework they bring with them. The interpreter also forms the linguistic link between the parent/s and therapist. However, the therapist cannot understand what the interpreter is in fact saying to the parents, e.g. is she interpreting only, is she adding her own thoughts? It is important to discuss the interpreter's role and boundaries before the work begins, and to monitor the working relationship during the therapy. At times the interpreter may also need support from the therapist, e.g. when she is exposed to traumatic information and feelings in the family.

Including other persons in the therapy or for consultation when the parent is reluctant

In exceptional cases, where the welfare of the baby is in question, the therapist may press upon the parent the importance of including other persons in the ongoing therapeutic work or for a consultation. This may be an alternative carer, e.g. father or grandparent, or professionals responsible for the provision of services to the family such as the health visitor or social worker. While engagement in parent–infant psychotherapy is voluntary on the part of the parent/s and they, in the usual course of events, are best positioned to know who should participate in the therapy, refusal on the part of the parents to engage with other important carers or professionals may be an indication for child protection intervention (see p. 50).

The focus of work with the baby and his parent/s

The primary work in parent–infant psychotherapy takes place between parent/s, infant and therapist. While the parent–infant relationship is held in mind throughout, the focus of attention and intervention may also be with either parent or infant, for a period of the session as appropriate.

Working directly with the baby is a fundamental tenant in this approach. This includes naming and scaffolding his affects, addressing his states of mind – including conflicts and phantasies, responding to and initiating play. The baby is seen to benefit from the direct therapeutic relationship with the therapist, as well as from his experiences of a more supported relationship with his parent/s in the presence of the therapist.

Working directly with the mother entails the therapeutic endeavour to understand and give meaning to past and current experiences and emotional states in the parent. This may include revisiting and working through unresolved experiences, constructing a narrative or linking past and present ghosts. In so doing, the therapist is attempting to help the mother address internal impingements on her relationship with her baby. However, when the therapist is working directly with the parent she will need to be aware of the infant's communications in the here-and-now about how the mother's state of mind is impacting on him. Sometimes, babies express relief and gratitude that the therapist is 'looking after' the mother, e.g. by playing quietly as though giving space, or by approaching the therapist to look intently at her. Sometimes the emotional tone in the room may worry the baby. The therapist may support the infant 'Mummy is crying now. You get upset too when this happens. We can help mummy and you to feel better.' The therapist will also bring the mother back to thinking about her baby, to reflect on the convergences between her personal material and their relationship.

Direct work with father does not differ in approach or technique from the work with mother. Father's needs and conflicts will be attended to in their effects on his mental state, his representations of himself as father and relationship with his baby.

When the *work is with the triad* there are the added dimensions of the father–mother–baby relationship. One of the important questions to consider is the coupling within the triad. Can the parents retain the mental representations of themselves as a couple, maintain intergenerational boundaries and parent their baby collaboratively? This is important not only for their relationship but for the baby's sense of safety within a developing notion of the parental couple and Oedipal triangle. A brief exception to the above is while the mother is in a state of primary maternal preoccupation, where the coupling could temporarily lie between her and the baby.

METHODS OF HISTORY TAKING

The parent/s

The parents' attachment history is seen to be crucial to understanding the pattern of their relationship with their infant and the development of a problem. The attachment history may be obtained via a structured questionnaire, such as the Adult Attachment Interview (AAI), or may be gathered spontaneously over the course of the sessions.

Structured: administering the Adult Attachment Interview

The AAI (George et al., 1985) is a semi-structured interview which addresses the parent's current state of mind and modes of mental functioning regarding attachment Hesse (1999). As a clinical intake tool[1], the AAI allows for the assessment of the nature of the parent's reported childhood experiences with her parents and the mental representations of the childhood experiences with them. The AAI also yields information about abuse, loss and other traumatic events and the extent to which these have influenced development and current personality organisation.

Patients are routinely told about the structured interview which explores their experiences of being a child and how they have come to understand

1 See Steele & Baradon (2004) for a discussion of the AAI as a clinical tool.

them. Introducing the AAI presents the parents with the therapist's thinking about continuity and links between their attachment experiences over the generations. The AAI is then conducted by the therapist in the second or third meeting, which is set up with the parent unaccompanied by the infant. When both parents attend the therapy, separate AAIs are conducted with each by the same therapist. In these cases the AAI material needs to be discussed between the couple so the therapist is not in the position of holding 'secrets'. In some instances, working towards more open communication between the couple may not be part of the parents' aims in undertaking parent–infant psychotherapy, and the respective points of view need to be straddled.

The AAI questions can elicit painful personal material for the parent, sometimes that which has not been spoken about before, and at the end of the AAI it is necessary to leave time to reflect on the process of the interview. This offers an opportunity for a clinical 'holding' of raw feelings and, if appropriate, the therapist may offer preliminary links between information that arose in the AAI and relationship patterns she observed in the initial session/s with the infant.

When using the AAI in the clinical work the therapist must avoid the assumption that because the material was brought in the interview the patient is in fact ready to work with it. This is an issue of timing that is always crucial in analytic work, but it is here befuddled by the availability of the material outside of the flow of free association. Another danger is that the therapist, well honed in the art of spotting the repetition of the past in the present, may be tempted to focus on links between the parent's experiences with her parents and the difficulties currently encountered in the parenting of their infant. However, elucidation of the past must serve the purpose of enhancing emotional functioning in relation to the infant, and is not an aim in itself.

Counter-indications to administering the AAI

It is important for the therapist to consider whether the AAI is appropriate for a particular parent at the point of referral to a clinical service. Parents should also be given the choice of refusing the AAI, for example a parent may feel that it would be too disturbing to 'revisit' her childhood. From a clinical point of view, the AAI is counter-indicated where rigid defences are crucial for the parent's short-term functioning with the infant, e.g. in the aftermath of a severe depressive or psychotic episode. The timing of the AAI is also important. It may be counter-indicated at point of referral in an antenatal referral, given the potential for highly conflictual material to rupture the mother's psychic organisation just before the events of birthing. However, the AAI may then be administered postnatally if the treatment continues.

Unstructured: gathering the attachment history within the free flow of the sessions

Where there has been a decision not to conduct the AAI, the parent's attachment history may be left to emerge in an unstructured manner in the sessions. Crucial material about relationships and their representations arises within the flow of free associations, evoked through the here and now of the interactions with the infant or with the therapist. The therapist will use the information brought as and when emotionally relevant to the parent–infant relationship.

The advantage of allowing the history to develop in this way is that material is disclosed at a time and pace of the patient's choice and can more easily be integrated into the flow of the therapeutic work. The disadvantage, in comparison to the AAI, is that important material, for example in relation to abuse or traumatic loss, may not be revealed at all, or may emerge very late in therapy.

Other background information

This includes information about the parental relationship, the nuclear and extended families, and the history of the conception, pregnancy and birth. This information is relevant to the representations, phantasies and expectations of the parent in relation to her baby, and can be gathered during the early sessions and supplemented as relevant as it emerges in the course of the work.

The infant

Developmental history and status

The developmental history and status of the infant is important information for understanding the problem/s and proceeding with the treatment intervention.

The *developmental history* describes the baby's adaptation after birth – establishing routines of feeding, sleeping, periods of alertness and play; his responsiveness to his parents and siblings and interest in the environment; achievement of developmental milestones. Particular vulnerabilities – motor, cognitive and emotional – are noted.

The *developmental status* of the infant is assessed in the context of the parent–infant relationship. It can be assessed formally through validated measures and/or by the therapist through observation. Attention is given to the affective tone of the relationship, the infant's attachment behaviours, self-regulating behaviours and interactive regulating behaviours, and the presence of relationship risk behaviours, such as fear and disassociation.

A model of age-appropriate, normative behaviour (within broad bands) is held as the base-line.

TREATMENT FRAMEWORKS AND CHOICE OF TREATMENT

A number of treatment modalities are available: parent–infant psycho-therapy with the individual family, within a therapeutic group, brief psy-chotherapeutic intervention and crisis intervention. This book focuses primarily on the individual and group frameworks although each of the modalities can be effective. The choice of treatment modality is determined clinically, with regard for suitability and patient preference (see also Chapter 8). However, organisational factors may come into play, e.g. in deciding between brief or opened-ended therapy with the individual family.

Individual family

The framework of 'individual' parent–infant psychotherapy, for the members of the individual family, is privileged when the parent and baby are very vulnerable, when fathers wish to participate, where a parent wants a more individually focused and private setting, or where it is thought that the parent will not be able to sustain a commitment to the group. Parent/infant and therapist agree a plan of treatment, which is open ended but subject to review and revision. The process of therapy in these cases is described in Chapters 5, 6 and 7.

Therapeutic group

The postnatal group is considered when the mother and baby are likely to benefit from sharing their experiences with other mothers and babies who model different ways of parenting and a variety of attachment patterns, and can challenge habitual patterns that are maladaptive for the baby. The assessment of mothers and babies for the group and the therapeutic process of the group is described in chapter nine.

Brief intervention

Brief intervention is a treatment of choice for families whose difficulties are circumscribed, or who wish to address only specific aspects of their diffi-culties, e.g. getting a baby to sleep. It may also be treatment of necessity if a family cannot undertake a longer-term commitment, e.g. live far away, or for organisational/resource reasons.

In a brief intervention the therapist and family may be able to accomplish dramatic change through focused attention to both strengths and disturbances. They may also have to forgo opening up material that cannot be held in the short-term work.

Crisis intervention

On the whole, parent–infant psychotherapy as a therapeutic modality is not geared to crisis intervention in situations of florid mental illness or immediate child protection situations. Mental health medical professionals or social services should usually be the port of call in such an event. However, a crisis may develop where there is already a therapeutic relationship in place, and the family may turn to the therapist as a trusted figure. Conversely, the therapist may be alerted to a critical flare-up in the patients' state of mind or situation because of her understanding of the psychic factors heralding a crisis. The therapist is then obliged to contact the network of professionals responsible for ensuring the patients' safety and care.

No treatment or deferred treatment

Parent–infant psychotherapy is counter-indicated where the parent cannot engage in a treatment setting, e.g. is psychotic, high on substance abuse or locked in a relationship of extreme violence. In some such cases treatment may be embarked on at a later stage, if and when the barriers to engagement have been resolved. Work with the caretaking agencies, particularly in representing the parent's and baby's attachment needs, may help to structure possibilities for a therapeutic setting to be put in place. In some cases, although an infant is involved and is affected, it is necessary for the parent/s to obtain additional help, such as marital guidance or individual psychotherapy before engaging in parent–infant psychotherapy. Parent–infant psychotherapy may not be the treatment of choice in cases where the primary problem lies outside the parent–infant relationship, e.g. substantial retardation.

ASSESSMENT OF RISK IN THE PARENT–INFANT RELATIONSHIP

Concern for the physical safety of the infant defines risk in the broadest sense. A small baby can be at risk of physical abuse (this would include sexual maltreatment) or his physical safety can be threatened by neglect. A particular kind of neglect ensues from a mental state of the parent wherein the baby is 'lost' from the parental mind because of other over-riding preoccupations; the normal attention to, and monitoring of, the baby's predicament does not take place and in this way the baby is not kept safe from accidents that would ordinarily be prevented.

> A teenage mother was relating to the therapist her claustrophobic experience of being assessed in a mother–baby unit. While she was talking her baby crawled behind the armchair. Mother did not notice this, nor did she check on her baby's whereabouts. The therapist expressed concern that the baby could get trapped between the chair and the radiator. Mother glanced over towards baby and said 'Get out of there, you'll get burnt'. Baby gurgled.

This baby was lost from her depressed mother's mind for an extended period in the session. She was also far too young to understand and obey mother's verbal instructions. The therapist assessed that she was at risk in the home environment where there was no other adult to keep an eye out for her safety.

Looking beyond physical safety, 'risk' is defined in terms of likely distortion or inhibition of the baby's normal development consequent upon factors within the caregiving relational environment.

Parent–infant psychotherapy is committed to supporting the parent–infant relationship as long as that relationship is deemed to be in the best interests of the child. To this end, the therapy will support the parent while working to facilitate change in the parent's mental functioning and in maladaptive parenting behaviours. However, in some cases parental change may not occur, or it may be too slow for the baby's developmental timetable. In such cases parent–infant psychotherapy needs to be aligned with the services representing the best interests of the child, and the psychotherapeutic work with parent and infant may be terminated.

What constitutes attachment-related risk?

Situations of risk in terms of the parent's mental state:	*Situations of risk in terms of the baby's precocious defensive constellation:*
The parent is preoccupied with her own affective state and is not able to recognise and/or attend to her baby's infantile needs.	The baby is learning to accommodate to parental unavailability by withdrawing from object relatedness and resorting to self-stimulation and soothing.
The infant has come to represent to the parent a repudiated aspect of themselves or a hated transference figure, resulting in hostility to the infant.	The baby demonstrates behaviours indicative of fear – freezing, disassociation.

Unprocessed trauma in the parent is passed to the infant through the parent's affective states, e.g. fear or panic, and particular defences, such as disassociation.

The baby becomes disorganised by the parent's mood/behaviour and/or resorts to behaviours as above – freezing, disassociation.

Habitual patterns of self-object relating, such as sadomasochistic or perverse, 'hijack' and distort the attachment pathways.

The baby 'joins in' with perverse modes of relating, e.g. laughs when the bottle is pulled out of his mouth.

How to assess risk in a session?

- Risk factors are played out in the parent–infant interactions. The therapist therefore uses her observations of the attitudes and behaviours of the parent to the infant and the infant's responses to the parent.
- The therapist should discuss her observations with the parent if this is at all possible.
- The therapist is further informed by her counter-transference, especially strong negative affects such as shock, anxiety or fear, in relation to what she is observing.
- While in the long run the therapist will need to assess the parent/s' capacity for change, in the immediacy of the session the therapist should assess the parent's capacity to engage in thinking about and planning for the baby.

Important questions in the assessment of risk in the session:

- Is the baby physically safe with the parent?
- Is the parent able and willing to recognise the baby's physical needs and (to be assessed separately) emotional needs?
- Is the parent's state of mind likely to be frightening to the baby?
- Is the baby showing signs of fear, withdrawal or self-harming, e.g. head banging?

Mother arrived at the centre in a state of extreme agitation and this increased in the course of the session. She shouted that she did not want to parent her son anymore and he crawled into the therapist's lap, clutching at her and unable to play. The therapist, too, felt alarmed by the violence in mother's voice. She talked to both mother and baby about how they were feeling with each other, but this did not seem to reduce their emotional turmoil at that point. Further probes about how mother would cope at home (e.g. what will you make for yourself and son to eat, how will you bath him, if you feel very bad in the evening, can you imagine what will happen with baby?) led the therapist to believe that mother and son would not be safe.

The following are key questions in relation for parental capacity to plan for the immediate care of the baby:

- Is the parent able to talk rationally about the baby's needs?
- Is the parent able to contemplate another point of view?
- Can the parent reflect upon their own state of mind and behaviours towards the infant?
- Does the parent feel empathy to the child as represented by the therapist?
- Are there supports in place – partner, friend, professional?

The threshold for action

When the therapist is concerned about the child's physical safety, she must act to ensure the baby's safety (in line with the institution's procedures) and alert the statutory services of the situation.

When the therapist is concerned for the emotional well-being of the baby, she will need to decide whether this concern is urgent and requiring immediate action in relation to the statutory services, or whether it is part of a longer-term therapeutic plan. On the whole, the aim is to work with emotional neglect or abuse as part of the therapeutic intervention, while the therapist assesses the parent/s' capacity for change in relation to the baby's developmental timetable. However, emotional abuse should not be allowed to continue indefinitely in the hope that the parent will change. Immediate action should be taken when there is an escalation in the threat to the emotional well-being of the baby to the point of physical risk as well.

Procedures

1. Discussion of the critical concerns with the parents

It is crucial for the clinical work with the family that the parents are party to the clinical intervention as far as possible. Counter-indications to parental involvement are situations where the parent is suspected of being a perpetrator. When the parent's state of mind is of concern to the therapist, it may be possible to contact the other parent/guardian of the baby and to make provisions for care of the baby with them.

2. Discussion with colleagues and clinical consultation

Consultation is integral to good practice and mechanisms for consultation in crisis situations as well as ongoing clinical provision need to be in place.

3. Consultation with and referral to external agencies

Concerns within the clinical situation about risk to the baby cannot be dealt with in isolation from other professionals who work with the family, such as the GP, health visitor and other agents (e.g. psychiatrist or social worker). The therapist would ordinarily be in contact with the professionals in the course of the work with the family (see p. 55). However, the therapist may also need to consult with/refer to these professionals while responding to an acute situation, for example, to instigate an emergency psychiatric assessment.

4. Crisis intervention

Legal procedures for child protection vary from country to country. In the UK, professionals are regulated by The Children Act 1987 and aligned social service procedures.

5. Assessment of risk in relation to the aims of therapy

A breakdown in trust of the therapeutic relationship is always a concern when the therapist actively engages the parents and other professionals/agencies in consideration of risk. Two prominent ideas can play into this. The first is that the baby will be taken away from the parents. It is important to clarify with the parents the steps that they will need to take to prevent this outcome. Such discussion with the parents can act as a catalyst for change. The second issue that frequently comes into play is the rage and disappointment that no one stepped in to protect the parent when she was a vulnerable baby herself. A discussion of the rivalry with their own baby and disappointment with the services from their own childhood can enable the parent to recognise the importance of giving her baby the protection she should have had.

WORKING WITH THE NETWORK

Parent–infant psychotherapy should be provided alongside and in coordination with any other services supporting the individual family. It needs to be viewed in the context of the service network and not as a stand alone activity.

The rationale

Families requiring parent–infant psychotherapy may need multilayered support from public/professional services. The more severe ranges of psychopathology are often associated with problems in functioning socially, educationally and economically. Moreover, coordination of mental health, social service and educational resources increases efficacy of provision, preventing duplication or falling between the stools. Inquiries into child deaths, such as the Climbié Report (Lord Laming: 2003), have emphasised the importance of interagency cooperation in preventing catastrophes.

Procedures for effective networking

At the point of referral the therapist is responsible for getting information regarding the agencies working with the family. The therapist will contact these agencies to gather reports and/or organise a preliminary meeting with the aims of: (i) creating a network around the family to include all services required and available; (ii) reviewing and coordinating the roles and responsibilities of the various professionals working with the family; (iii) locating the therapy in the network; and (iv) clarifying statutory responsibilities where relevant.

Routine contact with the professional network activity is an important therapeutic task as long as the family is engaged in therapy. With some families there will be minimal network activity, but where there is an infant at risk the therapist will work closely with the other services. The nature of the contact must be made transparent to the family.

With the termination of the therapy, either planned or unplanned, the other professionals and agencies involved with the family should be notified. This facilitates a 'handing over' of the family, where relevant, with discussion of any residual concerns (see Chapter 7).

CONSULTATION AND SUPERVISION

Both ongoing supervision and consultation have a place in this work. Working with primitive emotions and early psychological functioning (such as process of projection, splitting, disassociation) inevitably impacts on the therapist. Moreover, she can be faced with sensitive issues around assessing and managing risk. Clinical discussion within the parent–infant psychotherapy team can provide effective, supportive and challenging peer-group supervision. If team supervision is not available, individual supervision will be required.

The general aims of supervision are to:

- provide an emotionally supportive backdrop to the work
- develop and refine understanding and technique

- enhance expertise
- monitor the therapist's counter-transference and possible enactments
- develop a culture of organisational exchange in parent–infant psycho-therapy.

Chapter 4

Key techniques of intervention

Tessa Baradon

OVERVIEW

The over-arching focus of the therapy is on the parent–infant relationship as observed in the back and forth of the interactions in the sessions. Some interventions address the relationship directly; some techniques are directed more towards enhancing the quality of parenting, and others work more directly with the baby's experience. In any session, the therapist may move back and forth in her interventions between the baby, the parent and their relationship.

The choice of which intervention is used at any given point in a session can be a conscious one, but often a therapist may find herself using a particular clinical intervention without thinking it through (applied 'intuitively'). However, retrospective consideration of why she intervened in a particular way at a particular point often suggests that at a preconscious level the therapist is making a reasonable formulation of the problem and applying an appropriate response in the here and now of the session. Moreover, in the course of the work, the therapist and patients will evolve an understanding of what is more helpful in that particular therapeutic relationship. Consequently, a therapist may privilege certain techniques over others, depending on the personality, needs and defences of the patients, and the stage in the therapy.

There is a measure of clustering of techniques within phases of the therapeutic process. In the early phase of the work, the therapist is building up an understanding of the problems and the working relationship (therapeutic alliance) with her patients. In this, 'exploration and clarification', 'modelling', 'reflecting back' and 'parent guidance' play important roles. The therapist is also looking to effect immediate help for the baby in line with the urgency of their developmental timetable. In working directly with the baby, 'mirroring' and 'playing' are techniques that can promote this. In the middle phase, where there is already a measure of trust and a mutual therapeutic language – verbal and procedural – the therapist can utilise more challenging techniques, such as 'interpretation', 'linking past with present' and 'reframing'. While the techniques used in relation to the baby are still highly relevant, the therapist will hopefully find that the parent is taking over more of the scaffolding of their baby's states, indicating the progress of the work. In the final stage of the therapy, that of termination, 'recapitulation' is important for consolidation of the achievements as well as preparation for functioning without the support of the therapy.

TECHNIQUES

Although the techniques are presented as discrete, there is a considerable overlap between them. In other words, in applying any one technique there may be elements of other key interventions as well, and while the focus of an intervention may be on parent or infant it will invariably address both.

Clarification and exploration

The therapist will continuously attempt to understand the complex, and often multilayered, meaning of the patients' communications. This entails gathering information, probing, making links, making the unconscious conscious, checking and validating with the patient/s.

Clarifying and exploring information is a necessary part of creating and checking hypotheses and understanding of the parent–infant attachments and difficulties. The therapist can gather information from the patients in both structured and free associative forms (see Chapter 3) to create a shared appreciation of the reasons for the feelings and behaviours that present problematically in the sessions. The process of trying to understand the patient's thinking and communications conveys the therapist's interest and concern for the patients and at the same time assists in clarifying their thoughts and feelings. Sometimes this is the first experience the parent has had of another mind reflecting on their own, and they rely on the example of the therapist to (learn to) think about both their own and their baby's mental states. The process of clarification and exploration can assist also in the construction of a meaningful self-history, which is important to the coherent sense of self in the parent and in relation to their baby.

Working directly with the baby

A key intervention in parent–infant psychotherapy is direct work with the baby. The therapist may directly address the baby for two reasons. In the first instance, she offers herself to the baby as an interested, concerned person with whom the baby may wish to engage. The purpose in this is to open pathways of interaction which promote attachment and development where the parent may, at least temporarily, not be able to do so. In the second instance the intervention is aimed at helping the baby regulate his emotional state when the parent is not doing this. In this case the therapist will carefully attune herself to the emotional pitch of the baby and intensify or decrease her interactions with him to raise (e.g. where the baby is withdrawn), or lower (e.g. where the baby is hyperaroused), his emotional state as appropriate.

In both cases the engagement is primarily at an emotional level. The therapist borrows from the ordinary 'language' (in the broadest sense) of mothers and babies, which is developmentally most appropriate for emotional communication with the baby. The therapist will, at any given time:

- place her face at a distance that the infant can visually focus on
- use a lilting, rhythmic tone of voice
- amplify facial and body expressions
- take turns in conversation
- wait for the baby to re-engage when ready
- use a toy where direct engagement may be overwhelming to the baby.

The use of age-appropriate 'language' with the baby may be surprising to some families, e.g. where there is no accommodation to the infant's level of development or where it is contrary to cultural practices. In her intervention with the infant the therapist will thus also be modelling to the parent attachment-based, age-appropriate modes of engagement.

Reflecting back the interaction

The therapist relies on her observations to inform her understanding of the material of the session. Having noted, for example, a significant interaction between mother and infant, or states of mind in either, the therapist may choose to actively reflect back to them her observation/s.

This may be done when the therapist considers the parent is unaware or closed to (defended against) their own, or the other's, communication and the meaning of it. The aim is then to raise the parent's awareness of their state of mind or behaviour and thereby to open the issue for discussion. The therapist may also use reflecting back to the baby. The aim here is to scaffold the baby's feelings and behaviours and create meaning for them.

Modelling

In her very stance of observing and making sense of thoughts, feelings and behaviours, the therapist is modelling a way of 'being with the other' which acknowledges the importance and complexity of the other person's state of mind. In addition, the therapist may selectively engage in specific forms of play, communication, interaction with the aim of providing a model for the parent and/or baby which they may, in due course, assimilate and own.

Modelling is used primarily to enhance reflective function in the parent/s and to promote responsive parental behaviours towards the baby. Through her own behaviours the therapist addresses deficits in the parent's way of relating to her baby, for example in helping the baby regulate his emotional state.

Another common area for modelling is that of play, with the aim of helping both to establish mutually pleasurable play and playfulness. In the latter instances the therapist's modelling overlaps with her interventions of 'working directly with the baby' and 'playing'.

Playing

The therapist may initiate a sequence of play with the baby. In early months this rests primarily on face to face interactions, in later months it would include games, such as peek-a-boo, and toys. The choice of game is contingent on the theme in the session at that time and constitutes an elaboration of the theme in age-appropriate 'language'.

The aims in playing are varied. The therapist may be intending to model play, which is an important mutual pleasurable activity through which the baby learns about the social and object world (see Modelling, above). She may be using play as an age-appropriate language for clarifying for the baby events and mental states. Playing is also a way of introducing play-fulness, thereby preparing the way for taking an alternative mental perspective. This is particularly important where the parent tends to assume that the baby's state of mind is the same as their own (see Chapter 1) and the baby lacks experiences of his own feelings and behaviours being validated.

Mirroring affective states

'Mirroring' describes a process wherein the therapist reflects to the parent and/or infant their emotional state, with the aim of confirming the patient's experience of self. On the one hand, mirroring is a constituent of the overall therapeutic stance in that the therapist resonates the patient's emotional state and through this experience of 'seeing himself in the eyes/mind of the beholder' (see Chapter 1) the patient comes to understand her own mental state (Fonagy et al., 2002a).

Mirroring is an important tool in helping the baby recognise his own feeling state. In the process of mirroring to the baby the therapist highlights or amplifies an emotional or behavioural response that resonates with the baby's state of mind at the particular chosen moment. For mirroring to be effective the baby needs to recognise the reflected state as his own. In order to establish this recognition in the baby the therapist balances the high degree of similarity between the baby's state and that which is reflected by the therapist, but with the addition of an intentional subtle mismatch, e.g. through exaggeration of the emotion. This subtle mismatch enables the baby to differentiate the mirrored state as his own rather than a projection of the therapist's own mental state onto him.

Representing the baby's mental states to the parent

A key technique in parent–infant psychotherapy is the therapist's attempts to help the parent/s understand what their baby is feeling. Representing the infant's mental state has important functions for both the parent and the infant. On the one hand it works towards promoting the parent's reflective function in relation to the baby and their recognition of the baby's developing mind, different from their own. At the same time the therapist is scaffolding the baby's state for him, recognising his state of dependency and facilitating the infant's developing sense of self. In using this technique, the therapist applies her understanding of infantile emotions and impulses in relation to the state of attachment she observes between the baby and his parents. She uses emotional language, e.g. 'most beloved daddy', 'frightened baby', and explanations 'have you waited so long for your milk that you are too full of bad anger to eat it now?' In so doing she is trying to capture the primitive passions of the infant and their rudimentary cognition.

Reframing

The technique of reframing entails the therapist offering a different perspective to that held by the parent in order to help the parent review a negative position she may hold in relation to her baby. The aim is to recast the same event or behaviour in a more positive light, and thus open the way for the parent to be more accepting of the infant, allowing more positive interactions between them.

Interpretation

Verbal interpretation of intrapsychic and/or interpersonal conflict and defence

Interpretation in parent–infant psychotherapy carries the aim of freeing the parent and infant from impingements on their positive relatedness. To such purpose, interpretation may address conflict and defence in the parent (intrapsychic) inasmuch as it interferes with her relationship with her infant, or it may address conflict and defence between parent and infant (interpersonal). The therapist may also interpret dilemmas of the baby if these seem to be holding the baby back from seeking out his parent.

In the parent

Interpretation of conflict and defence in the parent is limited to those areas that have bearing on their functioning with their infant. In particular, the therapist may interpret mental states and patterns of defence that are being repeated from the parent's past. This may include scenarios where the parent attributes to the baby repudiated aspects of herself or negative characteristic that 'belong' to another attachment figure (transference to the baby). The latter include statements such 'he's got his father's aggressive genes', 'she consumes me with her demands and dissatisfactions, like my mother did'.

Between parent and infant

Interpretation can address conflict and defence between parent and infant as these are played out in the interactions observed in the session. The focus of the interpretation may be on the impact of the parent's conflict or defensive behaviours on the baby and the adaptations the baby is making in relation to the parent. The therapist may also address the co-construction of defensive behaviours, such as mother and baby using the same mechanisms to keep painful feelings at bay.

In the infant

The therapist may interpret the baby's state of mind where she observes the interference of defence in the baby's forward thrust towards attachment. For example, 'it is so frightening when mummy talks about her sadness that you go off to sleep'. The interpretation of the baby's dilemma also represents the baby's state of mind to the parent/s, and thereby is directed also to their relationship.

Enactive interpretation

This refers to interpretation constructed in the language of action and attitude. Interpretation in this form, through gesture, movement and expression, may be the most accessible to the baby insofar as it matches his level of mental functioning and development. For example, the therapist 'interprets' the infant's wish to be held by stroking the teddy. The baby looks seriously at her and then turns his gaze to his mother.

The *timing of an interpretation* is crucial. A well-timed interpretation can bring much relief to a patient who feels both understood in the moment and the possibility of transforming the inchoate experience into symbolic. An ill-timed interpretation can, at best, simply not be heard, or can increase the patient's anxiety and need to defend. The timing may be 'right' if what the therapist says pertains to what is emotionally in focus at that point, if the parent is sufficiently undefended to 'hear' the message, if it is being delivered without negative emotion from the therapist. It is not always possible to make an accurate judgement about this and, in a sense, the therapist is always 'taking a risk' in bringing into consciousness what has been defended against until then.

Linking past with present

Both adaptive and maladaptive patterns of relating incorporate repetitions from the parent's experiences of being parented in her childhood. An aim of parent–infant psychotherapy is to interrupt negative intergenerational patterns and to facilitate the co-construction of positive attachment behaviours between the parent and infant. An important technique in relation to this is linking past and present for the parent so as to bring the negative repetitions into consciousness, thereby enabling the parent to reflect and change.

The efficacy of linking is contingent upon capturing the past in the interactions observed in the session. Reference to the past without emotional and behavioural anchorage in the here and now can render it an intellectual, didactic or even preaching exercise, lacking in resonance for the parent.

Parent guidance

Parent guidance works to extend the parent/s' repertoire of responses to the infant through the therapist's joining with the parent in observing her own and her baby's patterns of behaviour and reflecting on the meanings of these, including cultural and religious influences in child-rearing.

Parent guidance is distinguished from the giving of advice in the position that the therapist adopts. Whereas in advice giving there is a position of expert knowledge, in parent guidance the therapist joins with the parent to create the expert knowledge together.

Recapitulation

The process of revisiting work done in the therapy is crucial for sustaining change. Through recapitulation the parent may gain a perspective on their initial difficulties and the solutions they have reworked to progress their relationship with the infant. Recapitulation can also enable the parent to assimilate a different perspective, whether their own in the present in comparison to their position in the past or whether that of another person. Although recapitulation is a primary technique in the ending phase of the therapy, it is used throughout to progress the work.

ADAPTATIONS OF TECHNIQUE

In the group

The techniques described apply to the therapeutic work in the individual family and in the group settings. However, the opportunities and emphasis may differ. In the group, these techniques are used to explore and develop both the dyadic/triadic parent–infant relationship and relationships amongst the mothers and amongst the babies. For example, interpretation in the group situation may address interpersonal rivalry between the babies which resonates with experiences of sibling rivalry for the mothers. Moreover, the group setting offers opportunities for intervention mother to mother and mother to baby (other than her own) and baby to baby. Thus, modelling, reframing and playing are offered not only by therapists but also other group members. Although not applied as selected therapeutic techniques by the members of the group, their use is effective in bringing about change (for a more detailed discussion, see Chapter 8).

Responding to patient pathology

At all times the therapist will try to adapt her technique to the patient's capacity to engage in the therapeutic work, and to be sensitive to the effects of guilt, shame and rage on the use the patient/s may make of her interventions. There are also particular mental states in the patient that require particular adaptations of technique. For example, a parent in a paranoid state may regard all the therapist's interventions that challenge her internal reality as attempts to disqualify her as a parent. A major challenge to technique is presented by parents with borderline personality disorder, whose difficulties in understanding mental states in themselves and others often precludes recognition of the infant as a separate being with infantile, but age-appropriate, needs. Premature application of techniques that challenge the parent's experience, such as representing the baby's state of mind or interpretation, are liable to increase the parent's confusion and sense of worthlessness in relation to the baby to the detriment of their ability to care for their baby. Techniques that are aimed at clarification and extending the patient's sense of efficacy in communication – such as mirroring affective states and engaging with the baby, may be extremely important for these parents/patients (see also 'Working across cultures' in Chapter 2, and 'Adaptation of technique' in Chapter 6).

Section II

The therapeutic process

Introduction

Tessa Baradon

The process of psychotherapy lies in the unfolding constructions between patient/s and therapist. These constructions are shaped by the patients' internal models of attachment (Chapter 1), the aims of the psychotherapy in relation to their current difficulties, the therapist's theoretical orientation and experience (Chapter 2), the setting (Chapter 3) and the interplay between these variables. The therapeutic process is therefore different for each patient–therapist unit – singular constructions that develop between individuals, at a particular time, in a particular mental and physical space.

The 'mind to mind' activity between therapist and patients is the fundamental activity in the therapeutic process. It broadly resembles the developmental process of stimulation, scaffolding and regulation for the infant through engagement with the adult mind. However, while the infant is constructing his representational world, the parent is revisiting it through the therapy. In so doing, parent and therapist straddle both undoing and rebuilding of adaptations and defences. Maintaining the parent's adult functioning and her position as parent, despite some possible regression in revisiting her own infantile needs, is vital for the well-being of her baby.

Much of what takes place between those involved in the therapeutic work is in the realms of body language, 'intuition', spontaneous gesture and enactment[1]. The dynamics of the interactions are complex and multi-layered, and often touch upon the unconscious of the patient and therapist. It is hard to capture in words the textures of experience and imagination that unfold in the arena of the therapy. Moreover, it is an attempt to describe in linear fashion processes that unfold simultaneously, at different levels of consciousness, in the declarative and procedural domains. Despite these limitations, the authors have delineated areas that the therapist may attend to, as pointers to the central spheres of the therapeutic process.

---

1 Although it holds the potential of being brought to awareness either through focusing attention (the descriptive unconscious) or through addressing the psychic defences (dynamic unconscious).

The process chapters encompass the work with individual families and the group. Chapters 5 to 7, describing parent–infant psychotherapy with a dyad or triad, have been divided for heuristic purposes into beginning, middle and end. In terms of a dynamic therapeutic process this is somewhat artificial, but the three chapters work as a whole in describing the application of theory to practice in the different phases of the therapy and in highlighting the therapists' thinking when using the different parent–infant psychotherapy techniques. The final chapter in this section describes conducting parent–infant psychotherapy in an analytic group, and elaborates on the unfolding process – beginning, middle and end – within this particular setting. This chapter has a separate introduction to elucidate 'group' concepts and the interface with working with babies.

Chapter 5

Parent–infant psychotherapy: engaging and beginning the work

Iris Gibbs

OVERVIEW

This chapter describes the beginning phase of parent–infant psychotherapy. It tracks the journey from the initial referral, through the intake, to a formulation of the problem and an agreed plan of intervention with the parents and their infant. Where applicable, the plan will also include collaboration with professionals who are already involved or are brought in as a result of concerns highlighted during the process.

The model presented does not include a formal intake stage and diagnostic procedures. The therapeutic encounter is seen to begin with the first contact with the family, and the psychodynamic formulations and the course of the work are informally revisited and reviewed (Chapter 2).

Engaging the parents is probably the most important aim of the beginning stage of parent–infant psychotherapy. It is first and foremost a collaborative process between the therapist, the parents and their baby. It encapsulates the ability in the therapist to draw the family into the therapeutic process. It also resonates with, or calls forth, something in the parent which enables them to take the first, tentative steps to accepting help.

The therapist's stance – of interest, concern, not passing judgement – is crucial in encouraging a parent to move from a state of anxious enquiry to accepting a first appointment. Where the therapist and the family are from different cultural groups, extra care has to be taken to ensure that early communications are clearly understood.

The process of engaging the family helps in promoting the 'treatment alliance' – the family's trust in the therapist and commitment to the therapy – during the initial period of seeking help and early phases of the therapeutic work, and may sustain the therapy at difficult times of challenge and change during the middle stages.

AIMS

The aims of the beginning phase are to:

- establish the intake process
- engage the parents
- establish the baby as a partner in the process
- assess risk to the baby in terms of his overall development
- assess the capacity for change in the dyad/triad
- reach a preliminary formulation of the problem
- agree the choice of treatment with the parent/s.

Establishing the intake process

The referral

The parent may be referred by other professionals or self refer. The initial contact is with the administrator, whose role is to ascertain the basic details for screening purposes. As the first point of contact the administrator will inevitably be faced, at times, with parents who are anxious and distressed. The manner in which she responds will be important in leaving the parent with an impression of the service as welcoming and potentially helpful in dealing with their difficulty.

The referral is considered in terms of whether the problem is appropriate to parent–infant psychotherapy. The central criterion is whether the presented problems (see Chapter 2) are likely to impact on the relationship between the baby and the parents if left untreated, with consequent risk to the infant's development. Responses to referrals need to be prompt, because the functioning of babies and parents in distress can deteriorate rapidly. It also enables the therapist to make a preliminary assessment regarding urgency and/or immediate risk to the infant.

> A mother and her five-month-old daughter were referred by their health visitor. In the letter of referral she stated that mother was very distressed because she was unable to produce enough breast milk to feed her baby. The other statement was that mother's thoughts had become 'disordered'.

This referral was seen as urgent and complex. The feeding problem, although presented predominantly as an issue for mother, would impact on her baby. This would be partly through baby being exposed to mother's distress and because feeding is an important part of the relationship between a mother and baby. The feeding issue alone would have, therefore, made it a suitable case for parent–infant psychotherapy. However, the reference to mother's disordered thoughts added information which suggested that mother might be suffering from mental health problems. Therefore before the referral could be further processed it was important to have a discussion with the health visitor. In this call, the therapist was interested to understand the health visitor's use of the term 'disordered', to discuss the appropriateness of parent–infant psychotherapy at this time, and to ascertain the level of support available to mother and baby.

'Inappropriate' referrals

It is important to think through the appropriateness of the referral beyond the presenting problem. This may happen before the therapist meets the family, or at some point after the first session/s. For example, a problem that appears to be environmental rather than psychologically based, such as poor housing, may be used to disguise other difficulties in the parents and or in their relationship to their child. Often a supplementary question by the therapist such as 'Are there any other worries about yourself or the baby' may be enough to allow the parent to acknowledge relationship difficulties.

Inevitably, some problems will not be suited to parent–infant psychotherapy, or the timing of the referral for parent–infant psychotherapy is not appropriate, or other interventions need to be put in place before therapy can commence (see Chapter 3). Where the referral is clearly outside the domain of parent–infant psychotherapy, as in the following example, the therapist will explore with the referrer and parent appropriate alternative services.

A mother contacted the service with a request for an assessment of her baby. In the course of the telephone conversation, the therapist learned that mother was engaged in court proceeding with her ex-partner over access to the baby. The therapist suggested that the parents consider coming together to discuss their daughter's needs and well-being. Mother refused the offer, wanting a 'witness' to present her case against the baby's father. The therapist understood that the parents would not consider parent–infant psychotherapy relevant to their interests at that point in time.

Gathering relevant information

The process of gathering information starts at the referral stage and continues both formally and informally as the parents and their baby engage with the therapy. If it seems that the dyad may consider/be considered for the group, the intake process will be completed by the group therapist (see Chapter 8).

Any information given is significant in that it informs the therapist of the family's thinking about their situation. Even when the AAI is conducted (see Chapter 3), much of the therapist's information about attachments is gleaned informally in the here-and-now of the sessions, through the inter-actions between parent and baby, the baby's adaptation to and defences against his parent's mental state, the transference to the therapist and her own counter-transference responses. In gathering information the therapist is also aware that culture and other differences, such as class and religion, may play an essential part in how the parents perceive and understand the referral difficulties. The therapist needs to explore the parents' expectations about treatment and should try to understand their personal–cultural perspective, avoiding fixed ideas about their culture. Language can play an important role in either clarifying or confusing understanding of cultural influences. The therapist should not assume that cultural issues are not important if they do not appear in the first contact with the family. Culturally based ideas or reservations may be avoided out of deference to the authority of the therapist or the feeling that she might not be interested. Inhibition of significant, realistic exchanges may lead to resistance in the parent regarding the treatment. Therefore, the therapist should remain open and alert and be prepared to ask about culture if she feels that the family is avoiding this.

In the process of gathering information the techniques of *exploration* and *clarification* are used extensively. These techniques may not only open up the process of exchange, but also *model* the reflective stance of the therapist (see Chapter 2) and may also help to contain some aspects of parental anxiety. Families may gain relief when, in the context of establishing this early contact, they begin to reflect on possible links in the material they bring and it acquires meaning through the therapist's attempts to under-stand and elaborate.

Putting the network in place

The role of the network is to support the family's functioning in all areas that impinge on the individual's and the unit's functioning. The network may be able to play an important role in helping the family access parent–infant psychotherapy, and/or in supporting anxious parents in taking up the therapy when offered. For example, a trusted professional could be an ally in the process of engaging with the parents by encouraging them to attend, or even accompanying them to the first session. Moreover, the network of professionals and agencies is crucial when there are concerns about child protection. The extent of contact with the referrer and network will depend on their role, responsibility and relationship with the family and their current or anticipated future involvement.

Engaging the parents

Steps in the process of engagement

Personalising the contact with the family

Personalising and individualising the referral starts with the therapist's first call to the parents. Her call links the parent to a named person who shows interest in their concerns about themselves and their baby. Depending on need, it may be a brief or lengthy conversation. Some parents contact the service with a good idea about what they want help with and the therapist's call will be in the context of arranging an appointment. Others may have been vague about the concerns and the therapist may need to have a more detailed conversation about the difficulties. A parent may spill over with concerns or try to engage the therapist in diagnosing the problems on the phone. The therapist has to be prepared to deal in an interested but boundaried way, maintaining an appropriate professional stance. She will, for example, desist from offering on the spot advice, but will express her interest in working with them and their baby in finding a solution to their difficulty.

The therapist will be aware that, at the same time, the parent is making assumptions and possibly an early transference to her. This may be based on her voice, accent, manner, or by the parent projecting onto her such attributes as kind and helpful or, in some cases, unhelpful. At this early stage a positive perception of the therapist may encourage the family to take the next steps in the process and in doing so, keep alive the hope of a satisfactory outcome to their difficulties.

Engaging the father

It is important that the father is part of the therapeutic process when possible, particularly if he is the other primary attachment figure for the baby. Persisting with an interest in father's attendance and flexibility in arrangements to accommodate him can lead to eventual engagement.

Sometimes the work of parent–infant psychotherapy goes ahead with one parent, usually the mother, and her baby. This may be the mother's choice, e.g. she may see the problem as pertaining only to her. The parents may not be able to work together for the well-being of their baby, as when there is extreme acrimony between them or continuing domestic violence. The father may be absent from the baby's life, e.g. for reasons of mental ill health, or out of choice. The therapist's task is to keep the father in mind from the beginning. This may be done in concrete ways such as asking what he would have thought about the referral/the problems, or may be dictated by the child referring to his father or attributing something in the session to him. The therapist thus addresses both the 'father in mother's mind' and the developing representations and phantasies of the baby about his father.

The first session

Where a referral satisfies the basic criteria for parent–infant psychotherapy, parents are invited to attend with their baby for a first meeting. In the first session the therapist will try to alleviate some of the anxiety in the family around the referral and to give them a sense of having entered into a safe, reflective environment. She will hope to achieve a preliminary under-standing of why the family is attending, what they are hoping to gain from coming, and to start to form an initial hypothesis of the problem and the possible origins.

The therapist attends also to the physical aspects of the encounter – the provision of a room that is welcoming and offers the necessary level of privacy, and which is laid out with the particular family in mind.

The initial greeting of the family can set the tone for the session. The therapist is careful to include both parents and their baby in her greeting, to observe cultural protocols, and to be sensitive to non-verbal communica-tions from each participant about their emotional state. In these first moments she will be adding to her information about the family such as noting the parents' appearance and manner and the level of anxiety shown. The therapist will also be aware of the baby's reaction to the new environ-ment and the responses of the parents to any alarm or distress in the baby. If a member of the family, including the baby, appears unduly anxious, the therapist may choose to address the situation (new person, new place) in general terms.

In the room, the therapist allows time for the parents to settle themselves and their baby. She may start by asking the family to tell her what has brought them to this point of seeking help. She will encourage each parent to give their version of the problem and at the same time she will be noticing who takes the lead, whether or not the parents refer to each other and what the baby is doing throughout the process. Individuals communi-cate and respond to feelings and difficulties in different and very unique ways. The therapist's task is to 'unpack' the different communications. She will use her observation and listening skills to attend to both what is said and what is suggested through actions. She will be clarifying and exploring statements and interactions that are unclear to her. In this respect she is putting the parents and their baby in the role of experts who are having to educate her into their ways of seeing and conceptualising their difficulties.

The therapist will also need to be aware of her counter-transference to the individuals and the family as a unit.

> In the case quoted earlier, it was mother who responded initially to the question about what had brought them. The story given was mainly about her and her illness, and in telling it mother spoke in a flat and barely audible voice. Her eyes remained on the therapist throughout and she appeared to be quite oblivious to her partner and daughter.
>
> At the start the therapist was quite mesmerised by mother's story and found it difficult to shift her attention to the other people in the room. She was moved by the mother's material and felt she needed to tread carefully. Her attitude was therefore attentive and unhurried. The silence of the partner and the baby's withdrawn state, however, spoke volumes and she also felt the pressure from them, albeit non-verbally at this point, to be brought into the process.

This example highlights the tug for the therapist's attention and identifications as the needs of each member of the family pulled in different directions. The therapist used her counter-transference awareness of mother's fragility to understand the grip of the mother's state of mind on the family and the withdrawal of father and baby. The therapist had to time her intervention carefully to bring the baby and her father into the therapeutic arena, as she did not want to cut across mother's story. This moment came with the first tiny sound from the baby, which neither parent appeared to hear.

> The therapist looked across to the baby and said 'You are telling us that you want to be part of this conversation'. Both parents turned to look at their baby, seemingly aware of her for the first time. The therapist then continued speaking directly to baby. She said she thought Mummy's illness was hard for everyone – mummy, daddy and baby.

The therapist acknowledged the feelings of each person in the family, and linked them with the other. She also offered a different way of being together where the father, too, could have a voice. She was *engaging directly with the baby* to scaffold her communications (her first tiny sound) and *represent them to her parents*. This technique supports beginning mentalisation and emotional regulation. The words the therapist used would have meant little to the infant but her voice and facial expressions, expressing empathy and interest, would have been impressed on the infant. She responded by making proper eye contact with the therapist for the first time in the session. This was a hopeful sign, in that baby had not given up on expecting a response.

The importance of the first session is thus twofold. The therapist gathers information through observation and *exploration*, which will inform her dynamic formulation of the problem and her thoughts about the appropriate intervention modality (see Chapters 2 and 3). She is also setting the scene for the therapeutic process: creating a facilitating environment for the therapy to take place, engaging each family member as a participant in the therapy, modelling new ways of being together that will promote the baby's development. For this she uses all that takes place in the room as intentional communication about the individual's state of mind and their relationships, tries to hold on to her mentalising stance in the face of conflicting needs and identifications, and draws upon her counter transference to elaborate her understanding. When attending at different points to individuals in the family, the focus of the therapist remains on the relationships with the baby and the baby's developmental outcome.

A further task in the first session is to put boundaries in place. Issues of confidentiality and action in the face of concerns around adult safety and child protection need to be addressed. The therapist will need to get parental consent for routine contact with the health visitor and other professionals and, separately, for the use of the video.

The Adult Attachment Interview

When the parents agree to the AAI it is conducted early in the intake, preferably the second or third session. The material raised by the AAI and the feelings that can emerge often make this interview an intensely personal experience for the parent and can forge a strong bond with the therapist.

At the end of the AAI, time is taken to reflect on the process of the interview and to draw out main themes that may link with the material from the first session. This may be helpful to the parent in making sense, early on, of patterns that concern them and in linking with further work to be done. At the same time the therapist must not assume that because the material was brought in the Interview the parent is in fact ready to work with it.

Some parents become engaged in the therapeutic work without the AAI. In these situations the issues unfold within the context of the ongoing therapeutic relationship.

Possible setbacks in the engagement process

Ambivalence or resistance in the parent

The therapist may have to reach out a number of times before making contact with the parent. Similarly, some parents attend once and are put off by an aspect of the procedures or contact with the therapist, which may evoke earlier disappointment, fear or suspicion.

> A mother cancelled her first appointment. The therapist called and another time was made. The mother came to this late. She spoke in a highly charged rush of words and the therapist felt that the mother was too anxious to take in any responses from her. After the session she received a message to say that the mother did not want to attend any further appointments but that the therapist could call her if she wished. She did, and on the phone the mother accused her of being cold and distant. The therapist had a long telephone conversation with the mother in which she addressed mother's disappointment, and mother finally agreed to give it another try. Thereafter the mother came with her baby and they had a successful engagement in the therapy.

Some immigrant families may have particular concerns about how the information will be used. With such families, the suspicion may have to be acknowledged and the issue of confidentiality addressed quite early on in the process. It is possible that over time and in the context of the therapeutic relationship, the suspicion or fear may subside and trust develops.

Secrecy

In certain instances the request for help may be kept a secret by the parent within the nuclear or extended family. Cultural factors may play a part, e.g. when turning for help outside the family is seen as shameful or dangerous. Personal anxieties about exposure or relationship stresses, such as domestic violence or intrusive grandparents, may also play a role. The attitude of secrecy may be known to the therapist from the outset, e.g. stated in the referral letter; in some cases she may be unexpectedly confronted with the secret, e.g. when phoning to make an appointment the telephone may be answered by a suspicious partner. In such situations the therapist is required to use her clinical judgement to sustain therapeutic contact. The issue of secrecy will need to be explored if therapeutic contact continues. In some cases it is the mother's own harsh self-judgement about the need for help that is played out in keeping knowledge about the referral from others.

Refusal to allow contact with the professional network

Not all parents immediately accept contact between the therapist and the professional network. This may be due to poor relationships with the professional/s in question, fear of stigmatisation, or a belief that the network is hostile, e.g. that their baby could be taken away. In the majority of cases, careful and sensitive exploration of these fears and a discussion about what contact with the professionals entails leads to permission being given. Where this is refused, careful thought has to be given to whether the work can proceed.

Refusal to allow videotaping

The parents may refuse to allow videotaping of the sessions from the beginning, or may consent to videotaping and then later retract, e.g. when disclosing sensitive material. This issue may need to be reviewed from time to time, given the meaning it holds for the family and the changes in the intimacy of the material and work over time.

> A father refused to allow the sessions to be videotaped. He also frequently appeared to take the therapist's observations and comments as criticisms of his parenting. The therapist took up his sense of her as a 'critical eye'. He agreed. The therapist wondered if he is often critical of himself. He confirmed that he was usually beset by self-doubt; thus he came to see that the first and strictest critic was himself rather than the therapist. He spontaneously made a link with not wanting the video, and suggested that the therapist might indeed use it.

However, the families' access to parent–infant psychotherapy is not dependent on their agreement to be videotaped and they need to be reminded of this.

High-risk, 'hard-to-reach' populations

The process of engaging becomes much more complex when reaching out to high-risk vulnerable populations who do not normally access perinatal and postnatal services, such as families living in temporary accommodation, women suffering domestic violence and asylum seekers. The therapist will need to work closely with the referring agency to plan the family's introduction to the therapist and service. She may need to persevere in initiating and maintaining contact with the family and be flexible in her approach.

> A refugee mother lost her way to her first session, the geographical confusion mirroring the emotional dislocation. The therapist responded by arranging to meet mother and baby to escort them to the centre.

Therapists at The Anna Freud Centre have been known to meet patients on the corner, visit accident scenes (see Chapter 6) and hold sessions in the back of a car.

Breaking off contact

Parents change their minds about proceeding with a referral to a service for any number of reasons. They may find the first session did not match their expectations, e.g. for direct advice on problem solving. Intrapsychic or interpersonal conflict – such as anxiety and shame about what may be uncovered, or concern about the impact on the couple relationship – can also deter parents from committing to a course of therapy. The therapist will have addressed as much of this as she can in the first session but it may not suffice. When follow-up attempts do not succeed in bringing the family back, the therapist does what she can to leave the way open for further engagement with the family.

The therapist will also take the appropriate steps to liaise with the relevant agencies. Where there are child protection concerns she ensures that the referrer is aware that the family is not taking up the offer of therapy. If the parents have self-referred and there are child protection concerns, the therapist will need to record her concerns with the relevant services.

Establishing the baby as a partner in the therapeutic process

The baby's importance as a partner in the therapeutic process needs to be established from the very beginning, no matter what the age of the baby or his familial or cultural status. The therapist's attention to the baby's state and his communications, her attempts to understand and scaffold his feelings, her readiness to privilege the baby's needs – impart to the parents, and to the infant himself, her perception of his centrality in the therapeutic proceedings. Her interventions in relation to this will be guided by the verbal and non-verbal information received from the parents and baby and her counter-transference to the baby.

The techniques used to engage the baby cluster around direct work with the baby and representing the baby to the parent/s. Working directly with the baby, as in talking and *playing* with him, involves adjustment of technique according to the baby's age and developmental stage. With a very young baby the therapist uses herself as the object of play. She may lean slightly forward to be in the baby's line of vision, use exaggerated facial expressions and speak in 'motherese'. Such actions are evocative for the baby and usually lead to increased social–emotional exchanges, with the baby taking turns in proto-conversation and regulating his state through maintaining and averting eye contact. In a slightly older baby the therapist may choose to incorporate a toy into the play. The therapist then follows the baby's cues, *modelling* pleasurable and playful interactions to the parents.

Baby, age seven months, was kicking her feet. The therapist tapped on the floor in matching rhythm. Baby paused, then resumed her kicking with her eyes fixed on the therapist. They played for a while and then father joined in. The following session baby kicked her legs, looking at the therapist. The therapist laughed and started tapping – looking at father. He also laughed and said it has now become a family game.

While, in this very early stage of the therapy, the therapist's attitude and behaviours with the baby establish his position in the therapy, it is important that the therapist is sensitive to the parent's feelings regarding her approach and interactions. In the previous example, the father was only too ready to learn about his daughter's capacity to join in and then to lead. In the case below, mother felt differently.

Six-month-old baby reached out to take a toy. The therapist said 'You like this toy don't you?' and placed it closer to him. Mother moved swiftly to stop this happening and spoke of her worry of germs and contamination. Baby's face fell and the therapist mirrored his disappointment in her facial expression. She then said to him 'Mummy is worried you will become ill'. This comment also acknowledged mother's anxiety and wish to protect him. The therapist was scaffolding both baby's and mother's states of mind and representing them in a non-judgemental way to each other.

The therapist's initial response in handing the baby the toy was an acknowledgement of his wish to interact through play. However, it is possible that she might have jumped in too soon with her desire to engage with the baby to meet his need to share and explore. This can happen in cases where the baby is eager for interaction and recognises a possible playmate in the therapist. It was also possible that the therapist was already picking up the baby's entreaty when his urge for play was being thwarted. In the early days of the treatment, this mother insisted on her baby playing with his own toys and the therapist had to tread carefully, with much sensitivity to the parent's feelings. Gradually baby's toys were replaced by the communal toys with no serious impact on his health.

In engaging with babies, therapists need also to be careful about competing with the parent. The therapist may unwittingly provoke feelings of incompetence or shame in the parents. If this is not recognised and addressed there is a risk of losing the family from treatment. Moreover, taking up the parent's response may open avenues of conversation about their feelings about themselves as parents, and may also alert the therapist to cultural morés that regulate their behaviours.

Working with the parent in relation to the baby also focuses their thinking on the importance of the baby in the therapeutic process. The therapist may *represent the baby's states of mind* to the parents by talking about what the baby might be feeling, or talking directly to the baby, as in the earlier case, when the therapist said to the baby 'You are telling us that you want to be part of this conversation'. Until the therapist intervened, the parents' preoccupations had kept her on the sidelines. At times, while engaging an anxious parent in the process of therapy, some *guidance* may be appropriate. For example, the therapist asked a mother who was struggling to comfort her baby 'Do you think she would like to face you and for you to talk to her now?'

Sometimes feelings of wanting to 'rescue' a baby are aroused in the therapist at this early stage in the therapy. This can be an indication that the baby's development is in trouble and therefore in need of urgent attention. In the same vein, a baby who is experienced as unappealing may have become so because of negative projections that he has incorporated. In such cases it is necessary to work both with the parent's representations of her baby, and with his adaptations to her negative projections, in order to engage the baby and establish him as a partner in the therapeutic process.

> Father continued talking to the therapist, over-riding the cries of his one-month-old baby. The therapist asked him what he thought was happening with baby. Father replied that he was used to crying, his mother and now his wife were the 'weepy sort'. The therapist realised that father was extending his derogatory anger across the generations (from mother to wife to baby), and was thus unable to recognise and accept his baby's age-appropriate developmental needs. She also wanted to help this very young baby to feel effective in bringing about a contingent parental response. The therapist spoke in a soft voice to the baby, repeating phrases such as 'Oh dear, you are getting so upset . . . you are very small and need your daddy now . . . what is daddy going to do?' Eventually father started rubbing the baby's tummy and then picked him up. Baby looked intensely into father's face and quietened. The therapist said, still addressing the baby 'The magic of daddy's face . . . your daddy'. Father replied 'I never thought . . .'

How a baby responds will provide clues to the security or otherwise of his attachments to his parents and will inform the therapist how to tailor her interventions. A baby who is able to smile at the therapist, but treats her with appropriate caution and who looks to the parents for reassurance already has a partnership with his parents. With babies whose predominant way of being is to disengage, the therapist has a more active role, both in her direct work with the baby and in working with the parents, to kick start the baby's skewed development. When babies are established as part of the therapeutic process, the therapist is in a better position to assess the appropriate treatment modality to address the difficulties in the parent–infant relationship.

Assessment of risk

The therapist is first alerted to possible concerns at the referral stage when she establishes the level of urgency for baby and parent. Throughout the engagement process the therapist observes and assesses the baby's development. The main criteria for this are behaviours in relation to expected social–behavioural milestones and adaptations and defences constructed within the parent–infant relationship. In addition the therapist will be looking at the parent's and baby's capacity for change (see below).

Where strains are developing, for example a baby who does not seek out his parent's face, this will be addressed by the therapist, and the parent's and baby's ability to create safer ways of relating will be monitored. The baby will be considered at risk if the parent is not able to work around the baby's strain and the baby resorts to increasingly maladaptive solutions despite the therapeutic interventions. For example, a baby who consistently avoids eye contact with the parent and slumps or arches when held is likely to be defending against strong negative feelings in the parent that are frightening to him. The therapist can address this with the parent and baby through a variety of techniques – exploration, mirroring, reflecting back, representing the baby to the parent, interpretation. She may find a gradual change in their relationship so that the baby is able to use the parent for comfort and safety, and the risk is then resolved. Where there is either no change, or change is too slow for the baby's developmental needs and timetable, this information will be crucial in the choice of treatment modality and in the decisions about involving the network.

Assessing the capacity for change in the dyad/triad

The changes that parent–infant psychotherapy seeks to facilitate in this phase of the treatment are towards safer, more pleasurable interactions and the repair of mismatches that cause fear and upset to the infant and parent partners. An acknowledgement in the parents that something needs attending to in their relationship with their baby is the first step. It is also necessary for the parent/s to feel responsible for, and capable of, making adjustments in their own behaviours. A parent who persists in blaming someone else – her own parents, partner or the baby himself – may resist reflecting on the difficulties they are bringing to the relationship with the baby and what they can do to improve it.

The therapist can promote change through supporting positive interactions and addressing the meanings for both parent and baby of the more negative interactions. In the beginning phase she may privilege the positive aspects, such as a baby's preference for mother, and choose not to comment on the negative aspects, for example a baby turning away. Alternatively, she may alert the parent to what their infant might be feeling, e.g. by *reframing* the baby's action as 'trying to find a comfortable place in mother's lap', or address the mother–infant predicament with a comment such as 'it is difficult for mother to know and impossible for baby to tell except by his actions'. A capacity for change can be seen to occur when a family begins to engage with new ways of thinking about the problem through their engagement with the therapy. It involves the family in learning new ways of seeing themselves and their baby. The capacity to change will need to be translated to the interactions between parents and their infants. For instance a mother who turns and scoops up her baby after she has been helped by the therapist to see her baby differently, or parents who are able to acknowledge that they have been attributing something to their infant that belongs to earlier troubled relationships, are well on the way.

The therapist's capacity to observe, reflect and model will be crucial to supporting the capacity for change in the parent–infant relationship. She will need to tread a careful line between intervening too quickly (sometimes out of her own anxiety), which may cause feelings of envy or incompetence in the parent, and leaving the baby too long in a difficult state. Careful attention to her own counter-transference will often be the crucial guide to the timing of her responses.

Reaching a preliminary psychodynamic formulation

By the end of this beginning phase the therapist should have a tentative working hypothesis about the dynamics underpinning the parent–infant relationship. This will include both nurturing and problematic aspects of the relationship:

- the parent's state of mind in relation to the baby
- past experiences that are unconsciously being replayed with the baby
- current attachment experiences that impact on the parenting of this particular baby
- unresolved loss/trauma for the parent
- the transference to the baby (including whom/what the baby represents to the parent)
- the baby's developmental status and adaptive strengths
- precocious maladaptive defensive functioning in the baby
- the capacity for interactive repair between parent and infant.

The therapist needs also to have a preliminary hypothesis about the relative strengths and weaknesses in the parents' current adaptive and defensive functioning, and their capacity for change. Finally, the therapist will have a grasp of areas of urgent concern in the relationship and child protection issues.

> In the earlier case of the mother described as having 'disordered thinking' the therapist's initial response was that the mother's difficulties might rule out the possibility of parent–infant psychotherapy. This view changed when the therapist observed the family's resources, such as the baby's tentative responses to the therapist's overtures, father's willingness to attend and the baby's capacity to use him as an alternative attachment figure. Observing the family interactions, the therapist was concerned about the lack of pleasure in their relationships and inhibition of spontaneity and play in the baby. The therapist's hypothesis was that mother's withdrawn and depressed state – related to unresolved conflicts with her own mother – was being echoed in her baby. Father, caught up in his own difficulties, was unable at that point to meet his daughter's infantile needs or support the relationship between his daughter and his wife. These issues in each member of the family seemed amenable to being worked with in parent–infant psychotherapy, as evidenced by the use each made of the first session.

Throughout the process of hypothesising, the therapist will be monitoring the transference to her – such as baby's and parents' neediness and fragility, and her own counter-transference feelings. The therapist's identifications may shift between parents and baby. She may feel anxious or overwhelmed. Throughout she must be able to reflect on these states in herself which are an inevitable and important part of the process of intuiting similar states in either parent or child. In addition the therapist must be able to distinguish what belongs to her from that of the parents and the baby. This will guard against her acting out her own conflicts through the parent–child situation.

Agreeing the treatment modality

The final piece of work in this phase is the choice of treatment modality. The therapist will have some thoughts on what may be appropriate for the particular family and will bring the subject for discussion with them.

The choice of modality will be influenced by a number of factors – their suitability for parent–infant work, their wish to work individually or in a group, the intensity of the bond they have established with the therapist in this phase.

The first question is whether parent–infant psychotherapy is the treatment of choice. The parents will already have indicated their ideas about this, either in their evident commitment to the process (attending regularly, expressing relief) or in voicing their doubts. In some cases they may have expressed their feelings through lack of engagement and/or actual with-drawal. The therapist may think that parent—infant work is not appropriate at that point because, for whatever reason, the parent seems unable to engage or sustain the engagement in therapy, or another course of action (such as hospitalisation, or marital therapy) is needed.

If the wish is to proceed with parent—infant psychotherapy, there is a decision to be made at this stage whether the group or individual therapy is preferred. The criteria for selecting/joining the group are set out in Chapter 8. The parents may request 'individual' family work, perhaps because they felt safe working with the therapist and sense that their experience of the therapeutic approach in the intake/beginning phase has been helpful to them. The therapist's psychodynamic formulation and assessment of the parent/s' and baby's capacity to change, and her counter transference to the family, will guide her in supporting the family's request or exploring it further with them.

A brief intervention may be planned out of necessity, e.g. moving to another area, or choice, e.g. the parent who does not want a longer-term commitment. A parent in this position may use the brief intervention to think with the therapist about the impact of the presenting problem on their child and to explore ways to address the situation. Here the aims will be limited and there may be less 'unravelling' of the different meanings of the difficulty.

A more open-ended course is frequently the treatment agreed upon. The parent may feel reassured that help will be available as needed and that the pace of change will dictate the length of treatment. Whether or not this, in fact, turns out to be the case will then depend on the shape of the therapy as it progresses.

The end of the beginning phase

The beginning phase sets the parameters for the work of parent—infant psychotherapy: building a trusting relationship in a safe setting, where the strengths of the parent—infant relationship can be reinforced and the difficulties in the relationship can be addressed. The therapist will have developed an initial working hypothesis and some aspects of this psycho-dynamic formulation will have been discussed with the family, as the basis for engaging in the work and the chosen modality. The end of the beginning phase of parent—infant psychotherapy is not a discrete entity. Many of the techniques used in this phase will continue to be relevant in the middle stages. There is nevertheless a change in the nature of the therapeutic encounter as the therapy becomes more established: it settles into a regular pattern of appointments and the process of work in the sessions for both the baby and his parents is more taken for granted.

SUMMARY OF THE THERAPIST'S ROLE IN THE BEGINNING PHASE

- Establishing the setting for therapeutic involvement with the parents and network.
- Engaging the parents and baby in a collaborative process to understand their difficulties and address them.
- Modelling the therapeutic process through her mentalising stance and application of appropriate techniques of intervention.
- Reaching a preliminary psychodynamic formulation about the strengths and difficulties in the parent–infant relationship, past and present personal and cultural influences, the participant's capacity to change and areas of risk to the baby.
- Reaching an agreement with the family regarding choice of therapeutic modality.

Chapter 6

The middle phase: elaboration and consolidation

Carol Broughton

OVERVIEW

The middle of the treatment holds the key to change in the parent–infant relationship. Even if the therapeutic alliance – the shared commitment to find a way of understanding and addressing the problem – still feels shaky, there is a sense that the process of engagement and negotiation is ongoing. There is hope that things will get better despite possible tension between the slow groundwork needed to build a therapeutic relationship and the fantasies brought and acted upon by the parent. For example, the therapist may be faced with idealization and unrealistic expectations on the part of the parent for a painless, almost magical resolution. Inevitably there is disillusionment and moments of despair where the therapist has to hold on to hope. If the process of engagement is strong enough, the parents accept that they have to come back session after session just as they have to get up night after night with their baby, having done something with the powerful emotions in play. Where parent and infant have come reluctantly, perhaps urged on by a referrer, the therapist may have to create hope – that change is possible and that she can bear the tedium and the pain of the material that they bring.

The baby, too, absorbs and creates a sense of momentum in the work. He builds his own relationship with the therapist and expectations of her helpful responses. Babies seem quickly to understand the therapeutic space created for themselves and their parents, and to make use of it. For example, playing peek-a-boo to explore separation within the safety of the session, or turning to the therapist when mother is upset.

An appreciation of the positive therapeutic alliance may co-exist with other less conscious feelings, possibly anger, resentment, hurt or confusion that have yet to be addressed in the treatment. Such feelings are part of the ongoing therapy and take time to identify and work through. The important thing is that they form part of a process of engagement. In time, it may become possible to address directly something that earlier would have been left unspoken or barely alluded to. The therapist may also be aware that the parent has a different cultural background to her own. She may question whether she has understood well enough the relationship between the parent and infant and how the parent is engaging with her. Perhaps a parent finds the therapist's technique of including the infant in the therapeutic process quite alien, or that the therapist cannot really understand the complexity of bridging their different cultures.

In the session, the therapist has a number of techniques that she can use to facilitate the process of the therapy. These techniques are discussed below in relation to the specific aims of the middle phase of the therapy. As treatment progresses, the psychodynamic formulation and techniques are adapted to suit the current state of understanding at that moment between therapist, parent and infant.

AIMS

The aims of the middle phase are to:

- establish a sense of continuity, consistency, security and commitment
- work with the patients in the room
- interrupt maladaptive intergenerational repetitions
- consolidate therapeutic gains
- fashion a sense of the next session
- deal with resistance
- prepare for breaks and absences
- monitor the safety of parent and infant.

Establishing a sense of continuity, consistency, security and commitment

Continuity, consistency, security and commitment are essential components of the therapeutic alliance, in the same way that they are vital constituents of the parent–infant relationship. Parents and infants need to feel safe enough to admit to difficult feelings, risk shedding unhelpful defences and find new ways of relating to each other. The therapist uses her mentalising stance to offer an experience of another mind connecting with their own to process experience. She verbalizes affect to make sense of the confusing and sometimes frightening feelings in the room. She may use interpretation to regulate affect in both parent and infant. For example, she may interpret to the parent that he or she seems angry as a way of bringing negative affect into the open and dealing with it. For the treatment to feel safe to the parent and baby, the negative feelings must be dealt with as they arise in the room.

Security emanates from the understanding that the therapist attends to the workings of her own mind so that she does not intrude her own difficulties or prejudices, can bear the feelings and thoughts that are intolerable to the parent or baby, and will not retaliate. Security also comes from the sense that the therapist commits to the parent and infant, holds hope for them, but does not give false hope, patronize or condescend. She has to be thoughtful and attuned, and not offer glib answers or foreclose on difficult trains of thought.

The quality of the therapist's attention to the parent and infant's communications is central to sustaining the treatment alliance. It involves careful listening and appropriate turn-taking, including attending to silences and the capacity to be with the other without cutting across communications or defending against painful affect. The therapist must judge whether a question serves to clarify an issue or whether she is interrupting a difficult but possibly fruitful moment in the process. In the early stages, however, it is vital to avoid too many awkward silences that leave the parent feeling lost, bewildered or embarrassed. As the treatment progresses, the therapist can gauge whether a silence is destructive, leaving the other in a precarious, abandoned state, or beneficial allowing for reflection.

Working with the patients in the room

Who is the patient?

Insofar as all communication takes place in the room, in the presence of the other, the parent–infant relationship is at all times in focus. At times it is appropriate to work with the parent and infant directly. This can occur when both parent and infant may be able to hear a communication from the therapist. Sometimes, directly addressing the relationship in the therapeutic encounter may present difficulties. For example, the therapist may be acutely aware of the infant's anxiety but also sense that mother would feel rejected or usurped if she responded too precipitously to the infant's needs. Instead she could draw the mother's attention to the infant by voicing his anxiety: 'Are you wondering who I am? Are you checking to see if mummy thinks I am a safe person to be with?' This would allow mother to take the lead in responding to the baby. At other times, it may be necessary to work with one or the other in preparation for the work with the relationship. For example, when a baby is crying it is important to attend to his distress, or a mother may be so flooded with her own upset and confusion that she seems to need the therapist's attention all to herself. The therapist responds to the mother's material but at the same time she holds in mind its relevance for the parent–infant relationship and how she can bring it to bear on the needs of the infant.

The therapist monitors the responses of parent and infant to decide if her intervention is helpful. Are there changes in the parent–infant interaction in the room? Does the infant feel more able to approach his parent after the intervention? Does the parent respond differently this time?

As the therapy progresses through the middle phase, a process often takes place whereby mother and baby are able to share the therapist more and to recognize their relationship with each other as the 'patient', whereas when they start therapy each may be devouring of the therapist for her/his own needs.

Working with the parent–infant relationship

The affective tone between parent and infant is often a good indicator as to the quality of their interaction. Pleasure, playfulness, mutuality are qualities that strengthen the bonding between the infant and parent. A predominance of anger, fear and withdrawal suggests that the relationship is failing. Only when the mother recognizes and responds to her infant's need for her does he feel sufficiently secure to separate temporarily in order to play and explore the room for himself.

The therapist may use different techniques to further such aims. She may *represent the infant's point of view* to the parent, perhaps by speaking for the infant, for example 'Perhaps you are telling us . . .' 'I think you mean . . .' The therapist might *reframe the parent's attributions* to her infant; for example, she might take the mother's comment that the infant stays close to her side and lacks independence and present it in terms of the infant's trust in his mother and reliance on her better judgement. Another technique that could be used in such a case would be straightforward *parent guidance* – describing to the parent what might be expected of an infant at a given age and the way his behaviour relates to his developmental agenda.

Once the therapy is established, the therapist observes that parent and infant have characteristic ways of responding to each other. In the first instance, the therapist may need to draw attention to what is happening by describing what she has observed – *reflecting back the interaction*. This may bring home to the parent aspects of the baby's attachment – for example, his desire and need, of which the parent was not aware.

In the following example, a father is made aware of his own feelings and behaviours which were not conscious. The therapist reflects back the interaction and then links the observation with other material brought into the session by the father.

> Father placed a toy in front of his baby just as baby turned round to approach him. The therapist pointed this out: 'You just gave him a toy rather than yourself.' Father seems surprised, 'Really? I didn't notice.'

The therapist linked this with what they were just saying about father feeling suffocated by his baby's unremitting needs.

The therapist may also use *reflecting back to the baby*, with the aim of representing the baby's state of mind and linking his feelings and behaviour with that of the parent.

> Therapist: 'You started banging that toy just as mummy was telling me about getting cross yesterday'. Baby paused and looked at the therapist. Mother made an impatient click with her tongue. Baby started banging loudly again. Therapist: 'I think you are telling us how you feel about mummy's tone of voice'.

Reflecting back the interaction serves to disrupt the usual pattern of relating between parent and infant. It effectively 'winds back the tape', as in a video recording, to examine the frame more closely.

Mirroring may similarly address unhelpful patterns in the parent–infant relationship, as in the following example.

> Mother was describing her devastation at her own mother's recent death, while smiling brightly at the therapist and cooing at her baby. The therapist's face and demeanour were grave, matching mother's real feeling state. She said to the baby, 'Your mummy is very sad but frightened of what that will do to you'. Baby gazed at therapist gravely and mother burst into tears.

In this case, the mother's attempts to protect her baby from her distress were in fact confusing for the infant, who would have apprehended his mother's true feelings at odds with her behaviour. Addressing the relationship directly within the safety of the therapy, enabled mother and infant to recognize commonalities and links between their feeling states, behaviours and defences. It also helped to define what the feelings are and differentiate between what 'belongs' to the parent and what to the infant.

However, reflecting back and mirroring discordant situations can be exposing. The therapist has to judge the timing of such interventions and may decide to wait until the therapeutic relationship is well established. The therapist may feel that the parent needs to feel contained and understood before she challenges her to reflect on the meaning and effect of certain behaviours. At the same time, the therapist is aware that the baby does not have time to wait for changes in the parent's defences and habitual mode of relating.

It is also possible to interrupt maladaptive repetitions in the parent–infant relationship through *interpretation*. The therapist can make meaningful links between past and present through interpretations that lead to insight about 'ghosts' and conflicts. Unconscious assumptions and phantasies are often expressed through affect and behaviour, through the moment by moment transactions between parent and infant.

In the following example, the therapist addressed conflict and defence between parent and infant as these were played out in the interactions observed in the therapeutic session.

> Mother was changing her nine-month-old baby's nappy while he was squirming and shouting. Mother was getting increasingly tight lipped, clenching her face as she held him down. Baby's protests escalated and he twisted away from her. Then suddenly he stopped. Mother finished changing him and sat him up, away from her. He was motionless. The therapist said, 'You both got so angry there. I thought you were hating each other . . . perhaps it felt that the other one was also hating you?' Mother continued to look furious, but baby reached out to the teddy. Mother exclaimed that he had played with the teddy when they first came, and were both anxious then. She leaned over and kissed his head and baby collapsed into her.

Working directly with the infant

Babies are constructing their internal world and the attachment patterns that will guide their future modes of relating to others. It is vital, therefore, that the therapist consistently includes the infant directly in the therapy to provide functions that his parents cannot yet provide, and to enhance his efficacy in communicating and reaching out to the parent to meet his attachment needs.

The therapist uses various techniques to build up a therapeutic relationship that he experiences as including him too.

Playing is an effective way of communicating with the infant and addressing the relationship at the infant's development level. A game can become an important locus for pleasurable sharing between the baby and the adults in the room. Furthermore, it is one in which the baby can take the lead, initiating and terminating the game as he wishes.

> Baby was clutching a ball but lost his grip. It slipped out of his hand and rolled in the direction of the therapist. She said 'Hello ball. Shall I roll you back to baby?' and did so. He chortled and tried to return it to the therapist. The game continued for a few minutes and the therapist suggested 'Shall the ball go to mummy too?' and rolled it to the mother. Mother joined the game and they played as a threesome. In the next session, the baby initiated the game. The therapist suggested 'I

know who plays best with you – it's your mummy!' and left most of the rolling to them, although watching with interest and joining in when the ball came her way.

By including and handing over to the mother, the therapist avoided presenting herself as the better parent, or implying that the mother did not understand the infant's wishes and intentions as well as she did.

The therapist may help an infant to regulate his affect through *mirroring* the infant's state of mind.

The therapist observed that a baby seemed frightened by loud noises but that mother was dismissive of his 'edginess'. In an early session he startled at the sudden slamming of a door. The therapist gasped loudly, looking at baby and drawing his attention to her. He looked at her seriously. She said in an exaggerated voice, with widened eyes, 'That was very scary'. Baby's body relaxed. Later, the therapist linked the baby's startle with the noise of the parental rows to which he was exposed.

Through her use of mirroring the therapist helped the infant with his frightening feelings; she created meaning for the baby through her receptivity and contingent response, and for the mother by linking his 'scary' feelings to his experience of the parental relationship.

The therapist may *interpret* the baby's state of mind where she observes a precocious defence interfering with his dependency and attachment needs.

Baby, four months old, was biting on his fist as mother tearfully described feeling depressed and overwhelmed. Ignoring his mother, he fixed his gaze on the therapist. She said to him, 'Your mummy is so sad . . . you can't ask her to hold you when she's crying like this. Are you lonely and scared like mummy? Are you asking me to help you and mummy?' Mother and infant looked at the therapist. It seemed a thoughtful pause.

Interpretations that are made in the here and now of the interactions between parent and infant challenge preconceptions and create a rupture in habitual modes of relating. Arising out of the immediate heightened emotional context, they are in effect appealing to the parent's capacities for reflection and linking.

The infant's use of the therapist

The therapist's work with the infant is facilitated by his growing 'use' of her to promote his development.

In the early stages of the therapy baby responded to father's angry recriminations towards his partner, baby's mother, by very quietly staring at the lights. As he became accustomed to the therapeutic work, baby continued to play even when father's voice took on the particular strident tone that still triggered his anxiety. After a more reflective period, father came again in turmoil. Baby rushed over to the therapist and threw himself into her lap. Father expressed amazement 'I think he is asking you to help'.

The infant had come to see the therapist as someone who could help with the frightening anger between his parents. She also introduced a reflective, regulating 'third', which facilitated his experience of a safe triad, rather than an explosive one.

Working with the parent

Scaffolding the parents' self-reflective function

The therapist uses her capacity for reflection and mentalisation to make sense of the parent and infant's states of mind, to give them shape and meaning and to locate them in a therapeutic process. Through her reflection on the parents' material, the therapist fosters a sense in the parents of the importance of reflective functioning for their relationship and how states of mind impact on the parent–infant relationship. The therapist makes her own thinking available to the parents as a means of scaffolding their reflective capacities. The parents take in the model of a thoughtful adult mind engaging with the vicissitudes of another mind and, in turn, are able to offer this capacity to their own infant. In the following vignette, the therapist observes the minutiae of the interaction and reflects on what she sees, offering her thinking to both parents and infant so that each has his or her own experiences represented as part of a wider set of meanings.

Baby was held by father, facing out, while the parents and therapist talked about the mother's extended period in hospital, separated from her baby and partner. The therapist leaned towards the parents, attentive and empathic to their pain. As mother spoke about her guilt at leaving her baby, she reached out and took him from father. The therapist noted the timing of mother's claim on her baby and that father handed him over silently. She thought that the silent movement of the baby from one pair of hands to the other was a replay of the undiscussed separation at the time of mother's hospitalisation. She watched the baby's body as the transaction took place. He stiffened briefly, before relaxing in mother's lap. He, too, did not make a sound. The therapist reflected on the baby's experience of rupture as, without warning and with no reference to his internal state, he had to accommodate to the unexpected change in his physical and emotional holding. The therapist addressed all three of them, saying: 'I think that these separations have been so sad, and have made you feel so guilty, that there has been no way for you to think about them together. Each of you, perhaps, has suffered silently and alone.' Mother stroked baby's cheek as her eyes filled with tears, and father put his arm round them both.

Each member of the family had been struggling with their own feelings in relation to separation. By contextualising their feelings and giving them a shared meaning, the therapist enabled the parents to scaffold their infant's experience so that his sense of separation and loss is made bearable by their expression of tenderness towards him.

Working with conflict

A parent's attachment representations may engender conflict and defence at the interpersonal level. A parent who is ambivalent and unresolved in relation to her past relationships brings the same ways of relating to her infant and to the therapist. The therapist may find that a mother cancels at short notice, but then rings the therapist and wants to talk extensively about her difficulties. The therapist may feel confused and uncertain about the status of the therapy and the nature of her engagement with the mother. She may note that in the room the infant seems anxious, dissatisfied and difficult to comfort. The therapist offers the mother an understanding of her dilemma: that she both wants and doesn't want the therapeutic engagement and how difficult it is to feel anxious and uncomfortable when she is in the room and anxious and unsupported when she isn't.

A parent may also carry negative feelings about herself at an intrapsychic level and these too may impinge on the relationship with the infant.

A mother, outwardly attractive and successful, described her own mother as finding her ugly, disappointing and defective. She was referred because she persisted in an unfounded view that her infant's head was misshapen and that he was brain damaged. In this case, the mother transferred repudiated aspects of herself on to her baby to the point where she was compromising their relationship and his development by being unable to look at him with affection so that already he was gaze avoidant.

The therapist worked with the interactions in the room while linking past with present in order to separate what belonged to mother and what to her infant.

The therapist has to judge the timing of her interpretation. There has to be sufficient trust and understanding between therapist and parent, otherwise at best the interpretation will be ignored or at worst it will reinforce the parent's defensive manoeuvres or leave him or her in a vulnerable state.

The therapist may not feel that a parent is open to interpretation at all and choose to stay with the directly expressed dilemma, perhaps around the exhaustion or confusion of being a new parent. It may be that a new mother, finding herself isolated and without the support of her own mother, for example, is looking for a positive relationship with another person who can take on a supportive 'grandparent' role. In that case, the therapist would decide to work with the positive transference and give less weight to ambivalence in the mother's relationship with her infant. A brief intervention, together with support from the network (see Chapter 3), might be sufficient to help the mother. In another case, negative feelings of hostility, blame and guilt towards the infant might emerge during treatment and the therapist would address these through the deepening therapeutic relationship.

Working with the father, mother and infant

Wherever possible, fathers are included in parent–infant psychotherapy. The therapist works with the material brought by each person in the room and the relationship of each parent with their infant, with each other and with the therapist. Inevitably, working with a triad is complex because each individual or combination within the triad may be simultaneously needy for the therapist's attention. At times, the therapist may feel she can hold all participants in mind, at times she may feel that she has 'dropped' one of the members of the family. It is important that the therapist attends to her own functioning in the situation and, when necessary, she may slow down or halt the proceedings in the room to make sure that all are gathered in again.

The therapist has to be sensitive to dynamics in the parents' relationship and how they impact on the infant. Where parents are able to work collaboratively in the sessions around co-parenting their infant, the therapeutic work with the baby is supported. In some instances, the therapist may recognize a pairing within the triad so that the third is subtly excluded.

Mother's disability prevented her from carrying her baby. However, she felt that all other maternal functions were also taken away from her by her able-bodied partner, who was the baby's primary carer. Observing the interactions in the room, the therapist noted that even before baby had completed a communication his father was moving in to respond. Thus father was cutting across possibilities for baby and mother to reach out to each other. Closer observation also showed that the baby avoided his mother, whose hostile and teasing remarks to the baby alternated with reaching out and grabbing him to her.

A conflictual relationship between the parents may be played out with the infant. Perhaps the therapist will observe how the infant cannot move freely between mother and father in the room as if he senses that there is no comfortable place for him. The therapist can represent the infant's experience to the parents, and explore with them the difficulties in being a threesome. The therapist might address the infant with a comment on how when he wants to be with mummy he feels that his daddy feels left out and when he wants to be with daddy he feels his mummy is upset. In situations of conflict the therapist has to monitor her own responses to each parent carefully so that she is not pulled into supporting one over the other or repeating a particular aspect of their relating.

Even when the father is absent, the therapist works to include him in the room. She explores the mother's feelings about him and the attributions that she makes to the infant in relation to him. A mother who experienced her partner as a bully may perceive ordinary infant behaviour, such as mouthing, tugging at her hair, or accidental flailing, as deliberately aggressive. The therapist can reframe such behaviours so that the mother can reflect on where her own feelings come from. The therapist may talk to the baby about his anticipated thoughts about his father, 'We are talking about your daddy, you don't know him yet but you'll have lots of questions soon, like "where is he?" and "am I like him?"'

Adaptation of technique

Technique has to be used flexibly to help vulnerable or anxious families to continue in therapy. Technique is modified to fit the needs of treatment, including the stage of development of the therapeutic relationship – how far does the therapist risk presenting her understanding of what is happening in the session – and the vulnerability or defensiveness of the parent and infant? Not all parents will respond to the therapist's mentalising stance, some may be better served by a more active approach. A young mother might find it more compelling to look with the therapist at video footage of herself and her baby. Perhaps the therapist will have to go in search of the mother and infant in a concrete rather than a metaphorical fashion.

A mother who felt deeply ambivalent towards both her infant and the therapy telephoned moments before her session to say that she had crashed her car in a neighbouring street. Her baby was unhurt but had narrowly escaped being hit by glass from the broken window. The therapist, faced with what seemed an enactment of the mother's ambivalence, decided to locate the accident and find the mother and baby. It seemed more important to respond in an immediate, caring way than to keep to the boundaries of the therapeutic space, leaving mother and infant shaken and alone. The therapist was aware that interpreting the mother's conflict in relation to herself and the baby would have been persecutory to the mother; her cry for help had to be answered in a correspondingly concrete manner.

Working with the relationship with the therapist

How the parent and infant experience and relate to the therapist is central to the therapeutic process. The ways that patients relate to the therapist depend on their preconceptions, habitual modes of relating to others, as well as the real figure of the therapist in the room. Thus a parent may be relieved to find a therapist who is able to accept their anger and help make sense of it, while another parent may be infuriated or shamed by the therapist's seeming ability to stay calm and continue thinking despite angry outbursts. The therapist conjectures that in each case she has triggered a transference response. In the first case, to a benign, helpful parental figure who makes the parent feel safe. In the second case, to a superior, triumphant, persecutory figure who makes the parent feel infantile, inadequate and out of control. The therapist takes up the negative transference in order to protect the therapy.

> The therapist noted that mother disagreed with every comment she made but at the same time expressed her rejection in an appeasing way 'You may be right, I'll have to think about it, but I don't think so.' After some time the therapist suggested that mother experienced her comments as critical and intrusive, much in the way she described her reactions to her mother in all their telephone contacts.

The therapist also uses her counter-transference to understand how such feelings play into the parent–infant relationship. Does the infant's anger and frustration seem intolerable to the mother? Does the infant feel frightened by mother's outbursts? The therapist is also aware of her relationship with the infant. His attachment representations are in the process of formation but hopefully he is still open to new experiences, both through the interventions of the therapist that speak to him directly and through mother's different ways of thinking and behaving towards him.

Interrupting the repetitions

Rupture and repair in the parent–infant relationship

Both the parent–infant relationship and the therapeutic relationship between parent–infant–therapist are subject to rupture and repair. Close observation of the interactions, and sensitivity to their affective tone and to her counter-transference, can aid the therapist in locating the ruptures in the minute-to-minute interactions.

The therapist observes the 'dance' between parent and infant – where there is attunement, disruption and repair. How long it takes for repair to take place and whether the infant is left for long periods of time in a disregulated state. Do the parents pick up on the infant's distress and offer reassurance either through words or touch or do they allow the infant to become tearful, disconsolate or enraged before intervening? Only if there is a failure to repair does rupture follow. In the room, the therapist models interactional repair through attempts to regulate the infant's and the parent/s' affective states.

> A visit from maternal grandmother had left the mother greatly dis-tressed but the therapist noted that she was keeping a tight lid on her emotions. Towards her baby she was calm and gentle, the strain showing only in her reluctance to allow him to get close to her. Baby, for his part, was unable to play as usual and sought his mother's lap with increasing sadness and anger. The therapist suggested that baby was extra clingy today because he was aware of her turmoil. Mother looked upset, as though the therapist had added to her burdens. She replied that she was keeping her feelings away from him. The therapist suggested that she was trying to do what she had wished, as a child, her own mother could do – protect her from her moods – but that just as she was very clued in to her mother's moods, her baby was to hers. Mother was thoughtful; apparently unaware of her actions, she shifted her position to make it easier for baby to climb into her lap. Later the therapist suggested that linking baby's mood to mother's had initially been hard to take, but that mother had indeed been able to use it to comfort her baby.

Over time, the therapist works to make the ruptures less violent by enabling the parent to be more sensitive to disruptions and the baby to become more effective in communicating his need for repair. This extends the periods of attunement, in the parent–infant relationship and in the relationship between parent, infant and therapist. In a well-regulated state there is potential for reflection in the parent and for the growth of self in the infant.

Rupture and repair in the therapeutic encounter

The therapist has to be attentive to the to-and-fro of interactions in the room, changes in behaviour and the affective tone of interchanges in rela-tion to the therapeutic encounter. She monitors the ups-and-downs in the therapeutic relationship, from slight withdrawal to outright ruptures. The therapist uses her counter-transference to monitor the feelings that may be evoked in the infant both by the mother and herself. She might pick up these feelings as they occur, naming and linking them to what has just happened between them, or to previous responses she has observed.

Timing is important in addressing unconscious repetitions from the past in the current parent–infant–therapist interactions. If the therapist can get hold of the disruption in the therapeutic exchange and take it up in the here and now of the session, repair may start to take place. If she fails to spot and repair early enough, the mother may not return. Too precipitate an interpretation may alienate the mother. Repair then may require active pursuit, telephone calls, letters, use of the network (see p. 55).

Consolidating therapeutic gains

Refining the psychodynamic formulation

Over time, the therapist's thinking about the parent–infant dyad or triad and the material they bring becomes more complex; new hypotheses present themselves and the original psychodynamic formulation is refined (see Chapter 2).

In the following example, a mother brought her infant daughter, who had recently been diagnosed with leukemia, for help with their relationship, which was under strain.

> The therapist observed that in the treatment room the mother kept an emotional distance from her daughter. The therapist's early hypothesis was that the distancing expressed an habitual mode of relating, as well as a defence against the fear that she might lose her daughter.
>
> As therapy progressed, the mother's anger and mistrust of the therapist seemed disproportionate and the therapist felt that mother was preventing her from speaking about the very things that had brought them to therapy. The therapist felt caught up in something that she couldn't possibly understand. When the therapist persisted in trying to understand and did not allow mother to push her away, mother was able to talk about the 'ghost' in her nursery: her own mother had died from cancer without anyone preparing her for the possibility and before she could say 'goodbye'. The therapist hypothesized that her baby's cancer had re-evoked the earlier unresolved loss and trauma, and that she was being subjected to the mother's anger towards her own mother for abandoning her and towards her infant for putting her through the anguish a second time. The therapist was also the recipient of the mother's projection of her powerless, confused and frightened self.

Through her counter-transference feelings the therapist extended the initial hypothesis framed in terms of attachment patterns, to include unresolved loss re-evoked by her baby's illness.

The therapist as a new object

In the transference the parent anticipates that the therapist will behave in the ways attachment figures did in the past. This is the basis for experiencing the therapist as, for example, critical, rejecting and hostile. Repeated disconfirmations of transference expectations allow the parent to experience the therapist as a new object (see Chapter 2), for example, an attachment figure who is accepting and empathic. The experience of the new object in the shape of the therapist enables the parent to develop more helpful, benevolent attachment representations.

The therapist is also potentially a new object to the infant, whose internal self-object world is still in the process of formation. The experience with the therapist free from impingements can enable him to experience his parent/s in a more benign way.

Fashioning a sense of the next session

The expectation that the therapy will continue at least for a given number of sessions is created at the beginning through the initial framing of the problem and the understanding forged between the parent and the therapist about how to proceed. The therapist conveys to the parent that she understands the therapeutic relationship in terms of a process in which therapist, parent and infant work together to think about the difficulties. As the therapy progresses the participants are creating an expectation of structure, coherence and a dynamic within the therapeutic relationship that enables one session to lead to the next, whatever the powerful feelings that come into play at any given point, positive and negative.

At the beginning of the session, there is a regrouping of the participants – a subjective sense in each person that some things are familiar and can be relied upon and that others are strange and unsettling. The treatment room itself, as described earlier, is kept as familiar as possible. The feelings of strangeness and familiarity are then focused on the therapist and the relationships in the room, in the same way that the infant experiences his mother as both familiar and safe and sometimes different and less predictable. The way that each participant responds to the others' seeming sameness and difference is the essence of the therapeutic encounter. Patient and therapist may learn to read each other's body language; a quickening of attention in relation to some material, a stiffening in posture suggesting

anger or disapproval, characteristic gestures of self-soothing when per-
plexed or worried. Similarly, the therapist, parent and baby establish a
pattern of welcoming and being received back and a store of shared
knowledge that eases them back into the session. The therapist is then able
to wait for the mother or infant to make the next move as she tries to
understand what has happened for each of them in the intervening time
since they last met. Perhaps the infant will choose a familiar toy or mother
will refer back to something that happened in the previous session. If so,
there is a sense that they are on the same track and working towards a
mutual goal.

When there is a sense that every session represents a new beginning, there
will be painful feelings of discontinuity and emptiness that need to be
addressed if the treatment is to progress. The therapist voices the anger,
disappointment or frustration in the parent that the therapy is not working,
and tries to help the baby find a safe way to be in the room with this
dissatisfied parent. Something may shift in the treatment as a result. Sometimes treatment is not successful or has limited scope and an ending is
agreed or the parent does not return.

As the therapy progresses, the parent and infant need to feel that the
therapist holds in mind the previous session and can make links with the
past, both in relation to the parent's history and to what has happened
previously in the treatment room, and has a sense of the future direction of
the work. The therapist finds ways of processing what has happened in the
previous session so that she can bring it back in a form that will be useful to
the parent and infant. She thinks about the material between sessions. She
may review the videotape of the session, often seeing things that were not
clear to her at the time. She may also consult with her colleagues or bring
the case to a team meeting. The important factor is that the parent and
infant sense that something has happened in the intervening period while at
the same time there is continuity in the treatment and the setting. Both
continuity and change are vital to the therapeutic and the developmental
process.

At strategic points in the therapy, the therapist may choose a formal
approach, beginning the session with a review recapitulating the progress so
far, identifying issues that have been dealt with, those that remain unad-
dressed and new issues that have arisen in the course of the work. This is
most useful where the therapist feels that a piece of work has been
accomplished or conversely where she feels that the direction of the work is
becoming uncertain. In general, the therapist waits to see what the parent
and infant will bring from the previous session, whether there appears to be
a change in their behaviours towards each other and the therapist. She
creates a sense in the parent that there is an ongoing process in which she
monitors change, reflects on the parent's and infant's responses, and looks
forward to further changes.

Dealing with resistance

Despite acquiescing to the requirements of the beginning phase, parents may not be fully engaged in the therapy. Resistance can take many forms: continual lateness, cancellations, or repeatedly informing the therapist that this is not the right place for them. Perhaps a mother says she wants something more practical, more structured. She can't see the point of sitting talking. The therapist is in a quandary. She may feel disconcerted, deskilled and useless. Does she take the mother at her word and accept that this isn't going to work, or does she press on, calling her to rearrange when she cancels, picking up on the lateness, looking for an entry into the therapeutic relationship. The therapist may take the case to her clinical team who, under the pressure of referrals, may also wonder about the value of continuing. The therapist has to consider all the available material. Would the mother be better suited with a different approach? Perhaps the mother is looking for treatment for herself and finds the emphasis on her relationship with her infant too difficult. The therapist may feel disappointment, anger, a sense of failure that her view does not match the patient's expectations. The therapist has to examine her own responses to the parent and infant in the room. She has to distinguish between her wish to continue or not and the patient's wish and psychic readiness at that point.

An important tool for the therapist in sorting out her own feelings in relation to a patient's material is counter-transference, which facilitates understanding of the unconscious meanings in the parent–infant's communications to the therapist, both verbal and non-verbal.

> The therapist had noted previously how uncomfortable the mother seemed in the room and her embarrassment, bordering on shame, whenever her infant made a mess, positing milk or leaving crumbs on the carpet. Mother entered the treatment room and ignoring the carefully laid out cushions in the middle of the floor, sat stiffly on the chair by the desk, keeping her coat on and her bag clutched in her lap. The therapist was left standing, unsure what to do. She was aware that mother's nine-month-old infant was on the mat, looking for attention. She felt the pull of the infant to sit with him. The therapist was caught between the mother's needs and the infant's needs. She felt awkward and out of place, and realized that the mother was not just resentful at being there but was communicating something fundamental about her way of being with others. As she sat with the mother the therapist felt like a small child, powerless and unwanted, and understood that this was in fact how the mother felt. She sensed mother as a child with coat on, belongings bundled up, waiting helplessly for the signal to leave.

The therapist used her counter-transference feelings – rejection, awkwardness and powerlessness – to inform her of the mother's underlying state of mind in relation to her seeming reluctance to engage. The therapist understood that the mother was unconsciously repeating in each session her expectations of loss and rejection brought from her childhood experiences of being passed from one inhospitable relative to another. The mother's resistance to treatment was then understood by the therapist as something that could be worked with in the sessions. The therapy in this case did not break down.

Preparing for breaks and absences

Breaks and absences such as leave, illnesses and holidays provide further instances of rupture and repair in the therapeutic relationship. There will be planned and unplanned breaks and absences in treatment. The therapist prepares the infant and parent by introducing the topic in advance and thinking about what it may mean for each of them and for their being together in her absence. Infants need to be prepared for breaks, as do parents, because they become attached to the therapist and to the therapeutic setting. If the parent is struggling to cope, or has specific difficulties such as a mental health problem, the therapist will talk about letting the network (see Chapter 3) know that there will be a break in treatment. Where possible, holiday cover is provided to deal with a crisis.

Feelings of abandonment and disillusion in parent and infant have to be dealt with after a break, especially if the break was unexpected. The therapist uses the feelings that are brought into the treatment room after a break to explore the parent's attachment representations around loss and characteristic ways of defending against anxiety and distress. The parent may defend against the feelings provoked by the absence by subjecting the therapist to a similar experience, for example, missing sessions, or behaving dismissively towards the therapist, or becoming angry and confused. It may feel as if the break has been 'catastrophic' to the parent. These ways of relating to the therapist's absence or perceived failure can illuminate the way that the parent's attachment insecurities is unhelpful to her infant.

> The first session back after a two-week break, baby and mother looked at the therapist with caution when she greeted them in the waiting room. Baby, normally unreserved in his pleasure at seeing the therapist, took his time before he approached: gazing from a distance and looking worried. After a while he gave a smile and the therapist smiled back and asked whether he was beginning to forgive her for the summer break. Mother, speaking for the first time, told the therapist that recently baby had not wanted to be picked up by anyone other than his parents. The therapist wondered whether she was linking baby's reserve with her to this. Mother shrugged and said, 'It's like being hit by a ball and then not liking balls afterwards'. The therapist

suggested that both mother and baby may have felt that she was a ball who rolled away over the break. Again mother shrugged, this time seemingly in agreement.

In this case, the baby, who was well acquainted with the therapist, may have acutely felt her absence. He would have needed his mother's encouragement to 'remind' him that the therapist was his 'friend' who had come back to be with them. Mother, herself feeling abandoned by the therapist, was not only unable to support her baby but also perhaps transmitted her hurt and resentment to him. Thus both were emotionally awkward upon reunion.

Monitoring the safety of parent and infant

The therapist must continue to assess any risk to the safety and well-being of the parent and infant as the therapy progresses.

Exploring risk in the observed interactions

The therapist assesses risk from the way that the parents talk about themselves or their infant, their behaviour in the room and the infant's response to his parents. As therapy progresses and the parents feels safer in the treatment room, they may feel able to trust the therapist sufficiently to admit more difficult feelings in relation to their infant.

> As her trust in the therapist developed, a mother was able to risk admitting to the therapist that she had been so provoked by her baby that she had found herself with arm upraised, glowering angrily at him. She prefaced this by taking a deep breath and saying that she wasn't going to tell anyone about the incident and seemed to surprise herself by adding that it was her father's angry face that she could see at that moment, her father's face contorted with rage as he struck her. She demonstrated that she was holding her arm in precisely the angle that he held his.

Through engaging with her reflective self-function, the mother was able to recall and put into words her long-forgotten memory. The therapist's measured but deepening intervention had enabled the unconscious procedural memory to find expression. Such an admission of vulnerability and the recounting of a shameful moment would have been impossible earlier in the therapy and was predicated on the empathy of the therapist with the mother's predicament and her linking of the here and now of the mother's experience of being with her infant with the ghosts in their nursery. Bringing this material for reflection, rather than keeping it out of the therapy, reduced the risk of mother acting upon her anger.

In the room, the therapist looks for signs of neglect or fear in the infant: tension, stilling or dissociation. She monitors the parent's mental state, noting depressive or psychotic ideation. Through clarification and exploration she tries to elicit a clearer picture of what the parent is conveying. She works therapeutically, using techniques designed to modify hostile or neglectful parent–infant interactions such as reframing, representing the infant, parent guidance and interpretation. The therapist watches to see how well the parent responds to the interventions and whether there is a shift in the pattern of relating between parent and infant. Decisions about whether a parent can continue to care for an infant with professional involvement may depend on the capacity of the parent to make use of the therapy.

The therapist is presented with a challenge to her capacity to work with a parent and infant in the event of a decision to call in social services. She may feel a tug of loyalty to a parent and baby and a wish to protect a parent who is trying hard to change from the apparently negative judgement implied in the referral to social services. The therapist may, on the other hand, feel very identified with a baby who is in emotional distress, and this can inadvertently be conveyed to the parent through the handling of the referral to the outside agency – it may be too abrupt and without sufficient preparation for the parent. The parent/s' relationship with the therapist is likely to be affected. The parents may feel unable to trust the therapist if the therapist was instrumental in bringing in outside agencies. They may feel that everything they say or do is being monitored and reported back. The perceived loss of a private, confidential relationship has to be addressed, together with the nature of what would be disclosed by the therapist to outside agencies. Parents may also feel relieved that their difficulties are being taken seriously. Often, for example, when parents were not themselves kept safe as children they will be both envious of their baby for being helped when they were not, and relieved that safe boundaries are being put in place. The therapist needs to be supported through supervision and/or consultation in these cases.

SUMMARY OF THE THERAPIST'S ROLE IN THE MIDDLE PHASE

- Strengthening the therapeutic alliance to maintain the ongoing work.
- Elaborating the therapeutic process through techniques such as mirroring, reflecting back, interpretation and scaffolding of the parents' self-reflective function.

- Supporting the infant's developmental moves towards separation, rendering coherent his self–other representations, and monitoring the safety of the infant.
- Supporting the parent's competence and enjoyment of parenthood through the exploration of self-representations and attachment behaviours and the provision of a 'new object' in the person of the therapist.
- Consolidating gains, towards ending.

Chapter 7

Endings in parent–infant psychotherapy

Judith Woodhead

OVERVIEW

Ending is a process and needs to be given time within the trajectory of the therapy. The decision to end parent–infant psychotherapy activates a final stage in the relationship between the therapist and the parent/s and baby. Raw feelings are often readily activated, anxieties about separation and separateness are close to the surface. It is necessary to be especially mindful of such affects, and possible concomitant risk factors. Whenever possible, it is recommended that a sufficient number of sessions are allocated in which to recapitulate experiences and developments over time in the therapy, and express feelings activated by ending.

When therapy proceeds from a beginning to a middle phase, and then to an ending phase, parents and their babies have an experience of a whole relational process that includes getting to know another person and also losing that person. Aiming for a 'good enough' ending, in which the feelings are processed, is important for both parent/s and baby. The baby is constantly facing separations, which he must learn to manage, even momentary ones such as when a parent goes out of the room, or leaves him to sleep, or does not come the moment he calls out. Throughout the therapy the baby and his parents experience the endings of each session and the goodbyes with the therapist – followed by reunions at the next appointment. The ending phase allows for a building-in of those experiences, leading to the final goodbye, when there will be no return for further sessions and therefore no reunions. The ending phase of parent–infant psychotherapy provides a unique opportunity for the baby, along with the parent, for the feelings about separation and loss to be perceived, named, understood, and digested. Experience within the ending process is likely to be felt for some time afterwards, depending on the kind of attachment built up in the therapy and the amount of working through of feelings that has been possible in the therapy. The family's experience of the process of ending will reverberate after the therapy ends. When faced with future separations and loss, experience of ending therapy may serve as an emotional resource.

Different cultures have their own traditions of managing separations and endings. Expressions of grief and mourning are culturally very diverse. It is therefore to be anticipated that parents and babies will have their own experiences and expectations. It is important that the therapist tries to bear in mind and respond sensitively to the parents' own cultural experience of ending and of saying goodbye.

AIMS

The aims of the ending phase are to:

- Enable the parent and infant to come to the end of their therapy and separate from their therapist in a planned way.
- Enable parents to work through their own and their infant's emotional states that are evoked by the ending.
- Interrupt the repetition of negative intergenerational patterns of relating in the ending phase and model new ways of ending.
- Assess risk in the ending phase.

CREATING A PSYCHODYNAMIC FORMULATION OF THE ENDING PROCESS

The therapist needs to prepare for the ending in terms of her thinking about its particular meaning to these patients and their likely reactions. She creates a psychodynamic formulation of the ending process: the kind of process that is likely to emerge and the possible pitfalls, defences and regressions that may emerge in the therapeutic encounter. Ending can reactivate patterns of thought and behaviour that were manifest at the beginning of the therapy and were seemingly worked through. The therapist, thus, has in mind all aspects of the beginning and the middle phases – the reasons for attending, central conflicts, affective states – that were worked with. She also draws on her current perceptions about the parent/s' and baby's functioning together and readiness to end. She will bear in mind, as she thinks about the likely length of the ending phase, the specific experiences of traumatic loss a parent may have had. She will, for example, be prepared to work with specific rigid defences against re-experiencing feelings of loss, this time in relation to the therapist, or the reactivation of overwhelming feelings. She will also bear in mind the pattern of attendances or missed sessions to inform her about whether the parent is likely to use non-attendance as a way of avoiding feelings about separation in the ending phase.

Signs of readiness to begin to end

Signs that the parent/s and infant are ready to begin to end the therapy may include:

Decrease in urgency

The sense of urgency with which the parent and baby first arrived at the point of referral has diminished. Initial concerns seem more in proportion and emotions are increasingly regulated. The decrease in urgency is likely to be linked to changes in the parent and baby's ways of relating, including their ability to tolerate frustration and distress with each other. The following example shows change.

A mother was exhausted and demoralised when she first came with her six-week-old baby. The baby was waking her several times a night. She felt her baby was demanding in order to annoy her and she broke down in tears of hopelessness in the first session. She voiced that she had never imagined that having a baby could be so dreadful, she had so looked forward to it. Slowly over her weekly sessions she was able to connect her current feelings with feelings about her own babyhood when she had experienced neglect. With this she began to be able to relate to her son and recognise his difficulties as separate from her own. As the work progressed the urgency evoked by overwhelming affect diminished. The mother was no longer close to tears all the time, was not full of emotion about the difficulty of being a mother. She was more able to tolerate the baby's waking and felt less persecuted by him. The baby in turn was less fussy, and able to settle more easily.

Development of healthier ways of relating between parent and baby

The therapist will have observed that the relationship between parent and baby has become 'good enough' in the sense that the baby is more able to communicate his needs and the parent is more able to respond contingently (see Chapter 1). Parent and infant show more pleasure and satisfaction in their interactions with each other. The new ways of relating, facilitated within the therapeutic relationship, are being transferred into the parent–baby relationship outside session times. Therefore, they are increasingly able to use ordinary local supports – parents, friends, health professionals and support groups.

Development of the parent's capacity to see her baby as a separate person

Parent's increasing ability to see their baby as a separate person, with his own needs and thoughts and feelings, is also a sign that an ending process can begin. For example, parents may increasingly differentiate between what their baby is feeling and their own feelings. The therapist is likely to have a sense that a transitional space has become established, in which there is a more spontaneous active engagement between parent/s and baby, and between herself (the therapist) and each of them. The parent/s may have gained a greater capacity to accept the baby's dependency needs while also accepting his developmental changes and his changing quests for relatedness. The therapist's perceptions are rooted in her observations of the interactions between parent and baby and in her countertransference feeling about her relationship with parent and baby as separate people. In contrast to earlier times when she may have found herself so involved in her interaction either with the parent or with the baby that she was unable to maintain awareness of the other, she is now able to be aware of the reality of both the baby and the parent in the room. For example, when interacting with the parent she is simultaneously aware of the baby making sounds towards her and finds herself reaching for a toy bus and pushing it towards him. The therapist is at that moment relating to each of them, simultaneously yet differently.

There will also be shifts in the parents' representations of their baby, as they become more able to see that baby's loving and aggressive impulses are part of his own inner world, not their own. This includes recognition that their baby is not a 'ghost' from their own past, nor a part of their own unconscious selves. As a greater sense of separateness arises so scripts that have been used to relate to the baby can give way to more spontaneous ways of relating. This brings a new receptivity to the baby's communications so that the baby's own growing sense of self becomes more supported.

> A baby put his hand into his mother's mouth, exploring the inside with his fingers. She told him to be gentle because it hurt. After a few moments of exploration he took his fingers away and looked at her solemnly. She asked him if he was interested in what the inside of her mouth was like and touched his mouth. He then went on to explore her eyes and nose, and she touched and named his own.

In this mutual activity the mother does not feel attacked by her baby as she might have done earlier in the therapy. She is able to accept the intimacy. She perceives his intention – to explore. She helps him distinguish between her body and his own, her mind and his mind.

Increased capacity for reflective functioning

Parents are likely to have developed their own capacity for reflective functioning through their experience of the therapist's mentalising stance. They will have also joined with the therapist in observing and talking about their baby, to understand his communications. They are thus encouraged to take a stance that has some relational distance from their baby. This allows the baby to begin to develop the capacity to perceive that his mother and father have a mind of their own, separate from his, which he will in time use as a reference point for his feelings and actions.

The capacity for reflective functioning underpins the capacity in the parent to use her own mind as a mirror for the baby, so that the baby can find his own developing self in the parent's mind. For example, a baby used to cry inconsolably when his mother tried to talk to him while feeling stressed and distressed herself. As she experienced containment in the therapy for her own distress she was more able to reflect to the baby his state of mind rather than her own. The therapist observed many subtle responses in the baby suggesting that he had begun to experience her state of mind as less frightening, and could be soothed and enter into reciprocal protoconversation. The development of the capacity for reflective function strengthens the awareness in both baby and parent of the other as an autonomous, but related, self.

Development of self in baby and parent

The therapist will be alert to the parent's perception of him-/herself as a parent and as a person with an identity separate from that of the baby. She will also hold in mind the parent's difficulties that brought the parent and baby into therapy, changes in their functioning, and increased conscious awareness of areas in which they still struggle. The therapist will similarly be alert to qualities in the baby's relating with the parent and with herself, and ways in which the baby is developing his own individual self, based on more diverse identifications. She will monitor the baby's adaptations and use of defences.

> In the first sessions of the therapy baby was unusually and worryingly still. He did not display curiosity about the therapist or the room. He resorted to self-comfort through rocking movements and did not respond to the therapist's overtures. The therapist had slowly to find ways of engaging him. His mother was filled with her own troubles from traumatic experience in her past and this seemed to be reflected in baby's frozen state. Through the course of the therapy, as the mother's own distress was worked with, space developed in which baby could begin to risk looking towards the therapist and make his own tentative

gestures of communication. Nine months later he related with his mother and with the therapist in a qualitatively very different way; when he was upset he could be comforted by his mother rather than comfort himself. His body posture had become more flexible, less rigid.

It was such signs, often subtle, that the therapist used to make a judgement about when to begin an ending process.

Development of emotional regulation

The parents' capacity to understand their baby's communications and recognise their baby's needs enable them to respond contingently to him. The therapist notes that when baby signals distress, mother or father is able to step in to prevent escalation, and when he is overwhelmed they are able to comfort him. In turn, the baby increasingly turns to the parent for emotional regulation where appropriate, expecting a helpful response, and is able to tolerate more frustration through soothing himself for brief periods.

When they began therapy, the three-week-old baby would move from apparent tranquillity to inconsolable cries within seconds. All mother's attempts to sooth – cradling, crooning and feeding – failed. The therapy addressed mother's intense emotional swings and her baby's sensitivity to them. At the end of the therapy baby was still acutely sensitive to his mother's mood. However, he and mother had developed identifiable patterns of comforting. When anxious or distressed he would crawl to mother's lap and she stroked his head. He remained there until he was more able to manage his feelings, and then he would go off to play again.

Signs of readiness in the baby

The baby communicates his psychic readiness to end the therapeutic process when he uses his mother for safety, comfort and play. At the same time, the baby shows increasing engagement with the outside world – objects and people – and, with the parent's support, more moderated anxiety in the face of unrecognised stimuli. The therapist may experience the baby as more robust, curious and playful. Often, in the countertransference the therapist will become aware that her sense of a burdened baby in need of protection has lessened. However, some infants may not achieve developmentally appropriate behaviours because of continuing developmental lags or disability, and the therapist needs to be realistic in her expectations of what a particular baby can achieve in his environment.

There may also be a situation where the baby is developmentally and emotionally ready to end but parent is not. For example, it may be the first time the parent has sought psychological support and she may still be in the midst of a process. Here the parent may be helped to end the parent–infant psychotherapy and seek individual psychotherapy.

Separating from the therapist and ending in a planned way

Separating from the therapist as attachment object

The ending centres on re-working the dependency that has developed during the therapy, and the separation of the parent/s and baby from this attachment figure and the therapeutic setting. In the course of the therapy the therapist has offered a reliable attachment experience that may be very different from the kind of attachment experience the parent/s had in their own infancy or more currently with the baby. With the ending in place, the baby and parents are faced with the task of leaving the attachment figure without this spoiling the positive attachment experience that they have had. If this can occur in a good enough way then there will be psychic development both for parent and for baby, impacting on their capacities to manage future separations from one another. However there are times in therapy when a parent finds the process of detaching from the therapist as attachment figure too difficult, and the therapy may collapse.

Talking with the baby and the parent about ending

Perhaps it is the parent who first brings up the question of working towards ending, or perhaps the therapist introduces the idea. She will seek to be responsive to the parent's view about the course of the therapy and what has been achieved within it. It is important that there is a sense of a joint decision about when it is appropriate to begin to work towards ending. Talking about ending must take place as a central component of the therapy and not be viewed as outside of the therapeutic process. The baby is included as soon as possible in the talk about ending, as he takes in the emotional timbre of the words and the affective tone of the exchanges. The baby may show through his behaviour his awareness of what is being discussed. For example, his play and vocalisations may become more disruptive, as though trying to drown out the adult talk. He may become clingy and demanding, or he may become solemnly silent and withdrawn, expressing shared feelings of being thrown out.

> After 13 months of therapy, the therapist and father decided that sufficient change had taken place in the relationship with the baby for an ending to take place. The father said that he felt that they would be able to manage without their therapy and suggested it was a real step

he and his baby needed to take. A date was set for three months later. During this ending period, difficulties that had brought the father and baby to the therapy were re-worked. To do this the therapist thought back to the beginning and middle phases of the therapy and supported the father in exploring earlier dynamics and events from those times. At the same time she was alert to communications through baby's play. When baby repeatedly went to the door the therapist suggested she was telling about how soon her daddy and she would be leaving and have no more sessions. When she brought her favourite toy, a bus, to the therapist the therapist said that baby had liked the bus and played a lot with it in the therapy. The therapist played with baby and the bus, driving the bus away and back again. She said to baby that soon she and her daddy were not going to be coming any more. They would be saying goodbye to the bus, to the therapist and the room. Father voiced his own memories of times in the therapy that had felt important to him. In particular he recalled how he and the therapist had come to understand that he and his baby daughter had missed out on the earliest bonding time. Father recalled the realisation that he needed to catch up on that bonding experience by allowing it to happen during the therapy. He remembered how he had been unable to look at his baby when she first came, and smiled when thinking of how this had changed. He expressed appreciation for the experience he had had. He thought about how tiny his daughter had been when they first came, how she became a crawler and a walker.

The therapist, by addressing each of them separately while in the presence of the other, and also both of them together, modelled a perception of them as separate individuals and also of them as a father–child pair. There was *recapitulation* of the course of the therapy. This demonstrated that the therapist had in mind the history of the father–baby relationship and was able to think about this. In speaking to the baby the therapist expressed her regard for the baby as a person with a mind of her own who needs to know what is happening. She treated the baby's play as communication that has meaning, thus *modelling* to the father ways of relating with his daughter that help the development of separation behaviours. The baby also experienced affective discourse between father and therapist, witnessing a particular kind of relating which she could internalise to help her develop her own ways of relating.

Including the absent father in the ending process

The father will have been present in the therapy from the very beginning, whether in the room or in the minds of the therapist, mother and baby. He may have been fully involved in the sessions and play a full part in the ending process. In such a case, the therapist will usually be saying goodbye to three people, each with their own ways of handling separation. It is more complex to include the father when he has been absent. The therapist needs to ensure that the absent father is not forgotten in the ending phase. She may refer to things the mother has related about the baby's father, or events that have occurred. This means including thoughts about what happened to the father, and thoughts for how the baby will learn about his father or get to know him in the future. The therapist's acknowledgement that he came from two people is important for the baby, and when she is no longer a part of the baby's life others will be required to provide him with an experience of being thought about cooperatively by two minds rather than by his mother's mind alone.

Arranging an ending date

Talking about ending leads to arranging an ending date. In brief work an ending date may be arranged at the beginning of the course of sessions. In longer-term work the therapist and parent arrange a clear ending date that marks the definite beginning of the ending process, and allows sufficient time for the ending to be facilitated and thought about. In particular there needs to be time for the therapist to explore and clarify with parent and infant their responses to the forthcoming separation from her.

Sometimes a parent may not stay the course through the ending phase, and leave early. On other occasions a parent may seek to prolong the therapy as a way of avoiding a final ending. When a parent requests more sessions, after the ending date, the therapist needs to think clearly about the reasons; these may reflect the parent's anxiety about separation. The parent may again rely on the therapist's reflective function to hold on to the gains of the therapy and work through the fears of no longer having the therapist's help. For example, the therapist may *reflect back* to the parent and the baby current interactions that differ positively from interactions in the past. She may recapitulate on their history together in the therapy and remind them of the changes they have made with each other. If she can address these issues it is likely that the parent will be able to keep to the planned time structure. The following example shows this process:

> A mother referred herself for parent–infant psychotherapy because her ten-month-old could not be left. In the course of the therapy it emerged that the mother could not bear to be without her baby and this was linked to her own abandonment anxieties. With this understanding, mother and infant were able to spend time apart. When the ending was agreed the mother suddenly felt she and her son would both be unable

to cope and sought to extend the therapy. The therapist was initially surprised because they had achieved a much greater degree of separateness in the therapy. She thought with them about the work they had done and helped the mother to see her anxiety as linked to the ending process. The therapist again helped the mother to differentiate between her mental state and that of her son. In this way she supported the infant's developing sense of self and showed she had confidence in the mother to use all she had gained in the therapy. They were able to end according to their plan.

Maintaining continuity and reliability in the ending phase

The loss of the therapist and therapeutic relationship is likely to evoke intensely painful feelings. The therapist needs to ensure that the therapeutic environment remains as facilitating as it was in the former stages of treatment. Continuity and reliability remain just as important as in the earlier phases. This is because the therapy needs to allow for the development of all feelings connected with separation, loss and mourning, so that the therapist can work with the feelings on behalf of the baby and parent. In an unreliable setting in the ending phase the processing and regulation of painful feelings would be impinged upon, with possible reconstruction of the habitual defences against recognition and experience of emotional pain. The availability of the therapist and consistency of length and timing of the sessions, provide necessary predictability and security at a time that may be filled with insecurity and anxiety about the unknown future.

Working through and regulating emotional states evoked by the ending

Throughout the therapy the therapist has been helping the parents to develop their capacity for reflection. This needs extra 'scaffolding' during the ending process so that it can be sustained in the face of the powerful emotions evoked by endings and the defences that parents may use in relation to these.

Understanding feelings in the ending phase

The therapist focuses on the parents' thoughts and feelings as they move through the ending process. She seeks to allow for the expression of emotion belonging to past experiences. She pays especial attention to the way a parent is viewing the present ending and the therapist. This includes noticing and speaking when appropriate about the parent's possible mixed feelings – simultaneously wanting to end (and to feel more independent) and not wanting to end (wishing to remain with the therapist so as not to experience a final separation). The parent's vacillating feelings about ending may be acted out in behaviours such as losing important objects such as her phone or scarf, and through the baby's unsettled crying and behaviour in a session. The therapist seeks to link the behaviour with its communication, suggesting that losing the phone may relate to feelings about losing contact after the end of the therapy. She draws the parent's attention to the expectation that the current ending will have similar components to past experience, and *reframes* this in the light of what is actually happening in the present. For example, a parent may be afraid of losing competencies they have gained when in fact their functioning is not affected. She also includes the way the parent views the infant as experiencing separation and ending. Perhaps the parents deny that the baby will notice anything or, on the contrary, feel that he will be overwhelmed as they are. Again the therapist will reframe as necessary, pointing to the baby's ability to tolerate sadness with his parent's help and representing the baby to the parent as a separate person.

Separation, loss and mourning in the ending process

The ending of therapy can be experienced as a developmental achievement, like age-appropriate separation–individuation (see Chapter 1), there will inevitably also be feelings of sorrow and regret, anger and denial. Understanding of mourning processes informs the therapist of dynamics likely to occur during the final phase of the therapy and alerts the therapist to the possibility of intense conscious and unconscious affects that impact on current relationships, and especially on relationships between parents and babies, where the affect may be raw.

Ending therapy activates parents' personal history of endings and ways of managing them. Previous experiences of loss of a significant attachment figure may need to be revisited. This includes, but is not restricted to, separation through death and other potentially traumatic experiences of separation – for example, migration. In circumstances where parents and children have lost their family and/or country of origin, mourning work may have been central in the therapy and sensitive thought will need to be given to the management of the ending phase.

Loss of the therapist as a new object and a transference figure

When the therapy is coming to an end the parents are about to lose their current relationship with the therapist as a new object with whom they have a live present relationship, and as all she stands for them in the transference. The therapist will need to help the parents mourn the loss of their current relationship with her as a friendly, interested and predictable person in their and their baby's lives. She will also need to help the parents reflect on their transference to her.

In the transference, parents are likely to experience the therapist ending the therapy in ways shaped by memories of their own parents managing separations and endings in childhood. Phantasies that arise about the ending will be linked to this. For example, the parents may believe that the therapist has lost interest in them and their baby and will replace them with another family, so forgetting them and the work that has been done. This may represent an unconscious childhood sense of being 'replaced' by a sibling, or of being erased from the parental mind after leaving home. The transference to the therapist may turn her into a rejecting or bad therapist and may also be defensive, so that the parents will not need to experience the pain of losing and missing the therapist.   .

Transferences to the institution

Both parents and baby will develop all kinds of feelings in relation to the institution in which they have their treatment, and these have to be taken into account. They may, for example, have enjoyed aspects of the institution, such as certain toys, rituals, and waiting room life with the receptionist. Parent/s and babies may have felt looked after by the institution itself. Alternatively, they may have felt scrutinised or let down by the institution perhaps repeating, from their perspective, previous disappointments. Whatever the nature of the transference, it is important to recognise that feelings existed and that the parent and baby may need help to say goodbye to the institution as well as to the therapy.

> Father and baby would arrive early for each session and sit in the waiting room. They evolved their own way of spending time before sessions, playing with the toys in the waiting room, talking with the receptionist, and eating the biscuits she regularly offered. The therapist was aware of this ritual. As part of the ending process she talked about it, naming how they were not only going to miss the therapy but also miss the waiting room and the receptionist – and the biscuits. Thus prepared, father and baby said a special goodbye to the receptionist on their last day.

Working with avoidance of emotional states in the ending phase

Defences and resistances may prevent effective work being carried out in the ending phase. In the ending process the psychotherapist seeks to perceive and interpret defences that protect the parent from overwhelming affect, so that feelings around separation can be experienced within the safety of the therapy. This work includes observing when no sad affect seems to be present. Emotional states can be hidden from consciousness by defensive behaviours in parent and infant, as in the following example:

> A mother and her baby were involved in a boisterous game in which the mother was tickling him and evoking high-pitched laughter. The therapist voiced aloud her thought that the mother and baby were filling the room with such laughter because they were afraid of quietness in which there might arise sadness and the pain of separating from the therapist. In making this interpretation the therapist demonstrated how meaning can be found in apparently random behaviour.

A parent may 'dissociate' from the knowledge that there are to be no more sessions and continue as if the sessions will carry on after ending, or another parent may relate intellectually to the ending and deny any particular feelings about it. The therapist may notice times in which a baby's behaviour expresses the parent's disowned feelings about ending.

> Mother was calmly telling the therapist about her plans, she seemed blank. Baby crawled to the door and sat there, whining. The mother sought to console him, then became cross. The therapist said: 'Baby seems to know that soon you will not be coming back for more sessions. Is he telling us how upset he is feeling about not coming back? I wonder about your own upset feelings – they do not seem to be here – maybe your baby is telling us about them instead?'

The therapist has drawn mother's attention to the baby's communications and related them also to her own emotional state. Her aim is to enable the mother to experience her own feelings directly, rather than through the baby. The therapist promotes the baby's coherent sense of self through representing to the parent their separate experiences of the ending phase.

Disappointments and disillusion

Disappointment about what has not been achieved is a part of the ending process, even where there is also an appreciation of what has been gained. The therapist helps the parents to express the disappointments and criticisms for things she did, or did not, say or do and mourn what could not be done. If the parents' criticisms cannot be voiced, or they fear voicing them will cause the therapist to reject them, negative feelings may prevail preventing the good experience in the therapy being retained and remembered.

> A mother who began therapy when her baby was six weeks old was coming up to the last session when he was 18 months old. She arrived at a session saying that she was in a bad mood. Her son was throwing

things around the room and she reported that he was impossible to deal with at home. She expressed with some bitterness her disappointment that the therapy seemed not to have helped change things. The therapist suggested that they were both angry and upset about coming to the end of the therapy and disappointed that things felt so difficult again. She reframed the child's 'bad' behaviour by saying to him 'You are showing us your feelings by throwing the toys rather than playing with them. You also feel angry and upset about leaving'.

Through giving meaning to both mother's and baby's behaviours the therapist was helping mother to regain her capacity to reflect on mental states and to contain and regulate her emotions around leaving. With this, more affectionate feelings towards the therapist began to emerge, along with renewed recognition of what had been achieved and the resources gained.

Gratitude

A parent and baby who feel helped by the therapeutic work are likely to feel affection and gratitude towards the therapist. The therapist needs to allow space for exploration of thankfulness. This helps consolidate in the parent's mind the changes that have occurred and the importance of the relationship that has developed with the therapist. The baby's own communications of thanks may be subtle, and also require the therapist's acknowledgement. This enables the baby to feel responded to as an individual with his own appropriate feelings.

In the last session mother talked about her difficulty in accepting she would not be coming to see the therapist any more. The therapist explored her anxiety of having insufficient resources to keep in mind the experience of the therapy. Mother then looked at the therapist and said she actually wanted to say how much it had meant to her to be able to come for this therapy with her son. She recalled how difficult things were when they first came. She said she felt they had been listened to and understood and that their relationship had been helped. The therapist responded to this by saying she had also appreciated the work that had been done and the way mother and baby had always got to their sessions and worked hard to develop their relationship. While mother and therapist were expressing these things, baby came to the therapist. He leaned his back against the therapist so that she supported some of his weight. He then turned and touched her face for a moment with his hand, looking up at her. The therapist felt tender feelings for him, and felt that he was expressing his own appreciation of her. She spoke to him softly saying he was telling her he was going to miss coming for his therapy, and that she had enjoyed working with him and his mother.

Feelings that lead to breaking off the therapy in the ending phase

The therapist will strive to contain overwhelming affects in parents and babies as the ending phase commences. However, some parents may find ending too difficult and simply cease to attend sessions. Affects may include rage associated with unconscious early experience, and there may be defensive denigrating of the therapy ('it was useless anyway') and the therapist ('she was not any good'). There may be a defensive kind of hopelessness that masks anger ('there was no point in coming for therapy in the first place – I knew she would ditch us in the end'). It may feel safer and more manageable to leave the therapist by not going through to the end of the therapy. This serves as a defence against feeling abandoned by the therapist.

There is a particular danger of prematurely breaking off the therapy when intergenerational ghosts manifest. In the first instance, the therapist will try to capture the affects while the parent is still attending. If this fails to hold the parent (or frightens them into further retreat) she will try to enable them to return to say goodbye on terms they will find manageable. She may try to speak with the parent on the phone, and/or write to them, showing that the parent and infant remain in her mind and that she has not enacted the phantasy of abandonment. If no further work can be done, the therapist may try to suggest where else help may be sought, and will work with the network so that support is offered through other channels.

> Mother had experienced a turbulent relationship with her own mother, with whom she had dramatic breaks and reunions. In the therapy mother and baby were intensely involved and came on time to all their sessions. After nine months it was agreed, with much thought in the sessions, that sufficient work had been done and a leaving date was set for two months later. All seemed to be progressing well. However, the therapist received a short letter saying that mother had decided no further therapy was necessary – she had returned to work leaving the baby with her mother. The therapist eventually managed to talk with her on the phone and found that she (the therapist) had become the bad abandoning person and maternal grandmother had become 'good'. An intergenerational repetition was enacted, in that the ending process was sudden and total, as happened often in separations from maternal grandmother.
>
> The therapist had difficult counter-transference feelings, for she had invested a lot of thought and commitment to helping this mother and

baby and felt suddenly rejected. She tried to contact the mother and left answerphone messages. Her calls were not returned and she wrote a letter referring to the work they, including the baby, had done together and suggesting that they meet once more to say goodbye, and that they could arrange a time for her to do so if she wished. The therapist heard no more. She continued to speak with the health visitor, who subsequently talked with the mother and reported that the mother felt she had moved on and a goodbye session would clash with her work.

This example shows that although much therapeutic work had been done leading to changes in mother's relationship with her son, termination had thrown the mother back to patterns of relating that were embedded in her life experience with her primary attachment figures. In such cases, where termination cannot be worked through, the baby is at risk of internalising troubled dynamics and becoming the next generation to re-enact them.

The therapist's counter-transference feelings

The therapist can feel enriched by good enough endings and rewarded in the gains of the parent/s and baby in the work together. But ending inevitably touches upon the therapist's own experiences and representation of separation and loss. The therapist needs to be aware of the particular dynamics that are touching her in the ending phase of each therapy, and to be on the lookout for her own difficulties in separation and ending processes. She, too, will need to mourn the ending of each therapeutic endeavour, and work with any collusion on her part with the parent/s' defences against pain or regret. She also needs to be alert to any tendencies in herself to avoid endings and keep parents and babies in therapy when it is no longer necessary. This could be due to the therapist's own attachment to the parent and infant and her wish to go on seeing the baby's development, or omnipotent feelings that she can help a parent and baby change much more than is possible.

Interrupting the repetitions and modelling new ways of ending

In the process of the therapy, intergenerational repetitions will have been addressed and hopefully modified. However, 'ghosts in the nursery' may be particularly difficult to resist at the fraught time of ending, where the new modes of adapting are severely challenged. The therapist will try to help the parent think about traumatic separations that could become entangled, in the parent's mind, with the current loss. Cues for this may be gained from what the parent says or from the way the parent is relating to the baby.

With the ending in sight, father started to miss cues from his baby about her need for him. She brought him the doll's bottle but he did not notice. She then threw the bottle on the floor and was sharply reprimanded by him. She burst into tears and father said to the therapist that he was being driven mad at home by her tantrums. The therapist wondered whether the baby was upset because he was preoccupied. Father looked blank. The therapist reminded him that the ending date was approaching and that he might be preoccupied with this. Father replied that even as a child he had never known the time or date. Laughing, he said 'I never knew when my parents were going away or when they were coming back'.

In this example, ghosts from the past haunted the present through the father's 'cutting off' in the face of pain, even though good therapeutic work had been done over a period of nine months. However, a planned ending did take place as he and the therapist worked through his habitual defence, and thought through his responses to this ending. They also addressed possible internal scenarios after therapy ended.

Father expressed his worry that he did not feel any anger for the therapist, only gratitude. But what if suddenly anger erupted? He recalled being furious with his mother when she came back from a trip and not talking to her for days. 'I can't not talk to my baby, just because I remember to hate you!'

Anticipating feelings that he was not currently in touch with facilitated a more authentic emotional experience for this father and his daughter. The extended process of recognising feelings, understanding their history and locating their enactments in the parent–child relationship reinforced the place of this ending as a new model for others.

Assessing risk at the ending phase

Central to the ending phase is risk to vulnerable babies who will no longer be monitored by the therapist after ending. In the ending phase the therapist works with the parent, and the network where necessary, to think about the baby's physical and emotional safety. In some cases the difficulties the parent and infant brought to the therapy will be reactivated and need reworking in the ending phase. The therapist uses her experience of the beginning and middle phases of the therapy to distinguish between this necessary reworking and dynamics in the parent–infant relationship that will require intervention or continued support by other services.

The anxiety about the future for the parent/s and infant and their relationship has to be borne by the therapist as part of the ending process.

Assessing remaining concerns includes thinking about whether the act of ending may spark anger that becomes directed towards the infant. The therapist will work with the parent/s to plan for the time after the therapy has ended when there are feelings about no longer having therapy, and there is no longer the therapist with whom to think about those feelings. This situation should be discussed with the parent/s as part of thinking about support that may be needed after the ending.

No current risk

The therapist draws on her knowledge of the referral factors from the beginning phase and any concerns she has about risk or child protection that arose within the course of the therapy. When there have been no risk-related concerns, contact with the referrer should take place to communicate the plan to finish the therapy by a certain date so that others can provide support if the need arises.

Remaining risk concerns

When the network has been involved in the organisation of the therapy the therapist will activate it in preparation for ending. It is essential that communication is clear with the different professionals within it so that the family does not fall through a gap between services.

> Mother, an 18-year-old refugee, began therapy as part of a social service care package when her baby was born. Risk factors were thought to be high due to the mental state of the mother and a care order was in place. The therapist worked weekly with them until baby was two years old. She regularly convened network meetings, bringing together the professionals, mother and child. The ending was planned six months in advance and included preparation within the network. Home visits and access to local support groups were organised. Mother was given clear information on who to contact if she found herself in sudden difficulty in her relationship with baby. The therapist was thus able to work as usual in the ending phase within the security net of other provision being put in place.

There are times, however, when risk is very difficult to assess in the ending phase. For example, when improvements in the therapy are modest or fragile, the therapist will need to weigh up whether the improvements are sufficient to enable parent and infant to manage after ending. When there is regression in the ending phase, so that concerns and emotions flare up again, it can mask advances that have been made. It can then be difficult for the therapist to ascertain how parent and child will cope without therapy.

SUMMARY OF THE THERAPIST'S ROLE IN THE ENDING PHASE

- Helping the parent and infant recognise an appropriate time for ending.
- Addressing the feelings that arise in the process of ending.
- Enabling the baby to express, and the parent to acknowledge, the baby's feelings around the end of contact with the therapist.
- Facilitating a new experience of ending that does not repeat unsatisfactory experiences of loss from the past.
- Assessing remaining risk to the baby and, if necessary, ensuring that a professional safety net is in place.

Chapter 8

Analytic group psychotherapy with mothers and infants

Jessica James

INTRODUCTION

Mother and infant group analytic psychotherapy draws from the theories of group analysis (Foulkes, 1948, 1964) and the psychoanalytic model of intervention developed for individual mothers and babies described in this book. Individual and group perspectives are integrated to offer a therapeutic experience *in* the group, *of* the group and *by* the group, to include the therapists. In-depth explorations with individual mother and baby dyads are generalised into their meaning for the whole group. Co-therapists support and reinforce behaviours and attitudes that help mothers and babies to join into the group's shared psychic life. Interventions are framed to develop an intimate network of communications, so that the group becomes an attachment object for vulnerable mothers and babies.

The co-therapists keep practical boundaries to form a group environment that is on-going, coherent and indestructible. This is also a model for mothers in providing their infants with predictable care. As with parent–infant psychotherapy for individual families, the therapists are informed by their knowledge of the possible consequences for a baby's development if early caregiving becomes derailed (see Chapter 1). They are likely to intervene more actively than in conventional group psychotherapy to promote 'good enough' relationships as soon as possible, but in mature phases, as in all open-ended analytic groups, they are more likely to trust the holding capacity of the group process itself. Therapeutic material evolves out of spontaneous discussions and activities between mothers and babies. The therapists create a group culture where the babies are valued as equal contributors and they privilege interactions that involve engaging with babies and reflecting upon their affective experiences.

Mother and baby group psychotherapy has a curative function through fostering a sense of belonging, sharing of mutual concerns, a playful culture and a corrective re-capitulation of family and peer interactions. The therapists offer intervention techniques from parent–infant psychotherapy (see Chapter 4), and reinforce group members' positive contributions. As mothers and babies' involvement gains momentum, and their relationships in the group unfold and intensify, they often become accessible to work at deeper levels. The therapists recognise that there is extra bite and power when an individual's concerns are linked to the here-and-now of the group action. They use their counter-transference to help the group move between the past and to the present and between external and internal in their jointly held roles as group parents. Although fathers are physically absent in mother and baby group therapy, the therapists keep alive the fathers' actual and symbolic significance for each baby. They value the group's paternal function in providing co-operative thinking about its babies (see Chapters 1 and 2).

OVERVIEW

This chapter describes the structure and process of an analytic group as a psychotherapeutic intervention for mothers and babies. It describes the setting of the group, the processes of engagement, the elaboration of the therapy and the working through in ending and the roles of the co-therapists in this context.

AIMS

The aims in the analytic mother and baby group are to:

- Create and maintain a secure group context through which mothers and babies have a sense of belonging.
- Engage the group and the new mother and baby into a mutual process of therapy.
- Use the relationships formed in the group to explore differing per-spectives of mothers' understanding of themselves and their babies.
- Enable mothers, babies and the group to achieve 'good enough' endings.
- Monitor risk in the group.

The group context: creating and maintaining a secure group context through which mothers and babies have a sense of belonging

The provision of a predictable, planned environment is a fundamental backdrop to the survival and health of a psychotherapeutic mother and baby group.

Setting

Establishing and maintaining the group setting involves careful attention to its physical environment and organisation. The group meets at a regular time, is set up the same way and has routines for entering and leaving. The therapists, mothers and babies sit on the floor, with a mat set out for each baby. The mat remains there symbolically, even when a baby has grown out of staying on it or is going to be absent for a particular session. The therapists are prepared to conduct sessions with one mother and baby pair if necessary.

Boundaries

Mothers are asked to commit for at least six months to allow enough time to benefit and to ensure that the group membership remains sufficiently stable for the therapeutic process. Everyone is encouraged to use the group for talking over any doubts that they might be having about their attendance at any time. When someone misses a session, those attending are encouraged to think about that mother and baby and to consider the possible meaning of their absence. Once a mother and baby have joined, all communications between them, the therapists and other group members are brought to the group for discussion. Communications with other professionals involved with a family are also shared within the group.

Mothers are asked not to arrange to meet up with other mothers and babies whilst they are attending the group and, if they do meet unintentionally, not to discuss group matters and to bring it back to the group. The rationale is that participants need to be able to express themselves and to try out new ways of behaving, without repercussions like leaks of information outside the group's boundaries. Once a mother and baby have ended their therapy this rule no longer holds, although the implications of the changed relationship are considered in the group beforehand. Every situation that arises around the boundaries of the group is regarded as important 'bread and butter' material for its members.

Co-therapists

This model of mother and baby group analytic therapy benefits from two therapists. Mother and baby dyads bring complex unconscious processes and powerful projections. Conjoint working is supportive and helps to retain a therapeutic stance when states of mis-attunement and divergence inevitably occur. Each therapist brings their own background, gender, age, style and personality and this is both creative and challenging. When functioning effectively, the therapists represent a collaborative parental model for mothers and infants with inconsistent or absent experiences of parents themselves. They need to meet similar personal, professional requirements as for working individually with families (see Chapter 2). It is important that at least one of the therapists is trained in group analysis and has had personal experience of group analysis in order to develop the full potential of an analytic group as a treatment modality.

The therapists need to think jointly in retaining a working alliance about the group's progress. This involves a continuous re-assessment of the personal experiences of each therapist's participation in the group's ebbs and flows. The therapists need to build in structures to maintain collaborative functioning, such as talking together before and after each session, supervision, ongoing discussion about the group in the team and in the institution as a whole.

Assessing suitability

The first consideration is the mother's interest in a group, which evolves out of her early intake sessions. The difficulties mothers and babies bring to the group are similar to those who participate in individual parent–infant psychotherapy. What distinguishes those who are interested in a group is the mother's desire to belong and to think about herself and her baby alongside others who are struggling similarly. For some mothers, the intimate, full-on attention of individual parent–infant psychotherapy can be threatening and the group offers a more manageable access to psychotherapeutic thinking, where they can dip in and out of intense work and gain inspiration from others.

When a mother expresses readiness to consider a group, the following factors are considered:

- A constructive therapeutic alliance can be formed between one of the group's therapists, the mother and baby during individual intake and preparatory sessions.
- The mother is able to think about her hopes and anxieties for herself and her baby in a group setting.
- The group's current state and composition can accommodate the mother–baby's pathology.
- The therapists' own responses, empathy and sense of rapport with the mother and baby are important information for their suitability in the group and their likely impact on it.
- As far as possible mothers need to understand the importance of commitment to regular attendance.

Mothers and babies are not invited to join the group if:

- The mother's mental state, or defensive functioning, would impinge on her ability to relate to others and work within the boundaries of the group.
- The father is available for parent–infant psychotherapy, in which case his involvement takes precedence, although the mother and baby might transfer to the group at a later stage.
- The mother speaks poor English, as working through an interpreter would be too cumbersome for managing the speed and subtlety of group discussions.

In theory, mothers and babies can move from individual parent–infant psychotherapy to the group, but in practice this can be hard to achieve. The complications of transference, the loss of special attention and the baby's age after time in individual sessions, all contribute to this difficulty. Transitions from individual or family parent–infant psychotherapy to a group need to be supported by a thoughtful ending with the individual therapist, with careful liaising between the therapists around handover and timing.

The group process

Beginning phase: engaging the group and the new mother and baby in a mutual process of therapy

Preparing potential group members

When it seems likely that a mother and baby will be joining the group, the intake sessions take place with one of the group's co-therapists. When following the ordinary intake route (see Chapter 3), the mother and baby's forthcoming entry to the group is kept in mind. For example, when a mother talks about painful experiences the therapist will help her to think about what it would be like to share these with the group. If her baby becomes animated in an interaction with the therapist, the therapist will talk to him about the other mothers and babies he will be meeting soon. Mothers get a taste of parent–infant psychotherapy, including the experience of observing and reflecting upon their own and their baby's state of mind. Babies are introduced to the style of interactions and behaviour between their mother and therapist, and their participation in it.

The therapist's own countertransference and sense of rapport with a mother and baby are a rich source of data for understanding their likely impact on the group. If the therapist, for example, wants to rush a mother into a group in the hope that the group will manage them, it is unlikely that they will have a successful transfer. It suggests that a strong enough attachment has not been forged with the therapist, which is essential for containing the anxieties of the settling-in period.

The group is presented to its prospective members in ways that aim to be both attractive and realistic. It is important to avoid idealisation of group psychotherapy, but also to avoid mothers feeling pushed into joining a modality that seems second best. The therapist tries to bring alive what is involved in a mother and baby therapy group. She may say, for example, 'It is like is becoming a member of a family, which includes the positive aspects such as belonging, being missed and feeling cared for, but also involves the more complicated aspects, for example feelings that you have not had enough, are misunderstood or are being criticised. The group provides the chance to learn about yourself, to get feedback, to see others in action and to gain a perspective on your relationship with your baby as he grows and develops.'

A mother's response to this portrayal of group life is important information as to her suitability and likely use of the group, as is also her interpretation of the group boundaries. She might wonder whether she will get enough time for herself, or question the rule not to meet up outside the group. She may express a wish to try out the group and need further understanding as to why it isn't possible to 'give it a go'. The therapist describes the significance of commitment, 'A newcomer affects everyone and, since people are talking about private and painful things, they need to feel the information will be safe. Moreover, new members have to give the group time, as its benefits might seem incomprehensible at first. Doubts are inevitable and group members often go away from groups with questions unanswered. Bring feelings back to talk over the following week and you usually find that others have had similar ones.'

Preparing the group for newcomers

The therapists inform the group that a new mother and baby will be coming at least a few sessions in advance. The therapists encourage group members to share their feelings about the prospect of newcomers. There may be expressions of both interest and ambivalence. It is helpful to discuss the negative feelings as comprehensively as possible, so that the new mother and baby can be spared too many negative projections. The therapists may interpret recalcitrant group reactions. A baby grabbing toys, or discussions about sibling rivalry, might represent the group's anxiety about having to share with a new mother and baby. The therapists might prompt the group by asking its most recent members about what it was like for them joining the group, or the longer-standing members about what it had been like welcoming newcomers previously. This can be an opportunity for the group to take stock of its recent history and reflect on situations that have strengthened or disrupted group coherence.

The therapists can help mothers think about how to prepare their babies for newcomers. They are encouraged to talk with their babies about what is happening and to gain clues from their behaviour about the changes. A baby might seem to be especially active, as though claiming the group's physical and emotional space in preparation for having less room in it. A baby who becomes distressed could be expressing the group's insecurity.

Factors affecting group entry

Success in joining the group is affected by the interplay between an individual mother and baby, the group and the therapists at the particular point of time. Thorough assessment, engagement and preparation, a mature group culture and the therapists' greater experience and confidence, increase the likelihood of a smooth entry. During phases of cohesion, with regular attendance and established group members, the group may be more able to make an emotional space for newcomers and more risks might be taken if there are doubts about integrating a particular mother and baby. The therapist has to weigh up the situation in the group alongside a prospective mother's likely capacity to tolerate her own and her baby's frustrations in the group context. Sometimes the entry to the group is not successful (see p. 134).

Settling into the group

Transitions to the group are frequently not smooth and require the therapists to be flexible and responsive in relation to an individual dyad's particular difficulty. They may need extra support, even outside the group's boundaries, before their eventual establishment as committed group members.

> The group was suggested to a mother, who had come for help with her aggression towards her baby, and she agreed to join. She returned to her next session with serious misgivings. She was the youngest of nine children and lacked affection as the last of so many. Would the group give her the special attention she craved? Moreover, as a precocious child she had been rushed into situations that she had then struggled to process.
>
> The therapist became aware that she had colluded with this mother's difficulties. She had responded to her 'precocious' insightfulness into her difficulties by 'rushing' her and her son into the group. The therapist slowed down their introduction, gave greater time to thinking with the mother in preparatory sessions about the possible repetition. The therapist offered a further individual session after starting the group, in order to recognise their need for special attention in the transition and to ensure that the group was a positive treatment choice. The ability to

stop and reflect, rather than repeat, enabled this mother and baby to become engaged group members.

At first the mother and baby group can be shocking to newcomers. It can seem like chaos and it is difficult to concentrate on interactions generated from so many different angles and directions. Mothers' preoccupations are likely to include: 'Are my problems petty? Will my baby show me up as a bad mother? Will there be enough time to explore my concerns properly? I'm not sure that I've got anything in common with anyone else. Will it ever be possible to combine attending to my baby and listening properly?' Mothers take a while to fathom out how to make sense of the group and how to use it in a way that seems helpful to them. Babies often take their cues from their mother and may also express their mother's more hidden feelings. The therapists need actively to include new mothers and babies. They help them to express any difficulties in their adjustment and encourage other mothers and babies to make links with their predicament. They may also 'foster' skills for managing group life, which parallel those needed in ordinary family and social settings. These involve learning when to go with the flow, take risks, accept disappointments, trust that something can wait and allow oneself to be at a loss.

Establishing the baby as a group member

The therapists encourage the group to welcome new babies by fostering a climate of observing and noting their personal responses to the group. They might take the initiative to talk and play with the babies themselves, so as to convey that the group is a safe place. They point out any signs of interest that other babies show towards a new baby, they capitalise upon the new baby's reactions to them and those that they show in relation to being in the group.

Early dropouts

Both newcomers and established group members are bound to feel anxious at times of change. Sometimes that anxiety is acted out in the group, so that established members are covertly rejecting and the new mother and baby are over-defended, leading them to drop out.

It is difficult to know exactly why some mothers and babies do not give the group a proper chance, whereas others become committed group members even after shaky starts. The therapists reflect on what happened in terms of suitability and intake sessions. In some instances the mother's expectations and ambivalence have not been thoroughly explored. A sufficiently positive transference between the therapist, mother and baby may not have been developed. For the group, dropouts can be bruising but also strengthening. They are an opportunity to re-establish what the group offers and to share a mutual experience of rejection. The therapists try to ensure that the mother and baby who leave are thought about sensitively, that they are not scapegoated and that group members' own aggressive impulses are interpreted. However, sudden departures can leave group members destabilised, questioning their place and wary about future newcomers. All this is material to be explored.

Middle phase: using the relationships formed in the group to explore differing perspectives of mothers' understanding of themselves and their babies

While the group itself goes through phases of stability and transition, there are characteristic features of a dyad's trajectory in the group that may or may not overlap with the particular phase of the group. The middle phase of their therapy, by which time the individuals are more firmly established within the group, is a period in which more intensive intrapsychic understanding can take place. The therapists work in parallel with group processes, individual intrapsychic conflict (in mother, in baby) and dyadic relationship difficulties.

Reinforcing a culture of the group as an attachment object

The following are interventions that make links between individuals and the group, so as to reinforce a positive group culture:

- *Reframing problems in shared terms* to give individuals perspective and relief through a sense of themselves as 'not the only one'. This normalising experience provides a base from which group members develop further communication and frankness.
- *Exploring parallel experiences* so as to link the individuals' experiences. 'You have told us a lot about what it was like for you starting school. I wonder if it was at all like this for you when you started the group. Maybe others can make similar connections between their feelings beginning school and the group?'
- Making *facilitating comments* which value group members' contributions: 'Freddie (a baby) was peering into your face just then, he seems to be feeling for you.'
- *Talking directly to babies* about their interest in each other: 'Callum, you are really excited by Jane and her train,' and reinforcing his mother's role to assist him with this relationship: 'That's it, mummy is helping you and Jane to have a really good explore of that train.'

- Making *joining-up statements* in order to instil empathy and a common shared ground. 'We all seemed to be looking forward to hearing how you got on. I wonder what this experience means for others as well.'
- Adding *encouraging nuance* to non-verbal behaviour. This includes interested looking and nodding, eye contact, smiles or laughter, warm tone of voice and body language towards both mothers and babies.
- The therapists *include themselves* in their reflections on the group process, by saying 'we', such as 'We seemed to be struggling to know how to help Sam just now' – to emphasise the group as a joint enterprise.

A strong group culture is dependent upon its capacity to resolve disregulated group processes. The following behaviours signify when disregulating group processes are happening: mothers assiduously play with their own babies; babies whimper, cry and play unsatisfactorily; sub-groups are formed; discussions turn to dysfunctional families outside the group. The therapists need to be active in addressing the conflict. They label the underlying emotions, refer to them as shared phenomena and include themselves in their thinking. They might use what the babies are conveying: 'The babies seem to be having no trouble expressing their distress, but the rest of us seem quite stuck.' Or they might bring the discussion back into the room: 'I wonder whether the problematic families being talked about are also related to the problematic family situation we seem to have in the group right now?' Many group members have not experienced families who have been able to resolve conflict, which has led to fear and loss of contact. It is therefore a relief to find therapists can manage and that the group can survive. These types of interventions help to intensify the experience of the group as a safe attachment object.

Working with the mother–baby relationship

The mother's relationship with her baby is the focus of much of the therapeutic work. At times, the group may focus on an individual mother, as when her unconscious conflicts are played out in relation to her baby or another group member. The therapists may take these up and then extend the event to the group, or may invite the others in the group to consider the individual's material. This may entail, for example, *exploring* the mother's unconscious narrative, *linking past and present*, to give meaning to her feelings, moods and behaviours in relation to her baby.

At other times, techniques that address the relationship directly are employed:

Reflecting back the interactions in a group setting holds particular potency because it invites the group to take an observing stance vis-à-vis a sequence in the here-and-now of group life.

A therapist interjected to ask about what was going on between two babies and a mother who was playing with them: 'You are trying to relocate Jenny to her mummy. Do you want to say something to her?' The 'playing' mother said: 'She knows there is food in my bag. I felt sorry for her, as she seemed to want it. I wasn't sure what to do.' The therapist said: 'Isn't there a sense that Jenny finds the food more attractive elsewhere than with her mummy?' Jenny's mother: 'It's true she is a pain to feed. She eats if there are guests, but not if we are alone.' Another mother: 'I find that quite normal.' Therapist: 'You are attempting to make it ordinary. We are trying to understand what is going on. Perhaps you experience that as critical and challenging.' Jenny's mother: 'I find it embarrassing, it's as though she is stealing.' The 'playing' mother: 'And you bring such healthy food.' Jenny's mother: 'I guess I find it hard to believe that she will like my food, even though I know I am a good cook.'

The therapist's reflection back of her observation opened the way for thinking about Jenny's search for food-other-than-mother, and the reasons for it. Through the dialogue between the two mothers, Jenny's mother became more aware of her self-representation of not having 'food' that satisfies her daughter, and of her daughter as not being satisfied with her. This led to a linking with her experiences of feeding and being fed and the dynamic being played out with her baby.

Representing the baby's mental states supports both his mother and the other mothers in the group to reflect on the individual baby and babies' feelings and development in general. The therapists also help mothers to understand the emotional impact of the group process upon their babies, and their babies' own contribution to it.

Often the babies will bring attention to the feelings under consideration. Their finely tuned awareness and uninhibited expression of emotional undercurrents provide therapists and group members with a barometer to what is going on.

Pat was talking about her isolation at the drop-in group she attended with her daughter Katy. As she talked, Katy was playing with a box. Another child crawled over and pulled the box away. Katy lay down looking cross with her head on a cushion. A couple of mothers and Therapist A laughed. Pat exclaimed to Katy: 'For goodness sake!' Therapist B said: 'It was your box Katy, you were having a lovely game and they shouldn't laugh at your upset'.

Pat was not able to identify with her daughter's upset but the therapists used their different counter-transference understanding to reflect back and represent the baby to the group.

Later on, Therapist A brought the group back to thinking about what happened. Therapist A: 'Therapist B was right. We shouldn't have laughed as Katy was having a lovely time and suddenly it was gone.' Pat: 'Katy was stomping off just like I do.' Therapist B: 'But Katy wasn't stubborn or unreasonable, she was reacting to losing something she was enjoying.'

Therapist B refuted Katy's mother's projective view of her daughter by describing Katy as an individual with her own inner world, and reframing mother's understanding of her own feelings and behaviours.

Another mother said she felt cruel. 'I would feel bad if someone laughed at me when I hurt. Babies can feel that way.' The therapist asked Pat what she thought got in the way of feeling for her daughter at that point. Pat replied 'I guess I don't like her to be pathetic, which is what I am when I sulk.' The therapist wondered about her 'sulking'. Pat said she could never talk directly to her mother about distressing feelings. Then she would be angry with mother and not talk to her. Pat reached out to Katy looking at her warmly. A mother made a link about herself and her mother whom, she had previously felt, suddenly stopped loving her. 'It probably felt like that for Katy.'

In this segment of the session the focus was on helping Pat disentangle her baby from her representations of rejected aspects of herself. The therapist used exploration of the mother's feelings to help her link past and present. Some other mothers, while allowing the work with Pat to take place, found they could identify and address their 'ghosts' as well.

The reflections of other mothers and babies can be disturbing and experienced as persecutory and unbearable. The group creates limitless possibilities for an insecure mother to look at the other mothers and babies through her own distorted mirror and resulting projections, and for her own self-critical and isolating tendencies to be exacerbated. For example, another mother may seem like a better player with her baby, or her baby's snatching or whingeing becomes a shameful reflection of her own infantile urges. The therapists need to be alert to these dynamics and their impact on the recipients of the projections. They encourage group members to share their perceptions of the same situation, which helps understanding the disturbing emotions of a particular baby and/or mother. The group offers the sense of 'being in it together' since everyone has, at some time, been in the spotlight and emotionally churned up, especially when reflecting upon their baby's unmet needs.

Parent guidance may be used by the group to address a mother's diffi-culties in relation to her infant, where mothers offer information and ideas, as might a benign extended family. The therapists help the mothers to reflect on the meaning of the different ideas for individual dyads, including those that may be cultural or religious. However, guidance *per se* is not productive, as groups can get into a solution-led, symptom-relieving mode. The therapists may need to help the group to overcome their defensive stance at that point. They might ask the group to reflect on what is happening, or make a direct statement such as: 'We've heard a lot about the physical reasons, how about the emotional ones?'

Summary of techniques addressing the mother–baby relationship

- Encouraging *observations* of the babies' behaviour, to *represent their mental states* to their mothers, *scaffold* the babies' experience and help understand their unconscious meaning for the whole group.
- *Reflecting the baby's state to the mother* to help mother differentiate between herself and her baby.
- *Interpreting* negative transference and projections that impinge on mother's responsiveness to her baby.
- *Using contributions* from all group members to reflect on the meaning of events between a dyad at a particular time.

Forming a culture where babies are validated

Despite pulls in many directions, and even when adult discourse apparently dominates the room, the therapists aim to privilege communications and interventions with the babies.

Frequently, groups start with an atmosphere of attentiveness towards the babies, which includes apparently superficial chatting about them. The therapists understand this as representing mothers and babies' gradual transition into the emotional work ahead. This vignette characterises the beginning of group sessions:

> The mothers entered with their babies in arms, crawling or toddling and there were greetings, nods and quiet watching. One baby was placed carefully down and another was helped to reach a box of toys. A baby let out excited sounds as she grabbed and banged a rattle; a mother tried to peel her baby from her lap and sighed. Another mother exclaimed 'Gosh! What a lovely dress' and her baby moved towards the one with the lovely dress, and sat close by playing with a car. Mothers looked up fleetingly and smiled, soon returning to concern themselves quietly with the closeness of their own baby, except the one whose baby had left her side, who watched him and looked quite naked. The therapists, who are similarly 'without baby', observed this scene. A therapist responded warmly to a baby who showed her a toy 'Look

what you have got', or did sympathetic stretching with another who took time to wake up.

The silent act of observing the babies in itself sets the tone for the place of babies in the group. Sometimes this observing and playing goes on longer, either at the beginning or at other times. This may signify a particular need and a developmental turning point for a baby and mother, or it may also be a way of avoiding painful issues and, if so, needs thinking about. As the adult discussions intensify the babies move, sometimes seaminglessly and sometimes not, from fore to background in the group's multi-dimensional layers of helplessness.

The therapists employ the parent–infant psychotherapy techniques, described in Chapter 4 and adapted to the group setting, in their direct work with the babies. In due course, these ways of addressing the babies may be taken on also by the mothers in the group, and become shared adult–baby interactions.

'Talking' with babies occurs both verbally and non-verbally in the group. Part of the noise in the group is adult conversations towards the babies. Therapists verbalise the babies' experiences by talking with them about what they are doing, how they are feeling and how they are interacting with others. Mothers might pick up and talk directly in similar ways, with their own baby or others. Babies pick up on the nuances of these conversations – they may approach or look at those engaged in the talking and they may seem relieved.

Non-verbal conversations are also a continuous part of the group. Babies, mothers and therapists make lip, tongue and mouth movements, push boxes, tap their fingers, wave their arms and nod their heads together. These are experiments with rhythms, turn-making. They match, mis-match and repair at the baby's pace within the group's action. Some mothers and babies fluidly initiate and partake in this group 'talking' behaviour, whilst others take longer and the therapists may need to be active in encouraging them.

Mirroring affective states: in the group there is a 'hall of mirrors' available for reflection between each of its participants. Mothers and babies can see themselves through the eyes and minds of the different beholders. Babies who are experiencing confused reflections of themselves through a mother whose own preoccupations lead her to respond impassively or with impingements, can find compensatory mirroring from someone else in the group.

> A baby waved his arms up and down. The therapist waved similarly and the baby waved back. Another baby looked at her mother and then back to the originally waving baby. They waved together and there were smiles. A few minutes later, the first baby waved again but got no

response. Much later on in the group he tried again and his usually static mother responded, they waved animatedly together for a few moments.

The experience of affective mirroring can validate the individual's self-representation. In addition, a mother's observation of her baby in relation to others, perhaps when held in another's gaze, offers her views from new angles. The mother gets a greater perspective upon her baby as someone in his own right. She might find that her baby is affirmed in a way that was inconceivable to her, and her baby can become increasingly sentient and human in her mind through these positive mirroring group experiences.

Playing with a baby: a lot of playing in the group takes place between mothers and babies and babies and babies. The play between babies and babies occurs naturally and is important for an individual baby's sense of belonging and learning from his peer group. A therapist will choose to play with a baby to stimulate that baby's capacity to initiate pleasurable inter-actions. The therapist must be aware of the other babies' reactions to special attention, as well as the baby's own mother and the other mothers.

Summary of techniques for working with the babies

- Validating *playful interactions* with babies and creating a mutually playful group culture.
- *Modelling* ways of being with babies that are emotionally resonant and reflective about the babies' experiences. The lead might come from the mothers as well as the therapists.
- *Talking to babies*, both verbally and non-verbally, in direct communi-cations.
- *Mirroring* affective states to validate the baby's self-representation and to affirm the baby in the mother's eyes.
- *Reinforcing attuned interactions* in the group when they happen between babies, their mothers and other group members.

Position of fathers in the group

The structure of co-therapy offers two therapists who can represent a parental couple, and this can be a positive model. The group itself provides co-operative minds for thinking about the babies and for sharing in their development, representing the perspective of the 'third'. Mothers can be helped to understand the babies' relationships with their fathers and to regard their own families' dilemmas, or past histories, in a new light. Thus although the fathers are not physically present the structure of the group helps to address the function of 'father' (see Chapter 1).

The real fathers are also alive in the group via the mothers' discussions and the babies' activities. At different phases the mothers are more or less preoccupied with their relationships to their babies' fathers, sometimes obsessed by talking about them and, at others, hardly mentioning their existence. The therapists need to be alert to either extreme and they may have to question what is being avoided or projected. At other times the real father is represented via mothers' discussing of the group with him. Mothers go home and talk things over and partners respond, sometimes even suggesting that contentious or anxiety-provoking issues should be brought up in the group.

Assessing risk

Mothers and babies whose situation is deteriorating are a concern for the whole group, not only the therapists. This may be expressed through heightened levels of anxiety in the group, greater dependence on the therapists and indications of fear in the babies who may, for example, stay close to their mothers or be fretful. If the therapists are concerned about a dyad they will talk to the mother involved, but they also elucidate the other mothers' perceptions.

> A mother talked in an obsessive way about the ever-increasing danger-ous substances that might poison her baby. The therapists tried to understand and assess the mother's panic and they also addressed the other group members' anxiety. They thought with the group about whether this mother and baby would be safe leaving that day and other mothers asked about what supportive arrangements could be made. They were relieved that the therapists acted to ensure their safety.

The therapist must consider the vulnerability and sense of exposure in the individual mother, and the need for group members to be able to rely on the therapists to act carefully and responsibly. This might involve individual sessions, bringing in other family members relevant professionals and referral to acute mental health services. The group is kept informed where appropriate.

Ending phase: enabling mothers, babies and the group to achieve 'good enough' endings

Each mother and baby brings their own personal and culturally diverse approaches towards ending, and the therapists can capitalise upon these to establish a setting where endings are a productive part of group life.

The meaning of endings

A mother and baby leaving the group are departing from a mini-community that will continue without them. For many mothers it is novel to go through a process of saying goodbye; they have little idea of how to proceed and are inclined to want to get it over with as soon as possible. They can feel persecuted by the group rules for ending, which may seem long and drawn out when they have decided to move on to fresh pastures, and they imagine putting their difficulties behind them. A group offers a variety of responses and perspectives that the therapists can mobilise. For example, mothers may fail to see the benefits of a 'proper' planned ending for themselves and their baby, but can be reminded by others in the group of the feelings of being left behind by previous members. The departure of a particular dyad may also have special significance for another mother and/or baby in the group.

The therapists need to be aware of the responses and projections that influence attitudes towards a farewell such as envy, a fear of abandonment and unresolved experiences of loss. The babies' departures are also often a source of mixed feelings. The group has usually accompanied their development from their early months and will not continue to be participating in it. All babies have their special place in the group, with their unique personality and ways of being, and there will be feelings to do with that loss – sometimes relief as well as sadness.

The therapists help to create an expectation that past members won't be forgotten in the continuing group. They notice the babies' awareness of each other's presence and signs of sensitivity to another's absence. A baby may seek out the absent baby by trying to play a familiar game, or by keeping a watchful eye on the door. The therapists help leaving members to keep the group in their, and their baby's, minds after departure. As one mother said: 'I am taking the group inside and baby and I are going off with it.' The group's regular time and setting can help bring these feelings alive, as in the following example.

> A mother was asked what she and her son would be doing at the group time during the week following their departure. It emerged that she had arranged to go to a play session in her local library. Saying this, she laughed at herself, and the therapists encouraged the other group members to think with her about what she was trying to avoid. Another group member suggested she left the time free for a few weeks in order to think about the group, to talk about it with her son, and to be sad if necessary.

Ongoing loss and separation

The routine experiences of separation and loss in the group are significant preparations for the final ending. These include the weekly comings and goings, the missed sessions and holiday breaks. An ordinary event in a session, such as when mother leaves her baby behind whilst going out to get a nappy, can be used to explore separation. The therapists may ask the other mothers about their observations and perceptions of this baby's experience. They may model talking to the baby about her mother's going and articulate the baby's responses or support empathic behaviour a group member displays towards the baby.

At first it can be hard for mothers to emotionally understand the idea that absences, or breaks, in therapeutic continuity have meaning and that they, or their babies, could miss others or be missed themselves. The therapists help them to note events and to label the affects involved. They use the heterogeneous range of responses to loss brought by its members. They encourage those who are able to feel and express sadness or yearning in relation to change and separation to do so and, in so doing, to speak for others and to assist them in exploring their own feelings. This helps to build a group culture whereby the feelings evoked by separations and losses become a dynamic part of its life.

Planning for ending

In deciding to leave, mothers take their cues from their progress in terms of the initial concerns. They might propose their ending and can ask fellow mothers and therapists for insights about their readiness. Once a date has been set, allowing time to work through this phase, the therapists help the departing dyad and the group to revisit their time in the group and the meanings it had for all. This involves a shared *recapitulation* of the mother and baby's ups and downs during their therapy, to include expressions of disappointment and gratitude. The therapists need to use their counter-transference to understand and label the affects and to help the group talk about any impulses that might be avoided. Sometimes the therapists raise the issue of ending for a mother and baby whom they consider 'ready' to leave the group (Chapter 7). They might need to question their own motivations in relation to a particular mother and baby to ensure that they are not influenced by any personal attachments or institutional requirements.

Engaging the babies in ending

Sometimes a mother seems to intuitively understand that leaving the group will be a loss for her baby that needs to be addressed with him. Other mothers may feel that their babies are too young to prepare them for the event. The therapists need to be alert to the babies' communications around the impending ending, and to help the mothers be so. The baby may also communicate group feelings in relation to an ending. For example, a baby spilt a cup of water and this became described as a bucket of tears shared by everyone at the prospect of a mother and baby's final departure. On another occasion two toddlers played peek-a-boo around the back of a chair at a poignant moment between the adults, as though suggesting that it is possible to recover from leavings. Another time a baby's mother was talking about their leaving and her son approached another mother and placed his face to her cheek.

Addressing the babies through talking or playing is an important way of scaffolding the changes and gaps in their lives to come, through the loss of the group. The therapists can speak directly to the babies themselves, or help their mothers do so.

> A therapist said to a five-month-old infant: 'You won't be coming here any more. You will be sad and mummy will be sad, as we have been coming here every week for a long time. We will miss playing together with the mothers and babies [who were named].' The following week his mother said to him shortly after they came in 'Today is our last time. Do you remember I was telling you on the way here?' To the group she asserted that she thought he understood because he was unusually quiet in his buggy.

Working through the ending process

Separation from the group as an attachment object will involve a reworking of the mother's and baby's dependency on it. Inevitably, painful feelings arise and many mothers and babies regress during this process of detaching. In the weeks leading up to their departure a baby's screeching might return, alongside his mother's inability to understand him. The therapists ensure that the group helps a mother and baby to explore their mixed feelings, including any inclinations to cut and run, or to spoil their attachment to the group. When disruptions are repaired, this not only helps individuals to tolerate and survive the inevitable mixture of loving and aggressive feelings, but this also helps the whole group to understand the complex emotional processes involved.

Monitoring risk

It is essential that the therapists keep in mind persisting concerns for vulnerable mothers and babies after ending group therapy. Whenever a mother and baby leave the group, a letter is sent to relevant professionals. They may offer a follow-up session in addition to notifying the referrer and network of the therapy's ending and the family's continuing vulnerability.

Psychodynamic processes in co-therapy

The co-therapists have to work continuously at maintaining a good enough collaborative relationship through their roles in the group. Potentially representing both a marital and parental couple, they receive projections that can veer between idealisation and denigration. Each therapist naturally brings her own professional style and personality, which is more or less sensitive to absorbing and resisting projections at different times. Like parents of new babies, it can be easy for the therapists to blame each other when under pressure, such as when the group feels stuck and incomprehensible. Similarly, it can be extraordinarily creative and enjoyable to take joint responsibility for the group's facilitating culture. For mothers who have had inconsistent, absent or hostile parenting themselves, the co-therapists can hopefully represent a positive alternative model.

On occasions, the therapists find themselves divided in their group functioning. Classically, splits occur along traditional male and female lines, such as when one therapist is seen as the nurturer, warm and supportive, and the other firm and questioning. Another split can be along generational lines, with one therapist playful and attentive with the babies, whilst the other is aligned with the mothers. These splits can be fruitful, for example when one therapist allows herself the freedom to attend to intense adult issues, knowing that the other therapist is keeping track of the babies. But the therapists need to be aware if their roles are becoming rigidly split and, if it happens, to think about how this has arisen and why. If a particular therapist carries the caring and sharing functions of the group, for example, the other might be left to bring in the more contentious issues. In such circumstances, the therapists may find it useful to consider how their personal predispositions interact with the group material.

> A mother attacked Therapist A for what she perceived as an uncaring phone conversation, in which the therapist had tried to talk to her about coming to the group despite having toothache. Therapist B sympathised with this mother since she had also recently been angered by a similarly perceived experience with her co-therapist. She recognised her own desire to use this mother's criticism as retaliation.

Therapist B, by understanding her identification with the mother, was able not to act on her destructive feelings. She neither encouraged nor refuted the mother's anger and was able to join with her co-therapist in helping everyone understand the conflict productively.

Collaborative working through

During taxing times in the group dynamics, it is helpful for the therapists to mobilise their different perspectives for thinking. Keeping eye contact is crucial, especially during sessions when they become out of touch with each other, and they can nod supportively or give a quizzical look to re-establish their connection. When the therapists find themselves emotionally playing into complex group relationships this gives important counter-transference information, but might result in the therapists sitting upon feelings in sessions and tensions flaring up afterwards. The therapists will need to spend extra time talking over a difficult situation and may need to consult with colleagues or have a supervision to understand their role in the group's projective processes.

When the co-therapists feel safe enough to discuss differences during a group, this can provide a useful parental model of disagreement. For example, the slightest disagreement between the co-therapists, such as when one therapist seems disapproving about the other's intervention, can provoke more fear in group members than the incident warrants. Some anticipate the kinds of 'disastrous' repercussions that occurred in their family of origin. In such instances, therapists help group members to appraise their perspectives on what happened. This is challenging for the therapists as their friction can be unnerving but, when they can risk and survive such situations, the resulting repair is often helpful for both the mothers and babies, and the group event usually results in renewed vigour and hope.

SUMMARY OF THE THERAPISTS' ROLES IN THE GROUP

- Establishing the group as a holding and containing environment.
- Prioritising the babies' participation in the face of competing group demands.
- Capitalising on emotionally affective events arising within the group's here and now, for individual and dyad's development.
- Maintaining a dynamic use of the co-therapy role.

Section III

Clinical papers

Introduction

Tessa Baradon

This section of the book illustrates the unfolding of the clinical process. The authors describe the therapeutic encounter – the constructions between patients and therapist – from differing angles. Within the same clinical setting, and drawing upon the shared theoretical base, the therapists describe the singular nature of the contact between individuals in the family and therapist. In each encounter, the mentalising stance of the therapist is applied to the constellation of adaptations, defences, imagery at that point in time.

The clinical material also illustrates the interweaving of the psychodynamic formulation/s with the material of parent and baby. The therapist's formulations, whether intuitive, conscious in the moment, or formulated between sessions or in retrospect, are the professional cornerstone of her interventions. These are made explicit to the reader, step by step, as the process of the therapy is described. The changes in the patient/s' material, woven into the interactions as well as enacted, validate or disconfirm her thinking.

The chapters also demonstrate the importance of the 'unconsciouses' in the room, and how addressing that which lies in the domains of 'not known' – procedural and defensive – can open up new intrapsychic vistas for change. What is noticeably difficult to capture, and is mentioned less, are the silences that accompany simply being with the parent and baby in the therapy room. Silence, in itself, may be an important intervention for an infant and parent, offering a transitional space for the development of new ways of being together. The therapist's silence – predicated on her reliable emotional availability – could facilitate for both mother and baby the developing capacity to be alone (Winnicott, 1958), as opposed to a habitual retreat from each other.

The progress of the therapy is incremental. The process of change is intensely personal for each, an individual and a partner in the dyad/triad/group. Yet for each parent and infant it can lead toward a state of togetherness, freer of impingements, where the parent can claim their baby, and the baby can anticipate being claimed.

Chapter 9

A brief intervention in the form of a therapeutic consultation

Angela Joyce

Veronica, a single mother, sought our help with her twelve-month-old son Peter. They lived a considerable distance from the clinic and could not travel for regular sessions so it was decided to offer them two long consultations over a two-day period. All I knew before seeing them was that Veronica was severely disabled and was assisted in her mothering of her son by a team of carers. On the telephone she posed her central question: 'How can I get my son to listen to my "no's" in the same way as he does to the others?' Not an altogether unusual issue for parents of older babies on their way to toddlerhood, but in the particular context of this family, it had multiple layers of meaning.

FIRST MEETING

Veronica and Peter arrived at the centre with one of the carers. This person did not take part in the consultation. Veronica settled herself down on the cushion on the floor in the consulting room, as I did. I was immediately faced with the impact of Veronica's congenital disability: she had short stumps for arms, no hands and was very small because she had short legs. She was an attractive woman in her mid-thirties and seemed open and friendly in her manner. Peter was an able-bodied, lively little boy who was nearly walking, and eager to do so. He gave me a wide berth at the beginning of our encounter.

Veronica used her feet to shake a rattle and attract Peter; he responded with interest, approaching her and beginning to explore the toys near her. She occasionally stroked him with her feet as he played. He looked intently at me and then retreated to his mother's body, using her to stand himself up and, with his arm around her neck, leaned against her and surveyed the room. After a short while he caught sight of something and crawled across the room to inspect it.

As this was going on Veronica was telling me what she wanted help with. Initially she described their difficulties in terms of herself and Peter being dependent on a team of seven carers to support her mothering her son (living very much then in the public eye). She said these seven made him sociable but that it was difficult for her to keep up 'the same ground rules'. Veronica's concern with the dynamics of this group, and how to get Peter to pay attention to her when safety was at stake, was quickly revealed to contain the issue of who comforts him, and therefore who was his main attachment figure. Her sense of not being his special person because of the limits imposed by her disability exposed her fear of him loving someone else the most, and the sense that they were taking her baby away from her. Her need of the carers and her hatred of her dependency upon them infused her attitude to the strong-willed, determined little boy she saw in Peter. Those traits had been indispensable to her as she grew up, and her need to foster independence in her son was highly over-determined.

Early on in the first session these issues were summed up in my comment to her that she was concerned with the question: 'Who is he going to love the most?' and hers to me: 'How can I politely tell the carers to get lost?'

Veronica wore a sleeveless dress on a winter's day, immediately challenging my affective response in the counter-transference. She was unable to hold Peter with arms, but used her stumps to respond to him, as she moulded her body to his in their interactions. Despite her short legs she was very dexterous with her feet and I was quickly impressed by her versatility and creativity around the limits of her disability. She seemed at ease with her body, certainly innovative in relating to Peter, and she made it available to him increasingly as the session advanced. However, I was to notice how she expressed her conflict over dependency by limiting her body's availability at times, as when she subtly withdrew from him.

The following transcript is about ten minutes into the first session. Veronica described how she used her voice to warn him of danger, but was anxious that the loud, disciplinarian tone that she used made her into a mother who just shouts at her child while the carers gave him the cuddles. She then talked about him being naughty, defiant, and as she did so Peter made a loud noise with the bricks:

V: But I sometimes think: am I giving more attention to the naughtiness?
AJ: More attention to the naughtiness?
V: Yes.
AJ: (*to P*) You do like making a lot of noise don't you? What's mummy talking about with me? . . . About when she thinks you're being a naughty little boy . . .

Peter carries on playing, appearing not to respond.

V: Defiant rather than naughty.
AJ: Defiant. And that is something you recognise from yourself?

V: Oh absolutely.

AJ: It's got you quite a long way?

V: It has.

AJ: Stood you in good stead?

V: Well it's why I don't want to quash it in him. But I obviously want to keep him safe.

At this point Peter hurts himself by catching his chin on the box of bricks. He cries out and Veronica goes close to him and speaks in a concerned but confident voice:

V: (*to P*) Oh, all right, all right. Is that your chin? Good boy . . . OK is that all right? Didn't hurt too much. Good boy. No, I know . . .

Peter quickly calms and turns to face her but she very subtly moves her body away from him. He makes a short protesting sound and then turns to the beaker. Veronica continues to speak to him and he takes a drink.

V: (*to P*) What? Are you thirsty? No sweetheart, it's the other way around. Let mummy turn it round then. (*She does so with her foot*) That's it, you do it, good boy.

I decide to address this sequence of action immediately in the moment.

AJ: (*to V*) You used your voice beautifully there to soothe him and he responded. Then he turned round to you . . .

V: Yeah . . .

AJ: Did you notice? He turned around and you backed away.

V: Oh right, I didn't know I'm doing it . . .

AJ: No, it's the sort of thing one doesn't notice oneself doing. But given you had just talked to me about being available to him to comfort him, I was wondering whether he wanted to come and cuddle up to you, and whether the anxiety you've been telling me about . . . well, it's obviously very alive between you and gets into these little details of your relating together.

V: I suppose I'm quite anxious about giving him his own space because of all these dynamics with other people. I'm very aware of him having his time for him and his space because I know that I need it. So maybe I backed off too quickly: 'Right he's fine now' so I can move away again and let him have his space.

AJ: And that links with your wish and need for him to be independent, self-reliant; so it conflicts with your wish also to be his special person, his mummy, to be the one who consoles him and cuddles him.

V: (*to P*) Quite confusing really.
AJ: Confusing for all of you.

Following this interaction Peter made his first overtures to me, offering me a rattle, and I acknowledged his beginning to feel safe with me, a stranger.

What issues are manifest in the interaction?

The opening ten minutes of this session contain the ordinary interactions of a mother and child, albeit in the special situation of a clinical setting. Peter shows us immediately that his mother is a safe base on whom he can depend for safety and reassurance in this strange environment. However, he goes off on his explorations rather soon into the session, making me wonder whether he is showing precocious independence. What then is the nature of his internal relationship with his mother? Externally, it seems that despite the anxieties expressed overtly, Veronica functions as an available, caring mother who is attentive to her son's needs, helping him settle by inviting him to play, making herself available to him, and then comforting him when he is distressed.

It is only in the fine detail of their interaction, picked up by the therapist/ observer, that the 'ghost in the nursery' becomes apparent. Peter's use of his body to hold onto his mother (rather than knowing that she can hold onto him) reflects the requirement upon him to be 'advanced' for his age. In my counter-transference I was thinking about him as a toddler when in fact he was just one year old. I presume that my image of him was shaped by the unconscious demands from Veronica, internalised by Peter, to outgrow his helpless baby needs.

In the sequence, as Veronica was describing her representation of Peter as a naughty, defiant boy Peter hurt himself, thus expressing his dilemma: his attempts to be the explorer developmentally propelled but also hijacked by his mother, and the strain it imposes. The strain of growing up too quickly.

We understand this kind of event as the way in which the unconscious transactions between the infant and caregiver get expressed. Peter's 'accidental' hurting of himself calls his mother to attend to him, which I took as a communication that his explorations are not rooted in an internal sense of safety. Veronica responds warmly to his call but then subtly withdraws. Peter protests momentarily before he reaches for a beaker as an alternative to the cuddle with his mum. This could be said to constitute a potential derailment in the parent–infant interaction, a derailment which is unconsciously intended by Veronica to promote Peter's precocious independence from her. Veronica longs for Peter to need and depend upon her, but she dreads it too – because to be dependent is so reminiscent of her absolute helplessness in her *disabled* infantile state.

Here we have the transference to the child – the unconscious injunction that he will not need her as she needed her carers so absolutely. Through my articulation of this dilemma, as expressed in the immediacy of the interaction, Veronica is able to recognise her 'too quick backing off'. I interpret the conflict she is in – her need for him to be independent of her, and her wish to be his special person in the face of all the competition from the carers.

We can see that Veronica's life-long struggle with her disability now has a new version as she has become a mother with an able-bodied son. The corollary for Peter is that he has to struggle with his own sense of himself as an able-bodied child whose mother is so damaged. The danger is that his core sense of himself will be compromised by the intrusion of his mother's conflicts about this, which form such an important part of his identifications.

How do you wipe your child's nose if you have no arms? How do you wipe your own?

A short while after the above sequence, Veronica commented that Peter needed his nose wiping, something he hated and about which he always created a huge fuss. I asked her if she wanted me to do it. She said yes, so I told Peter about what I was going to do. I spoke to him about his feelings about it: that it was horrible for me to do it to him; I was a stranger whom he had only just met, intruding into his body space. Afterwards he gave me a wide berth and I said he was not so sure about me now.

Unwittingly, by asking Veronica if she wanted me to wipe Peter's nose and speaking to him about it, I had disrupted the usual way Veronica and her team had of relating together in the care of Peter. My intervention was predicated upon an implicit model that I have of respect for the parent and of the mind of the child as an active, experiencing subject, requiring an emotionally sensitive engagement with the adult. This simple detail was to have an unintended impact – the effects of this was evident the following day.

Issues of limit setting and keeping safe – the representation of the child in the mother's mind

The complex issues around limit setting became alive in the session as Peter explored the new environment of the Parent–Infant Project room. Of interest to him was a sturdy stand, which Peter approached and pulled himself up on; his mother became anxious.

Veronica used her voice in an insistent, harsh way, saying 'No' several times, which he ignored. Quite quickly, she went over to him and using her teeth to hold his sweater at the back, she took him away, telling him that he couldn't do that. She could not see his face but I could. He was grinning, and he was limp like a kitten being carried by the mother cat. I felt that he was indicating that this interference with his play was a game in itself. I described this to Veronica, emphasising his pleasure in the close playful contact with her. She reacted in dismay as she felt this undermined her attempt to keep him safe, and his obedience to her prohibitions. He returned to exploring the stand and Veronica tried to distract him, as well as using a harsh tone to restrict him. She said at one point that he had her 'right where he wants her' – expressing her powerlessness in the face of his unfettered freedom of movement. What she was unable to appreciate then, however, was that in this complicated interaction he was indeed following her cues, and playing the typical junior toddler game of finding out who owns his body and what freedom of movement he indeed did have.

Very shortly after this exchange, as Veronica was despairing of having any impact upon him, I noticed a piece of interaction that was crucial. As he moved away from the stand, Peter looked at it, then at his mum, then back again at the stand, and then moved on to something else. I drew her attention to his use of her as a reference to decide what his actions might be. He then went onto further potential mischief, as he took the clock (a robust one) standing on the windowsill within his reach. He dropped it and immediately Veronica said harshly, 'Look, you've broken it.' Her rapid reaction was elaborated into a fantasy of a 'marauding two year old', which she dreaded Peter becoming. Interestingly, we did not talk about how her quick response interfered with his curiosity and exploration of the world. She did that piece of work on her own, and came back the next day much more able to bear her anxiety about what his curiosity would lead to and intervened at a much later point with the harshness much diminished.

Veronica's representation of Peter as a strong-willed, determined child also contained a sense of him being 'naughty' or 'defiant', and a much more difficult idea of him being a 'marauding two year old' whom she could not control. For Veronica, with her severe disability, this posed enormous problems at a conscious level. At a more unconscious level it related to her unremembered but never-the-less powerful experience of being a toddler. As these issues around limit setting were enacted in the session, I asked Veronica what she was like as a two year old. She replied with 'Pass . . . I don't remember.' But she did tell me that she had artificial limbs from six months that confined her rather than liberated her, and she did not walk until she was four years old. The fantasy of the marauding two year old contains perhaps a wish dating from that time in her own life when she had no possibility of using her body to express her marauding self. The fear for Peter contained a wish and also perhaps an inevitable envious reproach for his able-bodied-ness. The problem as a growing toddler for Peter was whether he could find his way of being an adventurous explorer without the alien intrusion of his mother's marauding self.

The end of the first session

Peter became tired as the long session went on, and Veronica spoke to him about wanting his cot, and to me about what would normally happen at home with the carers. A carer would pick him up and put him in his cot and she would feel 'the observer mum', but she was anxious if on her own with him in case she could not deal with what might happen. However, as the session continued and he became more tired, there was a prolonged period of Peter holding onto his mum and embracing her as Veronica embraced him with her voice and the stumps of her arms. Her voice was now soft as she spoke to him about how he was feeling. She spoke to me of how rare this was and how a third party always interfered with it. I drew her attention to the fact that I was such a third party but that something different was happening here. Peter, for the first time since he was weaned at four months, used his mother to fall asleep on.

AJ: He's never done that before?
V: No, he never had the space to do it. There's always somebody else who says: 'Oh, he's getting tired, so I'll take him.' It's always like, 'You can't cope with him and so I'll take over.'
AJ: Which is what I haven't done.
V: No, it's been really nice, it's been very refreshing. That sounds most ungracious, doesn't it? I know he would have been taken off me by now if I didn't have that 24-hour care.

THE FOLLOWING DAY: THE NEXT SESSION

Indicators of change – internal work

As I collected them from the waiting room, Veronica asked the carer who was with them to wipe Peter's nose and to make sure she told him what she was doing! Veronica told me of the surprise it had been to her when I asked her if she wanted me to wipe Peter's nose; this never happened at home. Also she had noticed me talking to Peter about what I was doing, acknowledging his feelings about it. She felt that this had made an enormous difference to him. She now asked her carer to do the same thing and Peter's cross-reactions to having his nose wiped had greatly diminished, amazing in such a short time.

Supporting curiosity and balancing it with keeping the child safe

The following vignette shows Veronica's increased capacity to bear the anxiety about Peter's safety so that his curiosity could be allowed some rein. Peter once again needed his nose wiping, and he crawled away rapidly from me.

AJ: (*to P*) You don't want your nose wiped. Want to come have your nose wiped?

V: (*to P*) You'll feel much better. Coming?

Peter approaches the plant stand.

AJ: (*to V & P*) Much more exciting things to do than have your nose wiped. Having a runny nose might actually feel quite nice; it's hard for us to . . .

V: (*to AJ*) I quite often have a runny nose and can't do anything about it . . .

AJ: What do you do about it?

V: I either have to ask somebody or stop what I'm doing, take my shoes off and say: 'Can I have a tissue, please.'

AJ: Very complicated. You know little children enjoy things like that, in a way that . . .

Peter starts to pull himself up on the stand.

V: (*in an escalating anxious tone*) Not the stand, Peter, not the stand. No . . . good boy. Good boy. Not the stand. It'll fall down; there'll be trouble. I'm not coming to get you, I refuse.

AJ: (*to P*) The world's full of interesting things, isn't it? How does it work, that stand?

V: (*to P*) Don't pull it down.

AJ: (*speaking as if for P*) But mummy it's so exciting, look, it's so exciting.

V: Good boy – ah, what's that? What is it? What's that? Not bored with that yet, then? If I ignore you, will you stop?

V: (*to AJ*) This is the thing I realise that I've got to learn. I need to know when to go bowling in and I need to know when not to, what do I do next?

AJ: How are you feeling now?

V: I'm feeling like I should be over there, taking him away from it.

AJ: And what's stopping you?

V: He's not actually hurting it or breaking it, he hasn't fallen. Maybe if I let the curiosity pass, he'll leave it alone. Every time I go over there and drag him away he thinks it's funny, playing a game. So am I just exacerbating the situation because he thinks it's a game and giving him the attention that he wants?

AJ: Little toddlers love playing games with their mums, don't they? And mums love playing games with their toddlers.

V: No! Peter. No, not that bit. Peter, no!
AJ: (*speaking again as if P*) But mummy I want to.
V: I know you do.
AJ: (*to P*) It's so interesting, it's so exciting.

Veronica's anxiety increases and she tries to distract Peter.

V: What have we got over here? Have something here instead.
AJ: No, not on your life. Oopsy! Peter.

Peter has begun to pull the stand quite strongly

AJ: Now I'm feeling that I . . . I might also . . . perhaps . . .
V: He's not getting bored with it, is he?
AJ: Perhaps now it's the time for you to . . .
V: (*getting up and going over to P*) I know, curiosity and all that over now, that's enough. Come over here. Not on your life. Peter, no! Good boy. I know it's interesting, I realise this. But it's not for you to play with. You can have a look, curiosity factor out now. We're bored with it, thank you . . . good boy . . . no! (*to AJ*) If I pull him, I'll pull the whole lot down.
AJ: Yes, I realise that. So it's actually quite a critical . . .
V: Yeah, because I would now be endangering him as well. He could pull the whole lot down on me. I need you to lift him up for me.
AJ: You want me to help?
V: Yes, please.

I get up and go over to Peter:

AJ: (*to P*) Peter, I'm going to wipe your nose and take you away from here.
V: Good boy, good boy . . . that's better.

I have brought Peter over to where his mum and I were near the toys, on the cushions. He immediately turns to crawl back to the stand.

V: There you go. What's in there, what can you find in there?

Veronica is at a loss to know what to do now and turns her head away from him.

AJ: (*to V*) I was wondering if rather than ignoring him, you could play with something . . . I don't know whether you can use the bricks.

She responds to me and tries to persuade Peter to return to play with her:

V: (*to P*) Come and look at these, Peter, look what I've got. What's
      mama got, look, what's this? Come and have a look. Peter. (*to AJ and
      herself*) I'm not good at this. (*trying to sound persuasive*) Come and
      look at this with mama. Peter, come and have a look, it's much more
      interesting. Pretty colours, look – reds and yellows and greens.
      There's no way. No!

She shakes the colourful toy with her foot. Peter has hesitated, clearly in
conflict about whether to return to the stand or to his mum. He then turns
back to Veronica and responds to her invitation by crawling back to her.

V: (*to P*) Good boy, good boy. Come over here then . . . Peter! What's
      this? What's this? What have I got? Makes a great noise – look. Then
      I shake it, fab! . . . great noise. Come on then, are you going to have a
      look? Come on then.

Peter pauses at the box of bricks. Veronica joins him there.

V: All right, shall we have a look at the bricks instead?

DISCUSSION

In this sequence we can see the possible beginnings of new ways of interacting between this mother and infant pair. These would contribute to
different structures of relating being established in this child's mind. The
procedures of 'being with the other' that gradually coalesce in the developing infant are consequent upon these interactions, which in turn are
infused with meaning from the internal self and object representations of
the parent, as well as from the emerging representational world of the
infant.

Veronica's sense of Peter as the marauding two year old, her own 'wished
for' self has been modified in this clinical encounter to allow him to take
some risks in a safe enough environment. Building on the interventions of
the previous day, I did not act, but attended to the affective and behavioural detail, the micro-events of this part of the session. This is the
mentalising function of the therapist, emotionally processing the experience
as it happens in the moment at a conscious and unconscious level. As a
consequence the mother was able to bear the anxiety of the risk of damage
to her child in this ordinary situation, a risk we could imagine as terrifying
to her. Peter was keenly attuned to the emotional nuances in the interaction
with Veronica and the outcome when he chooses to abandon the stand in

favour of playing with his mum is a moment of triumph for both. This whole sequence of interaction enables him to have a greater sense of himself as an active, exploring child who can rely upon his external and ultimately internal objects to judge what is a reasonable risk. This is a much sounder basis for him to enter toddlerhood.

This therapeutic consultation is also an environment where Veronica can request help from a concerned but non-intrusive other, the clinician who has provided her with a different way of being with, and which perhaps also contributes to some modification in her representations of the kind of help she can expect. There is already evidence for that in her request to the carer at the beginning of the second session to wipe Peter's nose and to explain to him what she is doing. These procedural aspects of the therapeutic relationship underpin the discursive, interpretive, semantic aspects, which form the 'to and fro' of the verbal discourse of the session.

CONCLUSION

Veronica had lived a public life since her beginning as a result of her disability. She created with me an experience of profound intimacy in a very brief therapeutic encounter, as I had the sense of her using every moment. Perhaps this reflected her ability to take what she could when it became available, honed by years of deprivation as a child. Despite the unusual brevity of this consultation, Veronica gained a greater capacity to be emotionally available to Peter in the moment. As a consequence he was able to be both an adventurous child and to relinquish the dangerous adventure in favour of closeness with his mother. What is clear is that time is of the essence as the infant's internal world is structured in the context of the relationships with primary objects from the beginning.

Formulations of change in parent–infant psychotherapy

Tessa Baradon and Carol Broughton

The psychodynamic formulation is the therapist's hypotheses about conscious and unconscious constituents of the parent–infant relationship and the pathology therein, the tasks of therapy and the interventions she may use (see Chapter 2).

In this chapter we examine the therapist's psychodynamic formulations and the ways they are titrated into the therapeutic encounter. Three sessions were selected in which themes around attachment develop and are elaborated. This elaboration represents the therapist's expanding formulations within the changing landscapes of the therapeutic encounter.

Therese and Anthony were referred for therapy because of her anxiety that she had damaged Anthony when separated from him during a psychotic episode after his birth, for which she was hospitalised.

SECOND SESSION (ANTHONY AGED TEN MONTHS)

Therese recalled that the therapist had said that sometimes the way things were for her as a child may have a bearing on how she is feeling now with Anthony. She said that she does not have many memories of the past. The therapist responded that she seemed to be protecting herself by not remembering. Anthony is playing with the bricks near the therapist.

TB: It sounds as though there are lots of ghosts along the way that you want not to be like. Perhaps you are in a situation of constantly monitoring yourself, worrying whether you're doing it right.

Anthony looks up from the bricks to the therapist.

Mother: I don't know if that's just a symptom of being depressed. I don't know why it is I need constant reassurance all the time. It's pretty exhausting really. (*Laughing*)

TB: Who's giving you the reassurance at the moment?

Anthony crawls towards Therese and, holding on to her, hauls himself up to a standing position facing her.

Mother: (*to Anthony*) Hello? (*to therapist*) I'm speaking a bit to my mum. I don't really talk to my husband about it; I don't think he'd understand.

Anthony sits beside mother, placing a rattle on the doll's head and being quite vocal.

TB: And what about Anthony, if he crawled up and held on to you. What did you think he was saying to you there?
Mother: I don't know really. He does that because he wants to practise standing up.
TB: Why didn't he practise that against the wall or against me?
Mother: He managed to come and sit next to me. I don't know.
TB: If he were coming up to say 'You're my special, beloved person, and I want to have an intimate, face to face gurgle with you'. Would that be reassuring? Flattering? Would it be a demand that you felt you couldn't meet? That you're too sad, too empty to do it?
Mother: Usually. Mostly it's a pleasure but sometimes, yes, there's an emptiness, like – how do I relate to him? She lifts Anthony to face her. He continues to vocalise and latches on to her long hair. 'Well, we're friends aren't we?' She murmurs gently: 'Yes, yes.' Anthony starts to fret in her arms, she puts him down.
Mother: (*to Anthony*) What's the matter? You look like you're stuck. Here we go. (*Gives him the doll*)
TB: But maybe sometimes it does feel – how does one have an intimate relationship with this little thing?
Mother: Yes. How do you build the proper foundations? Oh, Anthony, what's the matter?

Anthony is whimpering. He leans towards her and Therese picks him up. They both look at the therapist.

Mother: (*to therapist*) It's so hard, you don't know . . . (*to Anthony*) Is that better now?
TB: (*to Anthony*) Sometimes you just want a cuddle, don't you?

Anthony pulls his mother's hair.

Mother: (*repeats quietly*) A cuddle. Yes. (*Anthony tugs her hair, it seems to hurt mother*) I'm going to have to get my hair cut, or I'm going to have none left, am I?

Anthony nuzzles (or bites?) her neck

TB: I can see he's also started to kind of nibble at you.
Mother: (*Holding Anthony away from her as he stands on her lap, addressing him*) Yes, he gives me sloppy kisses and nuzzles me, don't you? Yes you do.

Anthony looks up at a mobile.

TB: So it's a mixed blessing – his being in love with you. It's both wonderful and it . . .
Mother: (*interrupts with vigour*) You know, I never think of him being in love with me though. It's weird. I don't think about that. (*She looks enquiringly at Anthony, who has his face sideways to her as he watches the mobile*) I don't think that he might love me. (*to Anthony*) But mummy loves you.

Anthony looks from the mobile to the therapist and back.

Mother: (*to Anthony*) Oh, you've seen that thing up there haven't you?
TB: (*to Anthony*) It's interesting, isn't it Anthony? It goes round and round and you can't catch it.

Commentary

The central issue is mother's anxiety about damaging her baby, and it is translated into a belief that she cannot be loved by him. This is mirrored by Anthony's lack of success in asserting his 'possession' of her – her lap, face. In the therapist's mind there are questions about how Therese and Anthony get to feel good about themselves in their respective roles as mother and as son. Is Anthony a source of reassurance or anxiety to his mother? What image of himself does he meet in her mind?

The therapist is alerted to a mutual turning away where there was potential for engagement. It is not yet clear what this pattern between them represents. Consider the meaning of Therese's conflict about intimacy with her baby and the possible roots in her own childhood relationships. For example, the therapist knows that Therese is ambivalent towards her mother – seeing their relationship as both special and destructive. Similarly in her relationship with her husband – he is present in her mind and yet rejected. The therapist suspects that Therese and her husband have not spoken about her breakdown and that she is afraid that he will not be able to embrace her psychotic part. The therapist is concerned that Anthony is over-riding his need for closeness in accommodating to his mother's emotional distance. The therapist's interventions are led by her under-standing that the urgency lies with Anthony for whom, in the counter-transference, she feels sadness that he is bereft of a maternal 'lap', and a wish to scoop him up. She suggests to Therese that she is special to her baby and he wants an intimacy with her that would not be shared with others. This is a statement that has the potential to reframe mother's representations. The therapist then wonders how that may feel to Therese – reassuring, or a demand that may confront her with her inner emptiness? The primary revelation for Therese is that her baby may be in love with her. This seems to amaze her, and to frighten her as well. Both feeling states in mother are translated into behaviours with her child: she holds him gently and she also distances herself from her 'attacker' (who will leave her no hair). Anthony, like his mother before him, tries to reach an internal accommodation with the love-object his mother is. The mobile at the window symbolically contained the intergenerational affective dilemma. 'It goes round and round and you can't catch it' the therapist says – you are yearning but cannot (yet) capture the passion of your mother's love.

THIRD SESSION (ONE WEEK LATER)

Anthony is asleep when they arrive. Mother wheels him into the therapy room, placing his buggy so that he faces away from her and the therapist as they sit down to talk (on the floor, as usual).

They hear Anthony stirring.

Mother: Have you woken up? (*She rises and approaches Anthony, talking softly*) Do you want to come and say hello to [*TB*]? (*She lifts him out of the pram and brings him to the carpet*) There you go, say hello to [*TB*].

She sits him facing outwards.

TB: Hello Anthony, you went to sleep and have woken up in a different place.

Anthony gets onto his hands and knees. He turns to look at the therapist.

TB: Do you remember me? I wasn't there when you went to sleep.

Anthony crawls after the ball away from the adults.

TB: (*to Anthony, in playful voice*) Where are you going?

Anthony is now across the room. He turns around, ball in outstretched hand. The therapist tracks his glance at his mother and says: 'What does mummy say?'

Mother: (*sounding flat*) It's very good.

Anthony drops the ball; it rolls back in the direction of the adults. Anthony crawls after it again.

Mother: Are you going to come back?

Anthony stalls at a cushion a distance away. He sags, head on the cushion, facing Therese, whimpering.

Mother: Are you still feeling sleepy, Anthony?

Mother and the therapist are watching Anthony. The therapist feels a strong wish to scoop him up, and wishes his mother would do so. Anthony gets into a sitting position and briefly handles the ball again. It rolls away from the adults.

TB: (*to Anthony*) Is it running away from you?

Anthony, intent on pursuing the ball, is in danger of banging his head. Therese and the therapist move to get him. The therapist, noting mother has arisen, settles back in her place. Mother picks Anthony up and carries him back to the playing space between herself and the therapist. She builds a tower for him. There is a silence as both adults watch Anthony play.
    After a pause, the therapist speaks.

TB: (*to mother*) What was the danger as a child in letting people know how you feel?

Therese describes being bullied as a child.
    Anthony moves across the room, and then stops and looks to the therapist and back at his mother. He whimpers and reaches out an arm towards the adults – it is pointing to the space between mother and the therapist. The therapist mirrors his outreaching movement, and momentarily holds her arm in that position. He watches, then starts crawling back towards mother in a circular route.

Mother: (*reaching out to him*) Do you want me? Do you want a cuddle?

She picked him up and held him against her chest. She talked about having a disturbed night as Anthony cried and was comforted only when put in the parental bed. She mentioned his father and conveyed that they were a couple in relation to their distressed baby. She continued in an affectionate tone, while stroking Anthony's head 'But you can't get angry because when you pick him up . . . he gives you this enormous smile'. The therapist was attentive to the affection mother was expressing but noted that throughout this exchange Anthony was reaching away from her. Therese offered him a toy, and then helped him onto the floor.

Commentary

There are already some changes in Therese's relating to Anthony – she risks considering whether it is her that he wants, and is more active in bringing him back to her. But Anthony's attempts to reach out to mother as yet carry no direct expectation of a contingent response. The question for both mother and baby in this session is how to have a robust and intimate relationship. Yet the therapist feels less torn in her identifications; she is able to mentally embrace both, and thus holds hope for them.

The ball, a spherical toy like the mobile, represents the unsuccessful dyad's attempts to grasp and hold each other. The balls lures, tempts and teases – it slips out of hand, is caught, rolls away again. The therapist, again using the toy metaphorically, says 'is it (the passion of maternal love) running away from you (eluding you)?' There is then an 'analytic enactment' (McLaughlin, 1991) between Anthony, mother and therapist: Anthony nearly hurts himself, mother and therapist rise to help him. The enactment resolves the situation: Therese brings Anthony back, recreating a space for him between herself and the therapist. Both adults join in watching him play. Dyadic constraints – mother baby/mother therapist/baby therapist – are regrouped into an analytic working space in which the parental couple 'hold' the immature infant.

The therapist hypothesises that Therese's difficulties in 'hearing' her child's cry to her is linked to her own experiences as a child (Fraiberg et al., 1975). With Anthony now safely anchored between Therese and herself, the therapist feels able to pursue the intergenerational patterns. Therese describes children who bullied her. At this point Anthony moves away and faces his mother across the room, whimpering. The therapist speculates that possibly in Therese's eyes at that moment Anthony is a bullying and frightening baby (and she an unprotecting therapist) and that Therese's emotional state is frightening to the baby. The therapist waits. Therese seems to move internally towards a recognition of Anthony as her infant, unlinking the association between him and the bullies. 'What do you need?' she asks him. 'You' he replies by crawling back (although the circular route he chooses suggests that he is still anxious). Therese responds, this time matching his affective communication, 'Do you want me? Do you want a cuddle?' She holds him to her yet Anthony does not respond to the spoken affection and the gentle gestures of his mother. This apparent mismatch – this time coming from him – suggests that Therese's doubt is getting in the way of Anthony's engagement. In the therapist's mind there is concern whether mother would be able to hold on to her emergent new representations and behaviours in the face of lack of reinforcement from Anthony, and whether Anthony would find his way to claiming through being claimed (Alvarez, 1992).

SEVENTH SESSION (ANTHONY AGED 13 MONTHS)

We will now present three shorter interactions from the seventh session through which we hope to track development and elaboration within the session.

Therese and Anthony are five minutes late for an early morning appointment. Anthony is not very well, says mother, he had not wanted her to touch him yesterday. The therapist notes that Anthony is back to playing today.

Five minutes into the session

Anthony turned and, vocalising, raised himself to standing position while holding on and facing his mother. He had a small ball in his hand.

Mother: Are you coming to show me this little ball? You like round objects don't you, Anthony? (*Therese encircles Anthony with her arm*) They hold nicely in your hand.

Anthony is a bit unsteady on his feet and Therese helps him balance. Anthony, vocalising, crawls over mother's feet, trailing his ball.

Mother: Where are you going?

Therese and the therapist watched Anthony chasing the rolling ball.

Mother: (*turning back to face the therapist*) He is livelier today, which is good.
TB: Were you worried yesterday?
Mother: It's when they are starting to get ill and they are just so unlike themselves. You do just get that sort of – is it a storm in a teacup or is it going to blow into something . . .
TB: So what did you feel?

Mother: Well, I suppose concern and a bit of that old anxiety. But not, you know, not . . .

Anthony had crawled back to Therese and she embraced him as he reached her. He vocalised and held on to her to stand up.

Mother: I suppose there are so many more axes on which I can judge him now because he's a more complex little person than he was.

Therese and Anthony face each other

Mother: Are you going to give me a kiss?

Anthony touched her face and she reached out to stay his hand. He sat down and played at her side.

    Therese talked about his eating quite well the previous day so she did not allow her anxiety to escalate. The therapist noted that she seemed embarrassed about the old anxiety creeping back.

Mother: Well, because I just don't want to be that woman again.
TB: That poor part of you, held so strongly in check. Is it allowed some expression?
Therese: Probably just privately to myself.

Anthony, who had been very focused on placing wooden people into a boat, looked up briefly and then went back to his play.

Mother: I think probably every parent has the same things but you can't be shrieking around (nervous laugh) undisciplined. This is about being grown up, isn't it? Feeling it inside but allowing one self to have control over it.

Anthony moves his bus closer to mother and she strokes his head. He is still playing with evident pleasure.

Commentary

Therese, alone with the sick, unresponsive child, was revisited by the internal 'undisciplined shrieking' that heralded her breakdown. At this early point in the session, Therese can only hint at it to the therapist. Yet, despite the anxiety, Therese is closely attentive to Anthony in the here-and-now of the session, and he is showing his interest and pleasure in her. She acknowledges that he likes round objects, and there is a sense of enclosure as she encircles him with her arm and he becomes the round object held in her embrace. He is in a safe place, as he was in the womb before the loss and separation entailed by her illness. Anthony is refuelled, he crawls off to play. It is then possible to touch upon her worry – was it a storm in a teacup or will it 'blow into something'? Mirroring the growing integration of her own complexity, Therese says that Anthony is a more complex person now; this seems to arise from their new, more satisfying relationship.

15 minutes later

Talking about a holiday planned with just her husband, Therese strokes Anthony's head as he sits at her side drinking from his cup.

TB: Are you a little bit apprehensive about the holiday?
Mother: Well, yes, a little bit. Of course, I know he'll be fine. He'll be well looked after. I hope he doesn't hate us too much when we come home (*nervous laugh*). My mother said to expect a bit of a cool reception and then you might be welcomed back into the fold after a couple of days (*laughs*). Anthony is watching the mobile.
TB: Does your mother recall a time when she went away and got punished?
Mother: I asked her. I remember them going away, but they apparently also went away when I was small and she was pregnant with my brother. She can't recall any sort of punishment then but I definitely recall missing them terribly when I [*sic*] went away when I was small and wondering why on earth they left us, but I was much older.

Anthony has stopped drinking and plays with a cloth nappy which he places on his head.

Mother: You want to play 'peep-bo' Anthony?

Therese opens the cloth and drapes it over his head, saying 'peep-bo'. Anthony pulls it off and, looking at his mother says 'pa' and she repeats 'peep-bo'. This game is repeated twice.

TB: Maybe you are a little apprehensive not only about Anthony missing you but also about how you will feel about him.
Mother: Oh, yes, I mean it is going to be very odd just going away with [husband] on our own – she rolls her eyes.

Anthony has continued to put the nappy on his head and look at his mother.

Mother: I'm just going to take a big stack of books and relax and enjoy it.

Anthony climbs up to standing position and then lowers himself, with Therese's help, into her lap. But he doesn't settle there; he continues to fret and she gives him a dummy.

Mother: (*to Anthony*) You're looking a bit sad today.

Commentary

Therese is contemplating a second separation from Anthony, this time voluntary. The therapist understands that the two are, as yet, conflated. She introduces a low-keyed affective adjective – 'nervous'. Therese locates her anxiety: she hopes Anthony will not hate her too much when she comes home. There is no physical distancing from Anthony as she says this. The therapist suspects that the anxiety is not confined to Therese's history with Anthony, and she refers to a possible transgenerational narrative by asking about separations in Therese's childhood. In Therese's confused answer, marked by grammatical faltering and time lapse, the abandoning parent and abandoned children cross the generations. Anthony distinguishes between mother and himself by initiating a mastery of separation through the peep-bo game, which is about losing and re-finding the object. The therapist follows his distinction in a comment that Therese is worried about how she will feel about leaving Anthony, as well as her worry about him. Therese seems to feel depleted by the conflict she is experiencing, and the playfulness is lost. Anthony finds it difficult to settle into his mother's lap. She offers him a dummy as a substitute for herself and says that he is looking sad today, a reflection, perhaps, of her own sadness and fears about the forthcoming separation.

15 minutes later

Therese is talking about not judging herself about the breakdown. The therapist takes up her (Therese's) perception of how the therapist may regard her. Is Therese worried that the therapist may think that there is indeed something wrong?

Mother: Well, I think that early on I was more scared.
TB: That I would judge you?
Mother: Yes, well, I'd had some bad experiences.
TB: Did that include your mother?

Mother: No, because I think that my mother, despite all her short-
comings and difficulties I had with her as a child and in the past,
she was the one initially who really took the bull by the horns
and said to [husband] – look Therese is ill and this is what has
got to happen.

Therese is talking with intensity here and Anthony, back to her, is unpacking her handbag and throwing its contents on the floor.

Mother: (*continues*) She was the one who said to the hospital, 'this
woman is suffering from puerperal psychosis and could you
please wake up here.' So, in that sense she understood the
situation most clearly . . . because I think she understood it a lot
more without even admitting because maybe she recognises
those feelings for herself at the time, but of course . . .
TB: She didn't get the help?
Therese: (*sadly*) No, she didn't get the help. No. I think my Dad said you
know you've got two beautiful children, get on with it. So that
was her way of, kind of . . . (*Therese becomes tearful*).

Anthony is babbling softly as he closely investigates mother's chequebook.

TB: It is very moving, as you describe it, for both of you – you and
your Mum.
Therese: Yes.

She is looking at Anthony, surrounded by her possessions. She reaches out
to take the chequebook from him, saying that no, he can't have it. Anthony
protests and crawls after the chequebook. His mother offers him a wooden
doll and he tosses it aside angrily. Therese laughs 'You don't want that!'
and gives him back the chequebook.

Mother: (*to the therapist*) As time has passed I've definitely got less hard
on myself about what happened.
TB: And less hard about your mother.
Mother: Yes.

Commentary

The therapist, by now, has a working hypotheses about Therese's use of
projection to expel the 'shrieking' mad bits of herself that she cannot
tolerate, which results in her feeling persecuted by others' judgement. This
has been addressed in some measure in previous sessions. The therapist

brings up the negative transference to herself, which has not, until now, been acknowledged. The therapist then chooses to take the transference back to Therese's representations of her mother. Therese talks powerfully and gratefully of her mother's intervention when she was ill. In this first re-examination of her ambivalence towards her mother, she moves away from recriminations to positive identification. She makes the intergenerational link that her psychosis mirrored her mother's unacknowledged breakdown. Her mother, she says, had drawn upon her own postnatal experiences to understand her daughter's condition, and Therese, in turn, shows empathy for her mother's lonely unhappiness when a young mother. Moreover, her mother had enabled her daughter to receive the help that she had been denied.

Anthony's play mirrors his mother's preoccupation – he is unpacking her personal belongings. He picks up a treasure from among his mother's things and refuses to part with it. Therese tries to placate him with a wooden doll, which he rejects as inferior and unconnected to her, just as he felt unable to embrace the wooden, unyielding mother of the early sessions. Therese lets him have what he wants, and there is a sense of admiring her baby for holding on to his desires. She says she has become less hard on herself and on her mother. She seems to be able to embrace the weakness, to find the greater strength in forgiveness.

The movement *in the session* is multilayered – encompassing present and past, representation and behaviour. In the early part of the session Therese hints at the 'old anxiety' that has resurfaced and her fears that its very presence again threatens to pull her back into a state of madness. The therapist conveys that she understands the effort Therese puts into main-taining the split, but in her mind the different aspects of Therese can be integrated – 'That poor part of you, held so strongly in check, is it ever allowed some expression?' By mid-session the anxiety can be explored and it is linked to attachment, separation and loss. Therese recalls her feelings when her mother left her, and draws on this to anticipate Anthony's and her own pain when she leaves him (a controlled separation this time). Mastery of the separation is played out in the developmentally appropriate game of peek-a-boo. In the final part of the session maternal abandonment is revisited with more compassionate eyes. Through this Anthony, as her 'treasure', is reaffirmed – with humour rather than guilt.

DISCUSSION

At the time of referral, Therese and ten-month-old Anthony were caught in an intergenerational dilemma where the gusto of parental love and infantile ruth (Winnicott, 1945) were associated in the mother's mind with damaging and being damaged by depression, madness and separation. The solution co-constructed by Therese and Anthony (Beebe, 2000) was to love from afar, without demands – a defensively avoidant attachment from which the imprint of passion is removed.

The therapist's formulations about Therese and Anthony's course from avoidance to finding each other can be described through the metaphor of the elusive 'round object'. In the second session, the circular mobile draws Anthony's attention and he is transfixed by an object rather than held in his mother's embrace. The mobile's endless spinning, like the transgenerational repeat of patterns of relating, conveys a message of being just beyond grasp, and each slips from the other's emotional grip and is left clutching at emptiness. In the third session, the round object is a ball that somehow also eludes Anthony. However, now it is in the room and it can be used to negotiate the affective space between mother and infant. The therapist tracks Anthony as he approaches and retreats; she voices his feelings as the ball gets away from him and he struggles to bring it back to his mother. The therapist felt a strong invitation from Therese to claim Anthony and from Anthony to pick him up. She cogitates this understanding until it can be offered – 'metabolised' (Bion, 1967) and in symbolic reconfiguration – as a non-verbal interpretation to mother and child. The therapist mirrors Anthony's outreaching movement and thus draws a line of communication between him, Therese and herself. Anthony is then able to begin the return journey to his mother and she responds to his wish to be gathered up. Presumably, at this point a representation of herself as comforting, and of her baby as being comforted by her, is taking form. Yet it is a transitional stage, as Anthony's squirming discloses, and there are still some emotional lengths to go. In the seventh session, Therese begins by acknowledging that he likes round objects. She extends the affective meaning by holding Anthony in her embrace and, thus, closes the circle.

The summary above illustrates how closely interwoven the therapist's formulations and interventions are with the material of her patients. The therapist is guided by the affective tone of the interactions in her interventions. For example, the therapist knew she was taking a risk in expressing her understanding of Anthony's desire for his mother so early in the treatment, but was led by the sense of urgency emanating from him. Yet, in the event, it was a key interpretation of the transference to the baby (Fraiberg, 1980), that transformed the mother's self-representation in relation to her infant and effected her move towards recoupling. Another transformational event took place in relation to Anthony when the therapist mirrored his gesture. This was an unconscious move that drew on her formulations about their mutual attachment needs. This interpretation, given in the language of action, created a symbolic triangle (Ogden, 1994) within which Anthony was able to make his way back to his mother. This 'moment of meeting' (Stern et al., 1998) in the relational field between therapist, baby and mother, rearranged their procedural knowing of how to be with each other. The repeated experience of finding himself safely represented in the mind of the therapist (Fonagy, 1999) was thus transferred to mother – closing the circle and heralding the completion of the work in the therapeutic encounter.

Chapter 11

Shifting triangles: images of father in sequences from parent–infant psychotherapy[1]

Judith Woodhead

Images of the father are central in the development of the psychological self during infancy. The symbol of the triangle is used in diverse cultures to depict father–mother–infant relationships (Tang & Smith, 1996).

In this chapter I aim to explore images of the father and the symbol of the triangle through case material of work with a mother and her infant son, in the absence of the father. The mother and father of the infant I shall describe had a complex history, including addiction and homelessness. They were referred when their son was nine months old as part of a raft of multi-agency support. Soon after weekly therapy began, the father precipitately left his partner, his son and the therapy and had no further contact. Clinical work continued with the mother and her infant son, along with a now 'absent father'. This work is the focus of this paper. I will refer to the mother as 'Shelley' and the son as 'Ben'.

Shelley expressed relief at becoming a twosome with her son Ben, which she felt offset the burden of becoming sole parent. She felt life as a twosome was easier than life as a threesome. This was a key statement, pre-figuring what was to develop in the therapy. Ben, aged nine months when the therapy began, also made his own non-verbal statement. He repeatedly lifted the edges of the rug beneath the baby mat and bright floor cushions of the therapy room, peering at the space he created between surfaces. I understand this metaphorically as a possible preoccupation with space between self and other.

FIRST SEQUENCE: THE MICROPHONE, THE TAP AND THE WASHBASIN

Above the rug hung a long cylindrical microphone. As Ben came into the therapy room, or whenever upset, he always looked up and gazed at it. He

[1] This chapter is an adapted version of a paper that was published in the *International Journal of Infant Observation* 7 (2 and 3): 76–90.

also managed the beginning of sessions by insisting that his mother lift him to stand in an armchair at a washbasin to play with the tap and the water. The combined tap comprised one handle that moves up and down to control the flow of water, and from side to side to control the temperature. The water flowed into the rounded white washbasin and down the plughole with a removable metallic stopper. Ben liked to pull this out and replace it so that the water ran away or stayed in the basin. He had no interest before the age of two in using the water for pouring activities. The water temperature brought an exciting element of danger causing Shelley often to shout at Ben to let her operate the tap while he felt the water.

Ben and Shelley would perhaps have stayed at the basin, in endlessly repetitive activity for the whole of the sessions. I felt that without my sustained effort to engage their interest in other objects and ways of relating, Ben would have remained at the basin or on the baby mat without seeking to explore and develop his capacities. I experienced many of these sessions as filled with tedium, a barely survivable emptiness, and my frequent sleepiness.

Comment

What is immediately striking at the beginning of the therapy is that Ben's activities link to powerful symbols of gender. He selects an inanimate phallic object to focus on. It is an interesting choice. The microphone's function is to record words so that they can be replayed and listened to for their meaning to be understood. Can it be that Ben is communicating that he lacks and needs an animated paternal mind that can listen to his difficulties, and provide him with new understanding?

The tap lever can also be seen as having gendered significance, with repeated lifting and lowering activities, giving Ben a sense of agency (Broucek, 1979). The liquid that cascades forth may for Ben be like body fluids from penis or breast. It is possible the washbasin, with the stopper in or out, suggests a preoccupation with what can be contained or lost. The basin suggests a womb-like or bladder-like object with a small plunger that can go in and out of the vagina/urethra pipe. This may serve a function for Ben's urethral eroticism (Tyson, 1989). It may communicate a bodily and interpersonal preoccupation with how male and female parts fit together. Interest in taps and water is an age-appropriate activity but the compulsive quality of Ben's activities suggests developmental difficulty. The combination of the phallic cylinder, the tap and the washbasin with stopper suggest Ben's concern with aspects of mother and father.

Another striking feature of the therapy is about the relationship between Ben, his mother and me. Together we form a threesome – a triangle that may be imagined as an equilateral structure, or as a multiplicity of different angled three-sided shapes, with one of us at each angled corner, according to where we are in the room and the relationship. At the washbasin Shelley and Ben are a pair and I participate from a distance. On the baby mat we form an equilateral triangle. The 'distances' between us – symbolic and physical – vary according to the lengths of the sides of the triangle. As Ben heads for the telephone wire the relational triangle shifts into new complex shapes.

SECOND SEQUENCE: THE TELEPHONE WIRE

Once Ben mastered crawling, at around a year of age, he frequently took himself away from the baby mat, toys, and cushions where his mother and I were sitting to go to the telephone wire that ran round the edge of the room. It was firmly tacked down. With persistent effort he tugged hard on it, so it pulled away, causing him to jolt from the sudden release. This activity occurred frequently during the next six months. Shelley would shout 'No' at Ben from a distance while remaining seated. Ben increased his wire pulling. Shelley would jump up dramatically and run to him, and shout loudly and sharply using words such as 'No Ben, don't do that, that's naughty – do you hear? That's naughty.' Ben would look excited, respond with piercing screams, and pull all the harder, or throw himself on the floor in a tantrum.

I intervened to suggest that Shelley's distant or dramatic responses were exciting him rather than helping him. I modelled how to go quietly to him, talk with him, say 'No' firmly while telling him it was because the wire was 'ouchy' and lift him away firmly but gently. I suggested Ben needed to know the safety reason for stopping his activity. Shelley 'learnt' how to do this through repetition, session after session, in which a sense of emptiness often prevailed. This can be understood as a working through of inflexible activities and processes.

There came the following situation. Ben, at two years, while sitting near us, looked towards the wire and then at each of us in turn, and then down at the floor. He made an unusual facial expression and body gesture, pulling in his shoulders and looking down at the floor, and raising his eyes slowly to look at each of us, from beneath lowered eyelids. He began to crawl towards the wire and then stopped to look back at us. He got very close to the wire, stopped and looked at us, then touched it but did not pull at it, all the while looking to see our reactions. We made little sounds such as 'uh uh', or 'ouchy' and so on. Then he came back to us. This was repeated on many occasions until he simply looked towards the wire and then at us, and made the body gesture, without having to go and pull the wire. Finally, he would occasionally simply look at the wire from a distance.

Comment

The telephone wire runs round the perimeter, the boundary, of the room, suggesting Ben's concern with separation of what is outside from what is inside, including the boundary around the therapy that protects the space within. The telephone represents communication, allowing two people to speak at a distance. Ben may be communicating his own preoccupation with speaking and being understood. The wire scenario evokes boundary setting. Shelley is at first ineffective and exacerbates Ben's behaviours. I have to set clear boundaries. 'No' is said in a deep paternal voice. 'Probably the voice's melody . . . is the most important melody we have to communicate a strong and solid image of the analyst' (Rosenfeld, 1992). Shelley and Ben become a pair in their excited game from which I keep a distance, observing and thinking. Through interpretation over time I interrupt their collusion, and form a pair with Shelley, who changes her behaviour. Ben's eventual bodily response, of lowering the head and the eyes, perhaps suggests a shame response. 'Shame represents this transition from a high arousal positive hedonic state to a low arousal negative hedonic state' (Schore, 1994) and suggests the development of a degree of separation. Ben develops more self-control and the triangle again shifts in shape. Wire episodes became part of the history of the therapy, to be looked back on at future times, part of a biography the three of us shared.

THIRD SEQUENCE: COMMUNICATIONS OF THE BODY

By 21 months Ben was beginning to take his first steps. Shelley began to have severe roving pains firstly in arms and shoulders, and later in her legs. The pains in her upper body prevented her from being able to hold Ben, and in two consecutive sessions the arm was not used, held as if in a sling. By the next week the pains had shifted from her arm to her legs, and she walked with a crutch, no longer able to push the buggy. Physical causes were ruled out. Ben became increasingly disturbed in the sessions, expressed through quietness and a worried expression, or through much throwing of hard objects. I felt at a loss to know how to help. Day-care was put in place for Ben to give Shelley respite and a taxi was provided to get them to and from their therapy. While this was necessary and helped, day-care also brought about experience of further separation from Ben. This brought Shelley to the brink of not being able to care for him. It took time before I was able to begin to understand and interpret that the root cause of her somatic difficulties may be the pain of separation from her son, who was becoming a toddler. I suggested that her loss of capacity to walk came at a time when Ben was gaining his. Shelley then wept that he was no longer her baby, and that she would no longer feel cuddled by cuddling him. I interpreted that leaving him with the child-minder gave her a glimpse into a family life in which Ben was included but she was not – a family life she herself had never had. She told me she hated leaving him at the door, not allowed in. I suggested it brought her own longings to be cared for and that when she had to go home, without Ben, she felt lonely and abandoned, without anyone. Such interpretations, built up over time, brought tears to Shelley, but seemed to reduce Ben's anxiety, expressed through less destructiveness. In time, Shelley's distress decreased and her somatic pains began to disappear.

Comment

This sequence suggests the use of the body rather than the mind for processing affects. The pains of separation seem to be expressed as pains in the body. We see the difficulty for Ben in being able to develop his own individual experience separate from his mother. It is possible that the baby Ben seems to be equated with her own baby self. When she looks after him as a dependent baby she feels looked after herself. When she leaves him at the child-minder she feels abandoned, as if she is the one being left by a parent. Ben shows the beginning of a manic defence through his quietness or over-activity. I perhaps demonstrate a paternal capacity in showing that it is my responsibility rather than his to provide his mother with empathic care and thought, and succeed in relieving their anxieties through interpretation that highlights their separation difficulties. Interpretation reinforces my place in the triangle, alleviating the anxiety and distress in the dyadic dynamic. I can be experienced by Ben as being in a relationship with his mother, while he is set apart observing the relating. 'The closure of the Oedipal triangle by the recognition of the link joining the parents provides a limiting boundary for the internal world' (Britton, 1989). It becomes possible to name 'daddy'.

FOURTH SEQUENCE: NAMING DADDY

Around the same time, the theme of 'the father' explicitly entered the work. Ben was seated between Shelley and me forming an equilateral triangle. Shelley rarely spoke of Ben's father, and when she did so it was in dismissive and derogatory tones. The theme arose of the different females in Ben's life but the absence of males. I suggested that of course he had known his father for a while and then suddenly lost him when his father left. Ben, on the mat between Shelley and me crawled towards me and looked up at me intently. I said directly to Ben that he used to have his daddy, and then he was gone. At the word 'daddy' Ben stopped playing and looked intently at my face. I then spoke softly about how his daddy used to be there but then went away. There was quiet as he gently pushed a bus closer to me. I said to him with sadness that he did not see his daddy any more. He reached towards my hand and stroked the stone in the wedding ring on my finger and then crawled rapidly away, seeming freer. It was a soft and intimate moment, in which Shelley quietly shared.

Comment

The absence of father had never before been spoken about or referred to in the therapy. But now it becomes important. Ben loses the possibility of a relationship with father who is different to mother. He lacks the representation of father as an alive, if absent, presence. I offer that image to Ben, which his mother is not able to offer. Hearing the word 'daddy' has immediate impact. The intentness of his gaze at me is new. It is as if he searches and tries to 'read' my face. He experiences my sadness through my expression and through my words. Touching my wedding ring he appears to communicate his concern about his mummy and daddy. Speaking of his daddy brings in the father's role. The father is physically absent but he is now psychically present as an Oedipal/symbolic third, which is important for Ben's construction of representations. Meanwhile, his mother extends her knowledge of ways of relating by the experience of my relating with Ben with a sensitive tenderness. The intimacy is a shared threesome experience that creates new thought accompanied by affect.

FIFTH SEQUENCE: COMMUNICATING THROUGH VIOLENCE

From 21 to 27 months old, Ben spent much time in disorganised activity, including throwing toys, sometimes hard across the room. On one occasion he came near to me with a brick he was about to launch through the air, I found myself putting my hands up to protect my face. I was in a dilemma between supporting Ben's need to express his aggression and the need for safety.

Ben still had little understandable language. He was developing many undecipherable sounds and strings of sounds, which lacked consonants. He did not appear to be using these sounds to make meaningful communication. Rather like the random throwing of bricks, that prevented anything being built, the sounds could not be used to build meaning between self and others.

During this period Ben frequently bit and pinched his mother. The bites were often to her face. He bit her particularly when frustrated, but also at times without apparent cause. Shelley would shout at him to stop. At times she cried. Ben would often then have a tantrum, screaming and throwing himself about bodily, making himself so he could not be picked up. I felt at a loss to know how to help. The therapy felt primitive and raw. I tried interpreting his strong feelings, and how he wanted to hurt his mummy, but this had no impact. All I could do was consistently and calmly name what was happening and connect this with the feelings of hurt and anger in him. At times, I drew in my breath, making a sound suggesting hurt and said words such as 'No' (while shaking my head), and 'ouchy' and 'not to hurt mummy like that, it is too ouchy'. I suggested that Shelley needed to tell him these things when calm. But the tendency to say 'No' to everything was limiting Ben's increasing wishes to explore. I worked hard to help her recognise when she needed to put limits on Ben's behaviour and when it was inappropriate for her to do so to distinguish those situations that required 'No' from potentially positive situations. I felt the despair of Shelley and Ben about the stuckness in their relationship and sometimes wondered whether the work could continue. Eventually, after many episodes of biting, Shelley arrived at a session in tears of hopelessness after Ben had bitten her in the waiting room. I suggested to them both that their difficulties were perhaps to do with Ben feeling they were too close, that maybe Ben felt trapped.

Comment

Ben is perhaps using biting and pinching to try and define himself through hurting others. The two acts are different – biting breaks the boundary of the other's body through the skin, making holes in the skin and leaving the mark of teeth. Pinching hard also attacks the skin. The mouth in biting, and the fingers in pinching pull the skin outwards while the teeth and nails sink inwards into the other's body. Both forms of aggression cause pain and leave red marks. Throwing bricks at close range causes a banging, bruising kind of harm to the body. Ben seems to express that he has difficulty with distance between self and others. The spaces between mother and infant in the triangle diminish until there is no space. In his aggressive attacks 'he becomes filled with what is bad or malign or persecuting. These evil things or forces, being inside him, as he feels, form a threat from within to his own person and to the good which forms the basis of his trust in life' (Winnicott, 1950).

Ben seems to show that he is missing a father figure who can contribute to boundary setting in ways that contain aggression, and who can reflect on Shelley and Ben's relationship from the outside and represent it to them in words. This is the function that I am being asked to provide, to protect the room and each other from damage. I can be perceived as staying apart from their merger. I model a boundaried mind that can think in the midst of their chaos, offering a lived experience of symbolising feelings through words, not acts. By linking my role to a father's function in this particular case, I do not intend to idealise paternity. In other circumstances, it might be the mother who served a parallel function in offering a perspective on a father–infant relationship. It is the provision of the symbolic Oedipal third that is required.

SIXTH SEQUENCE: FACILITATING SEPARATE IDENTITY

When Ben was 28 months old a game developed between us. It began when Ben was banging a brick on the floor repeatedly. I took a brick and banged it on the floor to the exact same rhythm as Ben. He looked up and smiled and repeated the rhythm with his brick. Soon we were in a turn-taking game, that we both found pleasurable. This occurred at a time when I felt something new needed to develop, against a background of delayed motor and language development. I decided, in discussion with colleagues, to provide Ben with his own box of toys just for him, a progression from having the communal toys, which also remained available. I put in the new box a large foam ball, which he could throw without causing damage.

Before the first session with the box, Ben was creating mayhem in the waiting room. Shelley was in tears as they came through to the therapy room. He had bitten her hard on the side of her face when she was trying to hold him. The following sequence unfolded. After tipping the toys out of the box and customary washbasin play, Shelley tried to persuade Ben to come down from the washbasin as he was soaking the armchair. He threw a tantrum, screaming and fighting, awful to witness. I felt at a loss. I suggested to Shelley that we had to find a way of helping him to calm down, and that she might try bringing him to have a quietening down time on the floor cushion. She lay him down and told me that at home she calms him down by lying with him and proceeded to do so on the big cushions, near to me. She lay with Ben beside her and he then climbed on top of her and lay stretched fully out. After a time of lying still with a vacant expression, he took handfuls of her hair and pulled very hard while watching her intently. She told him sharply not to do so because it hurt and then began to shout at him. He pulled harder, while also glancing at me. I felt a strong urge to intervene. I felt this could not go on any more. I suggested to Shelley that this was not a helpful way to try and settle Ben and that he was no longer a little baby that she may have laid with – that may have been appropriate at that time, but not any more. I went on to say directly that Shelley could not allow Ben to hurt her any more. I suggested she said 'No'. Shelley and Ben untangled themselves and sat up. Shelley told me that she had always comforted him by lying with him and there was nothing wrong with that. I suggested that it was too difficult and too exciting for them. Becoming upset Shelley said that she needed to lie with Ben like that for her own 'comfortability'. I felt very moved; especially by the invention of her own personally created word.

Shelley went to get the box of tissues and returned to sit down further away from Ben. Ben became calm. Soon he picked up an unclothed boy doll and fingered the penis, looking towards me and making sounds. I spoke to Ben about being interested in the boy doll's penis, and asked Shelley what name she uses. She said she calls it 'the mini'. Soon after this Ben went and picked up the doll's potty and played at trying to sit on it.

He then explored the new box of toys, exploring the different ones, and started to throw and catch the ball, with all three of us turn taking. In subsequent sessions we began for the first time to begin to build creatively with the bricks, and became interested in putting together wooden male and female pieces of train track. He experimented with how the magnets connected the trains together and began to say 'choo choo' as he pushed them. Within the next three months sounds began to form into recognisable words.

Comment

I bring in the box as a new resource, which symbolises Ben's separation from babyhood, and provides him with a symbolic container. Before he can use it Shelley and Ben show me their separation difficulty and how they use their bodies rather than their minds as a source of safety and understanding. 'If objects cannot be properly represented as thinking and feeling, they may to some extent be controlled, distanced or brought into proximity through bodily experiences' (Fonagy & Target, 1995). I suggest Shelley is using her son's body to calm herself, while Ben is fighting to hold on to a sense of self-learning to use his body rather than develop the use of his mind. As the third member of the triangle looking on at the twosome from a distant point, I bring in the 'No' of the father to help them to recognise that an important boundary is in danger of being crossed and to help them develop a more separated sense of self. My 'paternal' function is 'to woo the child and the mother away from too close a relation with each other' (Kramer & Prall, 1978) and to provide a shield from the mother's wish to keep her son in a state of symbiosis (Stoller, 1979). Their dynamic relational processes move between 'the poles of symbiosis and separation, with their associated affect states of merger anxiety and dread of isolation' (Brickman, 1993). I also serve to moderate Ben's aggressive impulses that are part of the complex affective state of 'father hunger' (Herzog, 1989). This separation process requires Shelley to mourn the loss of the son as mother's 'husband–father' comforter, so that individuation can continue.

Ben can now go and look for and find the boy doll, look at and touch the doll's penis, and hear what it is called. 'Mini' suggests a derogation of Ben's maleness and he needs to hear the proper name. There is no daddy at home with whom to identify. I suggest this paternal act of naming affirms that Ben is a little boy and serves to differentiate himself from his mother. In identifying with father, having heard his name in the therapy, he 'then becomes more aware of his penis, labelling all parts of his genital apparatus and beginning to integrate them as a part of his body . . . he now comes to seek father as an object with whom to identify' (Tyson, 1989). To sit on the potty suggests recognition of his own body, and also acknowledges the developmental task he faces of gaining control over his own body functions. The inanimate phallic microphone is replaced by recognition of an alive body part – his own.

Ben is freed to explore his new toy box, and throw the large ball powerfully and accurately, bridging the spaces within the Ben–Shelley–me triangle. With this development Ben begins to transform his defensive repetitive play and develop a 'hunger for new experience which is as strong as the urge to repeat' (A. Freud, 1965).

SUMMARY

My main objective in this chapter was to portray how an infant and mother constructed experiences with me to help them represent and manage their relationship with each other and with a physically absent father. Culturally defined images arose of father as creator of boundaries, structures and morality, who separates mother and infant, and stimulates thought and language. I explored how new relational opportunities evolved through triadic experiences. Mother and infant were afforded the opportunity to find an image of themselves as a pair and as separate people in my mind. I interceded between mother and infant creating a space in which 'the interpreting, self-reflective, symbolising subject' could begin to be generated (Ogden, 1994). The absent father became psychically present. Sufficient separation began to take place between mother and infant to allow for the beginnings of symbolisation that is fundamental to the development of the psychological self.

Chapter 12

Developing a culture for change in group analytic psychotherapy for mothers and babies[1]

Jessica James

In this chapter I will describe a phase in the life of a weekly slow open psychotherapy group for mothers with their babies. Clinical material is used to illustrate a group's therapeutic potential when its culture becomes sufficiently secure. We see the process of this development from a group session where the setting is tested but fails, to when four, eight and nine months later creativity and growth become increasingly possible for the mothers and babies who belong. I am a group analyst and my colleague is a child psychotherapist. The group's solidity has been mirrored by the refining of our own understanding and unfolding expertise. We have gradually made progress towards realising the full and rich potential of this therapeutic modality with mothers and infants.

INTRODUCTION

An analytic therapy group is an unfolding drama, not unlike the hurly-burly of family life. In our group we usually have four–five mother and baby dyads joining the group for as long as they need it, perhaps six to eighteen months. Comparable to the birth of a baby, at first the group may seem shocking. Behaviour – like that of a neonate – appears inchoate and requires therapists, and mature group members (babies as well as mothers), to create meaning out of seeming meaninglessness. At first, in the days after birth or early stages of group psychotherapy, this perception is a leap of faith. Without sensitive and confident handling, psychotic anxiety can proliferate. Early groups are compared to infants struggling to achieve a sense of being and unity in the first weeks of life (Nitsun, 1989). A good enough environment of a holding mother is required to meet the absolute dependence, to tolerate periods of deprivation, otherwise there is 'unthinkable anxiety'

1 This chapter is an abridged version of a paper that was published in the *British Journal of Psychotherapy* (2002) 19: 77–91.

(Winnicott, 1987) about falling apart and totally losing touch will occur. In mother and infant group psychotherapy, such imagery is particularly resonant with layers of dependency and anxiety interwoven literally as well as symbolically.

The clinical material that follows is taken from four sessions over a period of nine months.

'WE LEAVE THE GROUP UNSUPPORTED'

There are four mothers with their infants aged between six and sixteen months. One group member and baby joined six weeks previously.

> The newest group member is talking. 'Often we leave the session unsupported or misunderstood or, perhaps, left.' Her baby is in her arms. Another is being rocked by his mother, who is standing. As this is said, she sits down and turns to face away from everyone. She puts a bib on her daughter and proceeds to feed her. Another mother places her six-month-old on his front propped up by a cushion. Almost at the same time as doing this, she responds: 'Aren't they feelings we encounter in our relationships with our partners or in life anyway?'
>
> Then the baby on the cushion rolls off it and falls with a loud bang as his head hits the floor. He wails and is picked up and comforted. 'Oh, Oh, all right, all right'. The therapists watch and look concerned. Other mothers busy themselves with their own babies more avidly. The 'dissatisfied' new mother rocks and strokes her daughter. The 'feeding' mother glances round briefly, then turns back to resume the meal. The crying abates and is followed by a silence, which is broken by my co-therapist: 'He fell with a big bang almost at the very point you were talking about being unsupported by the group. You were saying that sometimes you leave with very painful feelings. I'm making a link between the fall and how you sometimes feel.' The fed baby crawls away from her mother towards others. Her mother pats her hard on the bottom a few times, tries to give her another mouthful of food, then returns to where she was sitting keeping her eyes fixed on her. The 'dissatisfied' mother continues talking about her concern for the mother whose baby fell. 'There was something you brought up at the last minute and I felt you were left unsupported. Then I couldn't remember what it was the next week.' She places her daughter on her back on the floor especially gently. She is facing her and she kisses her. The baby who fell is now in his mother's arms faced outwards. He is wide-eyed and looks into space with a dummy in his mouth and an uneasy calm.
>
> I ask the mother whose baby has banged his head about her resignation and its relationship with the resignation about the group.

'You say "Oh well, it's like that", then he falls. We're trying to work out if you're sensitive enough. You've told us that you're pushed to the limit in the middle of the night. When does it become too many bangs? Mothers feel worse and left in the air in this group. It's really important this is brought up. How can we help prevent this and the bangs?' Her reply is to tell us that her sister is also worried about the bangs. She says: 'I thought what can I do? I'm doing all I can.' The 'dissatisfied' mother wonders 'Has your sister witnessed what these particular bangs are like?'

This is a group that isn't safe and dependable at the moment. A relatively new group member is voicing the paucity of support available and her view isn't countered. No hope is expressed and aloneness, in the group or everywhere else, becomes regarded as inevitable. Backs are turned and own babies are attended to. The body language and activity are tacit agreement that no one wants to try to understand fellow group members' plights. Getting involved doesn't seem worth the risk if the security of long-standing participants is so precarious.

The baby's hurt expressed the group's pain with dramatic force. Others have become – perhaps like the baby herself – disconnected. The new group member's freshness of view is sensitive. The therapists are left to be concerned and to take up the meaning of this distress, whilst the other mothers give their own babies *ultra careful* attention so as to distance themselves. Their children are used as shields between them and the painful feelings. The fed baby gets a hard (cross) pat when she moves away, probably because she's leaving her mother exposed without her. The new member's baby is placed down lovingly, as if to say 'I'm not like you, I'm looking after my baby properly'. It is too dangerous to make contact between each other in this group. The web of relationships is fragile. Anxiety is free flowing and barely contained.

The therapists try to provide what's missing. My colleague has linked the painful feelings with the baby's fall. I'm attempting to improve matters by strengthening the whole group's capacity, as well as the falling baby's mother. But my comments veer towards being judgemental in their desperation: '*We're* trying to work out if *you're* sensitive enough.' My use of 'we' is intended to be inclusive so as to value everyone's contributions and the connections between them. As is also my positive affirmation: 'It's really important this is brought up'. Nevertheless, the tendency persists for the bang to be moved out of the group, with the new group member's question about whether the sister had witnessed the bangs. It's as though we're witnessing a crime committed by an offender, with whom we don't want association. The baby's pain is a reflection of mothers who can't protect their babies, and that is not welcome. Implied also are reverberating feelings about this 'intruder' member who has joined the group recently and, furthermore, expresses things we can't bear to see or hear. We're threatened by the possibility that this group is failing its members. Everyone, including the therapists, refrains from confronting this and insecurity reverberates. It has become too risky to talk about the bangs and distress happening *right now* to fellow group members.

'WE HAD BETTER SAY SOMETHING, EVERYBODY'

Four months later there are five mothers with babies aged between five and twenty months. The 'dissatisfied' mother has left (at that stage in the group's life dissatisfaction was intolerable) and two other pairs have joined.

A mother, who has an older daughter, is explaining about an outburst with her at her mother's house. 'She always misbehaves there'. She is talking energetically and loudly as she tells us about this. We hear that the row escalated into her going 'mad' and 'losing' it. The adults are listening attentively to this energetic talking about someone else's row. Another mother asks: 'What did your mother say?' And we discover: 'She didn't say a word. I was so upset.'

As this story is told, the babies are interacting with their own mothers, except for the baby whose mother is taking the floor. This baby is enabling his mother to hold forth by running to and fro with a toy to engage me. The mother of the baby who fell in the previous scenario is particularly interested in this story. She never had a mother remotely available for her. Her son (now ten months) crawls towards the mother and daughter (sixteen months) who were feeding in the previous vignette. The girl has a doll, which grabs his interest, but her mother ensures her daughter keeps it. She gives him something else and builds bricks with her daughter, separating her from the exploring and interested baby. This is a familiar scene at this stage in their therapy, that she views her daughter as requiring her total care and attention. However, unlike in the previous scene, her back is not turned to the others and she asks an occasional question.

My co-therapist says: 'So we had better say something, everybody'. Someone wonders what she wanted her mother to say. Meanwhile the action hots up between the exploring baby and the mother and daughter dyad with the bricks. Her daughter is taken onto her knee and she says 'that's yours'. She puts her arms across the front of this baby, between his unremitting desire and exploration, and her daughter. The baby's mother says: 'Come on, here's your pile', but doesn't move from her position against the wall some distance away. Her engagement is with the story being told. Attention to her son is perfunctory and the son, in turn, remains relentless in his interest elsewhere. Sympathetic noises continue about the distressing incident between a grandmother, mother and daughter outside the group.

Then we have an outburst within the group. My co-therapist says: 'Don't let's forget this discussion, but I think something happened here.' The 'protective' mother explodes. She gesticulates with her arms and shouts out to the mother of the 'exploring' baby (who was the one we saw fall with a bang as a six-month-old in the previous scenario): 'I wish you would take him away. It's upsetting her.' His mother calls out 'come on' and there's no response. She comes over, picks him up and places him on the floor between her legs. In silence she gets bricks and builds intently alongside her son, facing away from the outburst. I'm looking towards them and have forgotten about the baby I've been playing with, who reminds me of his presence by dropping a toy onto my lap. The mother who exploded is tearful. She stands up holding her daughter to get a tissue for herself. She jogs her up and down, then sits again. I say: 'It's upsetting you.' The mother is apologetic and says she doesn't know why it's upsetting her so much. 'I think she's this completely neurotic baby. If anyone comes near, she makes a fuss.' Then she becomes angry, turning towards the mother of the 'unremitting' baby: 'I was feeling just now I should ask you to take him away. But I couldn't because I thought you should notice what was happening'. The 'unremitting' baby's mother responds by retorting to her son: 'It's chaos and you don't even notice.'

There's opportunity to say more. We examine the replay in the group of the conflict from outside, which moved to the inside. My co-therapist points it out: 'You wanted your mother to take action, to give comfort either to you, your daughter or both of you. Someone needed to take control.' I agree: 'Action was required here.' All the adults' attention is grabbed by what we are saying. We dare to name what's happened now. The 'unremitting' baby starts crawling back to where he was. His mother swiftly pulls him back onto her knee. The 'outburst' mother is clutching her daughter with a doll on her knee. Co-therapist: 'Yes, there was something that you couldn't say here. Did you think it would sound too aggressive?' She replies: 'I thought it would sound rude. But it was silly, it ended up sounding more rude and aggressive than if I'd said something earlier'. The 'shouted at' mother is somewhat mechanically building bricks to keep her son occupied and out of nuisance. He is restrained behind his mother's legs, faced away from the highly charged emotion of the mother and daughter who are rejecting him. Someone comments: 'You seem a bit shocked'. She responds: 'No, well, it's just him, he doesn't understand. If I say no, he will want to go back there. I just have to divert him, basically.'

A dam of feelings has burst out. Their expression has been possible in this increasingly stable culture where connections have developed between group members. The individual's preoccupation and the topic under discussion – 'She didn't say anything' – have meaning for everyone. It is tipped into consciousness by a fight brewing between the mothers over their babies' behaviour. The message has been conveyed that strong feelings are permissible. Unlike these mothers' past histories and experience, violence neither escalated nor got swept under the carpet. Although the newer mothers weren't central players in this action, they are present within a setting that – unlike in the previous vignette – gives promise. This setting is sturdy enough to withstand difficult feelings. It is obvious that people care about each other.

This was a pivotal point in the 'rowing' mothers' and babies' therapy. It also provided a testing ground for this group's dependability as a secure base. The raw feelings – evoked by the babies – cut through niceties and provoked a rich seam of transference enactments for all to see and understand. It became a group event and part of its history to revisit, rework and hold in mind in the group's ether. The 'protective' mother was able to keep her anger alive for subsequent weeks. This differed from her usual tendency for going under, isolated with guilt, misery and depression. With renewed confidence, and much more effect than any therapist (with the full force of emotion), she expressed convincingly the attachment between the other mother and her 'unremitting' baby. This is how she put it the next week: 'Usually there's an invisible thread between mothers and babies, but in your case it seems to be missing.' The timing and accuracy of her insight is valued by the other members, including by the mother and her 'unremitting' baby. The incident and its aftermath faced this mother with her own contribution to the strong feelings in the group. Her life has been full of rejection, as portrayed by her baby's seeking of rejection, and the other mother's perception of the 'invisible thread that seems to be missing'. The ongoingness of this secure enough therapeutic environment offers reworking and change. Her strategies, by now familiar, of distancing herself – such as from the angry mother and daughter's orbit, or from her son's needs – are being exposed and questioned. Through other group members, the therapists and above all, her 'unremitting' baby's persistence, she is encouraged to find ways of renegotiating relationships, with less recourse to giving up, retaliating, or searching for more immediately fascinating distractions.

'ABANDONMENT: WE'VE BEEN PUSSYFOOTING AROUND IT'

A further four months later, it is the third week after a two-week break. There are four mothers and babies. The babies' ages range from six to nineteen months. A new mother and baby girl began three months earlier. This mother has a son whom she left behind when her marriage became intolerable eleven years previously, when the son was two years old.

The recent mother is telling the group about her current relationship with her son who is now aged 13. She tells us that her son avoids his new half-sister. 'He's not really interested in babies'. After a while my co-therapist asks about her son's name. 'You know I don't know the name of your son. It's always "he" or "my son".' We're told the name – which, for the purposes of this paper, is John – and others agree that they didn't know either. The mother looks towards her daughter and lifts her up. She squirms and is resisting. I look at her and also put out a hand to touch her. There is silence. Then a lively child captures our attention.

This lively child is the daughter (now nineteen months) of the mother who 'burst out' in the previous vignette. She is moving back and forth to a chair, saying 'chair' and pointing to it. We admire her: 'Isn't she grown up?' Then another baby crawls over looking intentional. He catches my eye and I say: 'Are you going to it now?' His wish for the chair evaporates and he returns swiftly to his mother. He found me intrusive. Another baby ventures over. It's the baby (now thirteen months) we saw first falling and then 'unremitting'. Last week the chair was one focus of his continuing insatiability. Someone says: 'We know you like the chair.' His mother tells us: 'He's better here this week. He didn't want to be here last week.' She says she is worried about her son's lust for new things in every situation and is concerned that he is bored. This idea is questioned. Co-therapist: 'Bored is a funny word for a child that age.' A discussion develops about the meaning of boring. We watch the 'bored' baby trying to get on the chair. He persists, but is frustrated and making noises. He looks a pitiful sight at the bottom of this unreachable chair. His mother goes over and puts him on it. Again he's not satisfied and sits with his mother reaching towards the window. He can't keep still and nothing seems good enough. His restlessness is settled briefly by a breastfeed that lasts one minute.

My co-therapist talks in relation to this material: 'Any child when he feels OK inside himself can create more and more interest in the same environment. I think that's true for adults as well, isn't it?' Group members are questioning the 'bored' baby's mother about her own contribution to her son's behaviour. She deflects us back to the unnamed son. Quite abruptly, she asks about a photo of John and more is told about him. Again it's reported that he doesn't like babies. Then John's half-sister alerts us to her by turning over. We look and lots of comments are made. 'Hold on tight.' 'Gosh she rolled over!' and her mother leans down towards her face and asks her 'Do you want to play?'

The mother of the baby who found me intrusive has been mostly quiet. Our engagement moves in her direction when she is asked about her silence. She says she's tired, but also unsettled and not sure why she can't join in. Looking at the mother of the 'lively' girl, she says: 'One thing that struck me last week was you saying you were a bit angry about the break.' This mother says: 'That's a bit of an understatement.' There's laughter and the quiet mother continues: 'It was frightening to realise how I'm not in touch with that anger.' We agree that another's anger has provided helpful recognition. Freed up by expressing her anger, she links her fear of anger to a disturbing sense of excitement with her father when she was growing up. It continued with her baby's father when their relationship went wrong. Then she reproaches me for something I said the previous week which felt critical and intrusive. Like her daughter, who moved away from the chair at my approach, she finds me intrusive.

The children are beginning to engage. They are clapping to a musical box, helped along by each other as well as the adults. The mothers talk about expressions of boredom being connected to fear. 'I used to go to mother and baby groups and think they were boring. It was an excuse to myself why I'm not enjoying it', 'I can't see a way to change this excitement that came from a terrifying background and spilled over into relationships.' The mother whose baby was described as bored in the group, is saying nothing. Her baby is becoming slightly more settled now. Instead of flitting from person to person, object to object, he sits on his mother's knee jumping with the rhythm of the musical box. The children are lively – plates are banged together, rattles are rattled energetically – and the mothers are quietly reflective. There is this silent moment, then someone says: 'This is quite important stuff'.

Up until this point we had avoided talking about the 'abandoned' son. As one group member put it later: 'We've pussyfooted around it.' Now the group is beginning to face thinking about this abandonment. A solid group culture, combined with this woman's emerging accessibility, meant questions beginning to be asked. I had reached out with my hand to touch her baby, feeling protective towards her mother whose daughter is manifesting her internal squirming and resisting. Our silence at that point suggests our awareness of their vulnerability and also, perhaps, our identification with John who was nameless. The lively child is a welcome release, especially as she is usually the one who clings, or is clung onto, by her mother. When the mother of the abandoned son brings her secret into the open, her daughter becomes animated and grabs our attention by turning over. We're all interested and, perhaps, compensating for her half-brother's lack of interest, as well as her mother's own struggle to risk becoming attached to her. Now her mother looks into her eyes and talks to her directly: 'Do you want to play?' She's daring intimacy with both her daughter and the group.

There's didactic talk about the idea of 'boring'. The 'bored' baby's mother resists contemplating this and bounces the discussion back to the abandoned son, who is also herself. She, too, was abandoned by her birth family. Like her 'bored' son, she tends to manage life by having a lust (often creative) for new things. Asking for a photo is another way of wanting to find out more and have the 'abandoned' son fleshed out and not forgotten.

Then abandonment comes into the group more directly. We abandoned them over the break and their anger – expressed directly by one woman last week, and now in silence by another – is alive. The juxtaposition of boring and exciting becomes meaningful in the here and now. This theme is developed. The developing engagement and attunement between the adults results in a similar experience for the children who become rhythmic and settled. Even the 'bored', hitherto flitting, baby is held in this moment of contact with others. There's mutual recognition of its significance: 'This is quite important stuff.'

'I WASN'T AS RECEPTIVE TO YOU AS I MIGHT HAVE BEEN'

Two weeks later this theme of abandonment is revived and pursued more energetically.

The 'intruded' mother brings up the subject again. She says she has thought about her silence and realises she feels hostile to the mother who abandoned her son. She makes the connection to her own experience. 'It's my problem, but you brought that issue into the group. I wasn't as receptive to you as I might have been. It wasn't just that you were new.' The 'abandoning' mother asks her to say more, indicating she can bear it. Others contribute their own feelings of hesitancy. It gets described as 'deep down criticism'. The therapists reinforce what is being said: 'This is really important. It's what you feared.' 'It's really good you brought it up.' Then we go further. The 'abandoning' mother: 'This is part of the reason people don't know about John. I've got to cope and deal with that.' She's tearful and is using her son's name as the feelings flow. Whilst talking, her daughter wobbles. She helps her fall gently and articulates what happening 'oops-a-daisy!' And another mother does interpretative work: 'Is there part of you that feels like that?' (self-critical). She replies: 'I think so', and leans back against the wall.

For a while we focus on helping this mother contemplate her own self-judgement. The babies let us talk. Two are pretending to make tea, babbling and responding to each other. She is assuring herself that her abandoned son isn't damaged. 'He hasn't been upset about it.' The therapists wonder if upset would be intolerable and bring upset back into the group. 'Do you think it would be helpful to hear more about the criticisms and feelings here? Or would that be intolerable?' She says she welcomes ideas to help her talk to John or make explanations to others. Another mother shares having had her own desperate feelings, which resulted in thoughts of killing herself and her daughter. She says: 'It's strange, I never thought of leaving her.' Then she's able to reach out to applaud this mother's efforts to do her best: 'It sounds as though you've been really thoughtful about him.' Other group members provide reassurance and comfort. This frees the therapists to probe further: 'Did your desperate feelings ever got to the extreme we've just heard about? Did you think of harming yourself or John?' Mother: 'No, not really. I planned the leaving all out. I was stressed and unhappy.' She's stroking her daughter and is tearful. Another mother: 'It sounds as though you saw that as the only solution.' Mother: 'It seemed the only way.' I say: 'You didn't have the words and no one picked up the signals.' Co-therapist: 'You must have felt abandoned by the people who loved you.'

This is powerful. Critical feelings are being acknowledged about each other inside the group. The 'intruded upon' mother's previous silence was not simply anger about the group or the therapists. After time to reflect, this mother has thought about her hostility towards the mother who abandoned her son. Judgement and self-judgement rebound. The 'abandoning' mother's disapproval of herself has become more pernicious since the birth of her daughter. As she declares this, she is in touch with her collapse. Previously we've noticed his mother's loss of contact with her daughter when she talks of John. This time, with the resonance in the group, she reaches tenderly, voices what is happening 'oops-a-daisy' and lowers her to the floor. Her own bodily movements are similarly responsive. Usually her place is in middle of the room, sitting stiffly and awkwardly with her big lump of a baby. Now she's accepting the support of the group and relaxes back into the cushions and wall.

This setting has enabled both empathy and analysis. Criticism hasn't been simply 'out there.' Mothers have shared their intolerable feelings generated by the past as well as the present. No one holds the monopoly on abandonment, in fantasy or reality and it has meaning for everyone. In our group, as well, we've seen – although not made explicit or interpreted at this stage – how this mother, who abandoned her son, took time to gain a position with her baby inside the group. Signals, through body language as well as words, became evidence that they were gradually available for intimacy and embrace.

CONCLUSION

I have used clinical material to demonstrate a culture of embededness as a pre-requisite for change in an analytic group with mothers and babies. In the first scenario, 'We leave the group unsupported', the group's identity was indistinguishable from that of its fragile members. Its potential for integration was unformulated. Mothers and babies displayed their fractured, disassociated and despairing modes of functioning and the group struggled to meet their needs. Refuge was taken in busyness with babies and talk that avoided the difficulties actually there in the room. The therapists also strained to address and stay with the events unfolding in the session, with their faith in the process diminished by the force of projections.

Following sessions portrayed a sturdier group culture, where a place of safety was formed with others who are 'in touch'. 'Falling for ever becomes the joy in being carried' (Winnicott, 1987, p. 86). 'Falls' occur both literally and symbolically, and are met by concerned others prepared and able to 'carry' each other. Cycles of collapse and recovery were repeated time and again as vehicles for engagement with the group as a reliable, sometime joyful, 'group-mother'. This passionate involvement was accessed from various angles. Mothers brought preoccupations from current and past lives, which were linked to the action in the room. The theme of abandonment reverberated and included babies being held insecurely there and then. With time to reflect, a few weeks later, judgements about abandonment were owned and borne between group members: 'I wasn't as receptive to you as I might have been.' This included venturing to question the behaviour of mothers and therapists within the setting. The thorough use of this (group) object, and the multiplicity of relationships within it, has been shown leading to movement and progression.

References

Acquarone, S. (2004) *Infant–Parent Psychotherapy – A Handbook*. London: Karnac.

Ainsworth, M. D. S., Blehar, M. C., Waters, E. and Wall, S. (1978) *Patterns of Attachment: A Psychological Study of the Strange Situation*. Hillsdale, NJ: Lawrence Erlbaum Associates, Inc.

Alvarez, A. (1992) *Live Company*. London: Tavistock/Routledge.

Ashe, J. and Aramakis, V. B. (1998) Brain development and plasticity. In: Friedman, H. S. (ed) *Encyclopaedia of Mental Health*. San Diego: Academic Press.

Balbernie, R. (2002) *An Infant Mental Health Service: The Importance of the Early Years and Evidence-Based Practice*. Report published by The Child Psychotherapy Trust, London.

Barrows, P. (2003) Changes in parent–infant psychotherapy. *Journal of Child Psychotherapy* 29, 3: 283–300.

Beebe, B. (2004) Co-constructing mother–infant distress in face to face interactions: contributions of microanalysis. *Zero to Three* May: 40–48.

Beebe, B., Lachmann, F. and Jaffe, J. (1997) Mother–infant interaction structures and presymbolic self and object representations. *Psychoanalytic Dialogues* 7: 113–182.

Belsky, J. (2001) Developmental risks (still) associated with early childcare. *Journal of Child Psychology and Psychiatry* 42: 845–859.

Berg, A. (2002) Ubuntu – from the consulting room to the vegetable garden. In: Raphael-Leff, J. (ed) *Between Sessions and Beyond the Couch*. Colchester: University of Essex, pp. 102–107.

Bion, W. R. (1962) *Learning from Experience*. London: Heinemann.

Bion, W. R. (1967) *Second Thoughts*. London: Heinemann.

Bollas, C. (1987) Extractive introjection. (ed) *The Shadow of the Object: Psychoanalysis of the Unthought Known*. London: Free Association Books.

Bollas, C. (1989) *Forces of Destiny: Psychoanalysis and Human Idiom*. London: Free Association Books.

Bowlby, J. (1969) *Attachment and Loss, Vol. 1: Attachment*. London: Hogarth Press and the Institute of Psycho-Analysis.

Bowlby, J. (1973) *Attachment and Loss, Vol. 2: Separation: Anxiety and Anger*. London: Hogarth Press and the Institute of Psycho-Analysis.

Brazelton, T. and Cramer, B. (1991) *The Earliest Relationship*. Reading, MA: Perseus Books.

Bretherton, I. (1992) Social referencing, intentional communication and the interfacing of minds in infancy. In: Feinman, S. (ed) *Social Referencing and the Social Construction of Reality in Infancy*. New York: Plenum Press.

Brickman, H. R. (1993) Between the devil and the deep blue sea: the dyad and the triad in psychoanalytic thought. *International Journal of Psychoanalysis* 74: 905–915.

Britton, R. (1989) The missing link: parental sexuality in the Oedipus complex. In: Britton, R., Feldman, M., O'Shaughnessy, E. and Steiner, J. (eds) *The Oedipus Complex Today: Clinical Implications*. London: Karnac, pp. 83–102.

Broucek, F. (1979) Efficacy in infancy: a review of some experimental studies and their possible implications of clinical theory. *International Journal of Psycho-Analysis* 60: 311–316.

Brown, G. and Harris, T. (1978) *The Social Origins of Depression*. London: Tavistock.

Carlson, E. and Sroufe, L. A. (1995) Contribution of attachment theory to developmental psychopathology. In: Cicchetti, D. and Cohen, D. J. (eds) *Developmental Psychopathology. Vol. 1: Theory and Methods*. New York: Wiley, pp. 581–617.

Cicchetti, D. and Beeghly, M. (1990) An organisational approach to the study of Down syndrome: contributions to an integrative theory of development. In: Cicchetti, D. and Beeghly, M. (eds) *Children with Down Syndrome: A Developmental Perspective*. New York: Cambridge University Press, pp. 29–62.

Clyman, R. B. (1991) The procedural organization of emotions: a contribution from cognitive science to the psychoanalytic theory of therapeutic action. *Journal of the American Psychoanalytic Association* 39, Supplement: 349–382.

Cowan, C. and Cowan, P. (1992) *When Partners become Parents*. New York: Basic Books.

Cramer, B. (1998) Mother–infant psychotherapies: a widening scope in technique. *Infant Mental Health Journal* 19, 2: 151–167.

Cramer, B. and Stern, D. N. (1983) Evaluation of changes in mother–infant brief psychotherapy: a single case study. *Infant Mental Health Journal* 9: 20–45.

Cramer, B., Robert-Tissot, C., Stern, D. N., Serpa-Rusconi, S., DeMuralt, M., Besson, G., Palacio-Espasa, F., Bachmann, J., Knauer, D., Berney, C. and D'Arcis, U. (1990) Outcome evaluation in brief mother–infant psychotherapy: a preliminary report. *Infant Mental Health Journal* 11: 278–300.

Daws, D. (1989) *Through the Night: Helping Parents and Sleepless Infants*. London: Free Association Books.

Daws, D. (1999) Brief psychotherapy with infants and their parents. In: Lanyado, M. and Horn, A. (eds) *Child and Adolescent Psychotherapy Handbook*. London: Brunner-Routledge.

Emde, R. N., Gaensbauer, T. and Harmon, R. J. (1982) Using our emotions: principles for appraising emotional development and intervention. In: Lewis, M. and Taft, L. (eds) *Developmental Disabilities: Theory Assessment and Intervention*. New York: S. P. Medical and Scientific Books.

Ferris, S., McGauley, G. and Hughes, P. (2004) Attachment disorganization in infancy: relation to psychoanalytic understanding of development. *Psychoanalytic Psychotherapy* 18: 1–16.

Fonagy, P. (1999) The process of change and the change of process: What can change in a good analysis? Keynote Address to the Spring meeting of Division 39 of the American Psychological Association.

Fonagy, P. and Target, M. (1995) Understanding the violent patient: the use of the body and the role of the father. *International Journal of Psycho-Analysis* 76: 487–502.

Fonagy, P., Steele, H. and Steele, M. (1991a) Maternal representations of attachment during pregnancy predict the organization of infant–mother attachment at one year of age. *Child Development* 62: 891–905.

Fonagy, P., Steele, H., Moran, G., Steele, M. and Higgitt, A. (1991b) The capacity for understanding mental states: The reflective self in parent and child and its significance for security of attachment. *Infant Mental Health Journal* 13: 200–217.

Fonagy, P., Steele, M., Moran, G. S., Steele, H. and Higgitt, A. (1993) Measuring the ghost in the nursery: an empirical study of the relation between parents' mental representations of childhood experiences and their infants' security of attachment. *Journal of the American Psychoanalytic Association* 41: 957–989.

Fonagy, P., Steele, M., Steele, H., Higgitt, A. and Target, M. (1994) Theory and practice of resilience. *Journal of Child Psychology and Psychiatry* 35: 231–257.

Fonagy, P., Target, M., Steele, M. and Steele, H. (1997) The development of violence and crime as it relates to security of attachment. In: Osofsky, J. D. (ed) *Children in a Violent Society*. New York: Guilford Press, pp. 150–177.

Fonagy, P., Gergely, G., Jurist, E. and Target, M. (2002a) *Affect Regulation, Mentalization and the Development of the Self*. New York: Other Press.

Fonagy, P., Sadie, C. and Allison, E. (2002b) *The Parent–Infant Project (PIP) Outcome Study*. London: Anna Freud Centre.

Foulkes, S. H. (1948) *Introduction to Group-Analytic Psychotherapy*. London: Maresfield Reprints.

Foulkes, S. H. (1964) *Therapeutic Group Analysis*. London: Allen and Unwin.

Fraiberg, S. (1980) *Clinical Studies in Infant Mental Health: The First Year of Life*. New York: Basic Books.

Fraiberg, S. (1987) Pathological defences in infancy (ed). *The Selected Writings of S. Fraiberg*. Columbus, OH: Ohio State University Press.

Fraiberg, S., Adelson, E. and Shapiro, V. (1975) Ghosts in the nursery: a psychoanalytic approach to the problem of impaired infant-mother relationships. *Journal of the American Academy Child Psychiatry* 14: 387–422.

Freud, A. (1953) Some remarks on infant observation. *Psychoanalytic Study of the Child* 8: 9–19.

Freud, A. (1965) *Normality and Pathology in Childhood: Assessments of Development*. Madison, CT: International Universities Press.

Freud, A. and Burlingham, D. (1944) *Infants without Families*. New York: International University Press.

Freud, S. (1920) Beyond the pleasure principle. In: Strachey, J. (ed) *The Standard Edition of the Complete Psychological Works of Sigmund Freud, Vol. 18*. London: Hogarth Press, pp. 1–64.

Garland, C. (1982) Taking the non-problem seriously (ed). *Group Analysis*, 15: 1, 4–14. London: Sage.

George, C., Kaplan, N. and Main, M. (1985) *Adult Attachment Interview (2nd ed)*. Unpublished manuscript, Berkley, CA: University of California.

Gergely, G. and Watson, J. (1996) The social biofeedback model of parental affect-mirroring. *International Journal of Psycho-Analysis* 77: 1181–1212.

Gerhardt, S. (2004) *Why Love Matters*. Hove, UK: Brunner-Routledge.

Glaser, D. (2000) Child abuse and neglect and the brain – a review. *Journal of Child Psychology and Psychiatry* 41, 1: 97–116.

Glover, G. and O'Connor, T. G. (in press) Antenatal programming of child behaviour and neurodevelopment: Links with maternal stress and anxiety. In: Hodgson and Coe (eds) *Perinatal programming: early life determinants of adult health and disease*. London: Taylor and Francis Medical Books.

Goldberg, S. (1997) Attachment and childhood behaviour problems in normal at-risk and clinical samples. In: Atkinson, L. and Zucker, K. (eds) *Attachment and Psychopathology*. New York: Guilford Press.

Goldberg, S. (2000) *Attachment and Development*. New York: Oxford University Press.

Green, A. (1986) The dead mother. *On Private Madness*. London: Karnac.

Herzog, J. M. (1989) On father hunger: The father's role in the modulation of aggressive drive and fantasy. In: Cath, S., Gurwitt, A., and Lunsberg, L. (eds) *Fathers and their families*. Hillsdale, NJ: The Analytic Press.

Hesse, E. (1999) The Adult Attachment Interview: Historical and current perspectives. In: Cassidy, J. and Shaver, P. (eds) *Handbook of Attachment*. London: Guilford Press, pp. 395–433.

Hopkins, J. (1992) Infant–parent psychotherapy. *Journal of Child Psychotherapy* 18: 5–17.

Hopkins, J. (1994) Therapeutic interventions in infancy. Two contrasting cases of persistent crying. *Psychoanalytic Psychotherapy* 8: 141–152.

Hopkins, J. (1996) The dangers and deprivations of too good mothering. *Journal of Child Psychotherapy* 22, 3.

Hughes, P. and McGauley, G. (1997) Mother–infant interaction in the first year with a child who shows disorganization of attachment. *British Journal of Psychotherapy* 14, 2: 147–158.

Karmiloff-Smith, A. (1995) Annotation: the extraordinary cognitive journey from foetus through infancy. *Journal of Child Psychology and Psychiatry* 36, 8: 1293–1312.

Klaus, M., Kennel, J. H. and Klaus, P. H. (1995) *Bonding: Building the Foundations for a Secure Attachment*. Reading, MA: Perseus Books.

Klaus, M. and Klaus, P. H. (1998) *Your Amazing Newborn*. Reading, MA: Perseus Books.

Klinnert, M., Campos, J., Sorce, J., Emde, R. and Svejda, M. (1983) Emotions as behaviour regulators: social referencing in infancy. In: Plutchik, R. and Kellerman, H. (eds) *Emotions in Early Development, Vol 2: The Emotions*. New York: Academic Press, pp. 57–86.

Klinnert, M., Emde, R., Butterfield, P. and Campos, J. J. (1986) Social referencing: the infant's use of emotional signals from a friendly adult with mother present. *Developmental Psychology* 22: 427–432.

Kramer, S. and Prall, R. C. (1978) The role of the father in the pre-verbal years. *Journal of the American Psychoanalytic Association* 26: 143–161.

Lord Laming, HMSO (2003) *The Victoria Climbie Inquiry*. Report presented to Parliament by the Secretary of State for Health and the Secretary of State for the Home Department by command of Her Majesty January 2003.

Lieberman, A. F. and Pawl, J. (1993) Infant–parent psychotherapy. In: Zeanah, C. H. (ed) *Handbook of Infant Mental Health*. New York: Guilford Press, pp. 427–442.

Liotti, G. (1999) Disorganization of attachment as a model for understanding dissociative psychopathology. In: Solomon, J. and George, C. (eds) *Attachment Disorganization*. New York: Guilford, pp. 291–317.

Lyons-Ruth, K. (1996) Attachment relationships among children with aggressive behavior problems: the role of disorganized early attachment patterns. *Journal of Consulting and Clinical Psychology* 64: 32–40.

Lyons-Ruth, K. (1999) The two person unconscious: Intersubjective dialogue, enactive relational representation and the emergence of new forms of relational knowing. *Psychoanalytic Inquiry* 19, 4: 576–617.

Lyons-Ruth, K. and Block, D. (1996) The disturbed caregiving system: relations among childhood trauma, maternal caregiving, and infant affect and attachment. *Infant Mental Health Journal* 17: 257–275.

Lyons-Ruth, K. and Jacobovitz, D. (1999) Attachment disorganization: unresolved loss, relational violence and lapses in behavioral and attentional strategies. In: Cassidy, J. and Shaver, P. R. (eds) *Handbook of Attachment Theory and Research*. New York: Guilford Press, pp. 520–554.

Mahler, M. S., Pine, F. and Bergman, A. (1975) *The Psychological Birth of the Human Infant: Symbiosis and Individuation*. New York: Basic Books.

Main, M. and Cassidy, J. (1995) Adult attachment classification system. In: Main, M. (ed) *Behaviour and the Development of Representational Models of Attachment: Five Methods of Assessment*. Cambridge: Cambridge University Press.

Main, M. and Hesse, E. (1990) Parents' unresolved traumatic experiences are related to infant disorganized attachment status: is frightened and/or frightening parental behavior the linking mechanism? In: Greenberg, M., Cicchetti, D. and Cummings, E. M. (eds) *Attachment in the Preschool Years: Theory, Research and Intervention*. Chicago: University of Chicago Press, pp. 161–182.

Main, M., Kaplan, N. and Cassidy, J. (1985) Security in infancy, childhood and adulthood: A move to the level of representation. In: Bretherton, I. and Waters, E. (eds) *Growing Points of Attachment Theory and Research. Monographs of the Society for Research in Child Development, 50*. Chicago: Chicago University Press, pp. 66–104.

Marks, M. N., Hipwell, A. and Kumar, R. (2002) Implications for the infant of maternal puerperal psychiatric disorders. In: Rutter, M. and Taylor, E. (eds) *Child and Adolescent Psychiatry: 4th edition*, Oxford: Blackwell Scientific Publications, pp. 858–877.

Mayes, L. C. and Cohen, D. J. (1996) Children's developing theory of mind. *Journal of the American Psychoanalytic Association* 44, 1: 117–142.

McLaughlan, J. T. (1991) Clinical and theoretical aspects of enactment. *Journal of the American Psychoanalytic Association* 39, 595–614.

Melhuish, E. (2004) Unpublished keynote paper. In: *Attachment Conference*. London: University College.

Murray, L. (1997) Postpartum depression and child development. *Psychological Medicine* 27: 253–260.

Murray, L., Sinclair, D., Cooper, P., Ducournau, P., Turner, P. and Stein, A. (1999) The socioemotional development of 5-year-old children of postnatally depressed mothers. *Journal of Child Psychology and Psychiatry* 40, 8: 1259–1271.

Nitsun, M. (1989) Early development: linking the individual and group. *Group Analysis* 22, 3: 249–260.

Nketia, K. (1966) Lullaby. In: Beier, U. (ed) *African Poetry*. Cambridge: Cambridge University Press.

Ogden, T. (1994) The analytic third: working with intersubjective clinical facts. *International Journal of Psychoanalysis* 75: 3–19.

Osofsky, J. and Fitzgerald, H. (2000) *World Association of Infant Mental Health Handbook of Infant Mental Health* (ed) New York: Wiley and Son.

Perry, B. D., Pollard, R., Blakely, R., Baher, W. and Vigilante, D. (1995) Childhood trauma, the neurobiology of adaptation, and user-dependent development of the brain, how 'states' become 'traits'. *Infant Mental Health Journal* 16: 271–291.

Piontelli, A. (1992) *From Foetus to Child: An Observational and Psychoanalytic Study*. London: Routledge.

Raphael-Leff, J. (1993) *Pregnancy – The Inside Story*. London: Karnac, 2001.

Raphael-Leff, J. (2000) Introduction: technical issues in perinatal therapy. In: Raphael-Leff, J. (ed) *'Spilt Milk': Perinatal Loss and Breakdown*. London: Routledge.

Raphael-Leff, J. (2005) *Psychological Processes of Childbearing, 4th edition*. London: Anna Freud Centre/Chapman & Hall, 1991.

Rosenfeld, D. (1992) Psychic changes in the paternal image. *International Journal of Psycho-Analysis* 73: 757–771.

Sandler, A. M. and Sandler, J. (1998) A theory of internal object relations. In *Internal Object Relations Revisited*, chapter 8, pp. 121–140. London: Karnac.

Sandler, J. (1976) Countertransference and role-responsiveness. *International Review of Psycho-Analysis* 3: 43–47.

Sandler, J. (1983) Reflections on some relations between psychoanalytic concepts and psychoanalytic practice. *International Journal of Psycho-Analysis* 64: 35–45.

Schore, A. N. (1994) *Affect Regulation and the Origin of the Self: The Neurobiology of Emotional Development*. Hillsdale, NJ: Lawrence Erlbaum Associates, Inc.

Schore, A. N. (2001) Effects of a secure attachment relationship on right brain development, affect regulation, and infant mental health. *Infant Mental Health Journal* 22: 7–66.

Spreen, O., Risser, A. and Tuokko, H. (1984) *Human Dvelopmental Neuropsychology*. Oxford: Oxford University Press.

Stechler, G. and Halton, A. (1982) Pre-natal influences on human development. In: Wolman, B. B. (ed) *Handbook of Developmental Psychology*. Englewood Cliffs, NJ: Prentice Hall.

Steele, M. (2003) Attachment, actual experience and mental representation. In: Green, V. (ed) *Emotional Development in Psychoanalysis, Attachment Theory and Neuroscience*, Hove, UK: Brunner-Routledge.

Steele, M. and Baradon, T. (2004) The clinical use of the Adult Attachment Interview in parent–infant psychotherapy. *Infant Mental Health Journal* 25: 284–299.

Stern, D. N. (1985) *The Interpersonal World of the Infant: A View from Psychoanalysis and Developmental Psychology*. New York: Basic Books.

Stern, D. N. (1995) *The Motherhood Constellation*. New York: Basic Books.

Stern, D., Sander, L., Nahum, J., Harrison, A., Lyons-Ruth, K., Morgan, A., Bruschweiler-Stern, N., and Tronick, E. (1998) Non-interpretive mechanisms in psychoanalytic therapy: The 'something more' than interpretation. *International Journal of Psychoanalysis* 79: 903–921.

Stoller, R. J. (1979) Fathers of transsexual children. *Journal of the American Psychoanalytic Association* 27: 837–866.

Tang, N. and Smith, B. (1996) The eternal triangle across cultures. *The Psychoanalytic Study of the Child* 51: 562–579.

Thomson-Salo, F. (2002) Working psychoanalytically with the infant in the consulting room. In: Raphael-Leff, J. (ed) *Between Sessions and Beyond the Couch*. Colchester: University of Essex, pp. 77–79.

Trevarthen, C. (1979) Communication and cooperation in early infancy: a description of primary intersubjectivity. In: Bullowa, M. M. (ed) *Before Speech: The Beginning of Interpersonal Communication*. New York: Cambridge University Press, pp. 321–347.

Trevarthen, C. (1994) Conversations with the infant communicator. *Winnicott Studies* 7: 67–84.

Trevarthen, C. and Aitken, K. (2001) Infant intersubjectivity: research, theory and clinical applications. *Journal of Child Psychology and Psychiatry* 42, 1: 3–48.

Tronick, E. Z. (1998) Dyadically expanded states of consciousness and the process of therapeutic change. *Infant Mental Health Journal* 19: 290–299.

Tronick, E. Z. and Cohn, J. F. (1989) Infant–mother face-to-face interaction: age and gender differences in coordination and the occurrence of miscoordination. *Child Development* 60: 85–92.

Trowell, J. and Etchegoyen, A. (2002) *The Importance of Fathers: A Psychoanalytic Re-evaluation*. London: New Library of Psychoanalysis/Brunner-Routledge.

Tyson, P. (1989) The role of father in gender identity, urethral erotism, and phallic narcissism. In: Cath, S., Gurwitt, A. and Lunsberg, L. (eds) *Fathers and their Families*. Hillsdale, NJ: The Analytic Press.

van Ijzendoorn, M. H. and Bakermans-Kranenburg, M. J. (1996) Attachment representations in mothers, fathers, adolescents, and clinical groups: a meta-analytic search for normative data. *Journal of Consulting and Clinical Psychology* 64: 8–21.

van Ijzendoorn, M. H., Goldberg, S., Kroonenberg, P. M. and Frenkel, O. J. (1992) The relative effects of maternal and child problems on the quality of attachment: a meta-analysis of attachment in clinical samples. *Child Development* 59: 147–156.

Von Klitzing, K., Simoni, H. and Burgin, D. (1999) Child development and early triadic relationships. *International Journal of Psychoanalysis* 80: 71–90.

Winnicott, D. W. (1945) Primitive emotional development. (ed) *Through Paediatrics to Psychoanalysis*. London: Hogarth Press and the Institute of Psychoanalysis, 1982.

Winnicott, D. W. (1947) Hate in the countertransference. (ed) *Through Paediatrics to Psychoanalysis*. London: Hogarth Press and the Institute of Psychoanalysis, 1982.

Winnicott, D. W. (1949) The ordinary devoted mother. In: Winnicott, C.,

Shepherd, R. and Davies, M. (eds) *Babies and their Mothers*. Reading, MA: Addison-Wesley Publishing Company Inc, 1987.

Winnicott, D. W. (1950) Aggression in relation to emotional development (ed). *Collected Papers: Through Paediatrics to Psychoanalysis*. London: Tavistock.

Winnicott, D. W. (1956) Primary maternal preoccupation (ed). *Collected Papers: Through Paediatrics to Psycho-analysis*. London: Tavistock, 1958, pp. 300–305.

Winnicott, D. W. (1958) The capacity to be alone. *International Journal of Psychoanalysis* 39: 416–420.

Winnicott, D. W. (1960) The theory of the parent–infant relationship (ed). *The Maturational Process and the Facilitating Environment*. New York: International Universities Press, pp. 37–55.

Winnicott, D. W. (1962) Ego integration in child development (ed). *The Maturational Processes and the Facilitating Environment*. London: Hogarth Press, 1965, pp. 56–63.

Winnicott, D. W. (1966) The ordinary devoted mother (ed). *Winnicott on the Child*. Reading, MA: Perseus Books, 2002.

Winnicott, D. W. (1971a) Transitional objects and transitional phenomena (ed). *Playing and Reality*. London: Tavistock, pp. 1–25.

Winnicott, D. W. (1971b) Mirror-role of the mother and family in child development (ed). *Playing and Reality*. Hove, UK: Brunner-Routledge, pp. 26–33.

Winnicott, D. W. (1987) *Babies and their Mothers*. London: Free Association Books.

Winnicott, D. W. (1988) *Human Nature*. London: Free Association Books.

Index